P S K E L ⎯ ⎯ A N

WHEN

TRUTH

AND LIES

COLLIDE:

THE POWER IN CONNECTION, COMMUNICATION AND RELATIONSHIPS

A CRIME...

He looked at her and didn't know what to say. There were no words, until he mustered the strength to find them, and then it was like water rushing through a firehose. But, you'll understand more about that later...

"Yes, I did it. Not the reasons you think. Life. Complications. Moral dilemmas. Judgment. The naked truth." Tears splattered across the tabletop. No windows, just four walls and concrete.

"Fear, torment, shame. Do you know the shame I have struggled with? I don't know how people carry it their entire lives for whatever reason, feeling less than good enough, made to feel they don't belong, or a bad decision, wrong turn, or yes, a crime. I don't know." His voice trailed off, he wiped his eyes, and looked directly into hers, with a cold stare he probably didn't intend for her.

He wiped his nose and held his head up high. "People, self-righteous people will judge, condemn, and crucify me. They don't even know me, but they'll do it anyway. And they will certainly never understand. You know how I lived with it every day? I knew I didn't have a choice.

"I challenge anyone faced with this. What would you have done? Really, what would you have done? I wouldn't be too quick to answer. It will require a courageous, raw, vulnerable, empathetic, compassionate, honest assessment to really know. Now here is my judgment - better make sure you have all that in you. Then, and only then, answer the question - what would you have done?

She simply stated in a barely audible whisper, "I'm not one of them. Help me understand."

CHAPTER 1

The brain, an organ acting like a muscle used for good, bad, evil, desperation and moral dilemma. The heart, the connector to navigate through it all. We have choices, at least most of us do…

* * * * * * * * * *

Why didn't she see it coming? Lindsay Thompson was usually better than that, sensing when something was about to happen, even if she didn't know what, how or why. She knew things, and yes, she had a habit of thinking too much.

She had awakened that morning with her mind racing like a double expresso on the brain and her heart was fluttering much faster than any possible normal rate. *God, is this a nervous breakdown or heart attack, or do I need to give up sugar completely?*

Lindsay didn't rest, spending most of her energy on other people or the work that was her life. It could be friends, colleagues, strangers she smiled at on the street, or her latest challenge of saving an Architect and Engineering firm from bankruptcy. But, she wasn't soft. Never soft.

On the way out of her condo that morning, Lindsay stopped at the hallway mirror for one last check. The humidity, her latest cut, or something had been wreaking havoc with her hair. She tried to fluff it with her fingers, but it didn't help much. She moved in closer, spotting a wrinkle that wasn't there a month earlier. *Ugh, the aging process.* Nothing could be done about the wrinkle, so she grabbed her briefcase and left the condo, pausing to listen for the door latch to click.

Driving in Washington D.C. was like maneuvering through an obstacle course even when the roads weren't wet and beaded with icy patches. She spent an hour in traffic, moving in and around fender benders. People yelled and motioned obscenities at one another. Winter weather on top of too much traffic and daily commutes brought out the worst in people. It wasn't exactly a testimony for the goodness of mankind. As for her, there was no road rage, just an annoying commute, too much time to think, and heart wrenching memories that popped up at random times. She had become good at shutting them down. She shook her head and let out a deep breath. *Not now. I've got some other work to do.*

After spending an hour in the car that felt like a bad road trip, she drove into her reserved spot and sat for a moment. Naturally, she left her umbrella in the office the day before. *Good place for an umbrella.*

Lindsay waited a second longer hoping for a break in the rain, but it gained momentum instead. Knowing that sitting in the car all day was not an option, she increased the speed of tapping her fingers on the steering wheel. Looking at her vacant left ring finger, she refused to think about it. *Really, right now? Love, commitment, age...who cares? It's all part of the same movie.*

Rather than endorsing a frivolous rant, she stopped herself, redirecting her mind to the good in her life. *Ah, the power of gratitude!* She was Vice President and Legal Counsel for the firm she loved, made a better than decent living, and bought anything she wanted, well almost anything.

And, enough of the positive self-talk. It's just annoying and all over the map. God, make up your mind. She yanked on the car door, grabbed her stuff, and made a run for it, with her raincoat flapping open all the way. *Ugh, winter.*

Little did she know it was the beginning of a rotten day that would change everything. And, it would affect everyone she cared about.

CHAPTER 2

Lindsay entered the foyer of the office building, pausing long enough to run her fingers through the front of her damp hair. She looked up and abruptly stopped when she saw him. Her mouth gaped open and she blinked hard. It took a second to figure out what was happening. *Oh please, no.*

She stepped in front of him. "No, please tell me no," she whispered, shaking her head from side to side.

He glanced up long enough to say, "Lindsay, I'm sorry." But, he didn't look her in the eyes and he always looked her in the eyes. "I promise you, it isn't what it…"

"Sir, let's keep moving," the twenty something police officer demanded.

The cop placed a hand on his back, giving him a slight nudge towards the door. He was led out of the building in handcuffs and sandwiched between an officer that looked barely out of high school and an overweight amazon that stood about seven feet tall. There was no conversation, just directing him through the door.

Lindsay turned and watched him leave, staring while the officer guided him into the back of the police car. She froze. Her mouth remained open, but no words came out. *This cannot be happening. How could he?*

She had believed in him, trusted him, protected him. He couldn't possibly have done this. Committed such a dreadful crime. Lindsay was wrong. And, she had never even considered it.

Her legs were weak. Forcing her feet to move a few steps, she dropped into a nearby chair in the lobby. Thinking back over the past year and a half, she couldn't believe she had missed the signs. With the emergence of the crystal ball, Lindsay realized the signs had been there all along.

Sitting on that wooden chair, she started to figure it out, remembering details, some related and others not so much. It went something like this.

CHAPTER 3

Several months earlier, spring was turning to summer and the sky was what some basketball enthusiasts might call Carolina blue. Lindsay was racing to work with the top down on her caspian blue metallic convertible, with the sun in her face and no humidity. Feeling the freedom of driving too fast in the open air and soaking in euphoric thoughts of what the summer might bring consumed her. *Someone really needs to figure out how to bottle that stuff.*

It was only a fleeting moment quickly overtaken by thoughts of the office. She hated when that happened. Her firm was in trouble, not a slow period, but actual trouble. They failed to meet planned revenue over the past couple of years, and drastically so over the last four quarters. Future projections looked even worse and their biggest competitor was obtaining design contracts they were accustomed to winning. Not only were they in danger of losing their status as a premier Architecture and Engineering firm, but their future existence was in question.

This led to insane pressure that brought out the worst in people from impatience, to altercations, to creating alliances against one another. It was easy to work together when there weren't difficult decisions to make, when money was flowing. Not anymore. Colleagues that were normally laid back and calm had become edgy and blamed others for budget problems. There were fewer times when the executive team laughed together or offered their assistance, like great teams do.

Until lately, there had been enough money to go around. There were lunches, coffee together, and even happy hours for the closest few. No real conflict or need to pass judgment, until things were different. No one was safe and they were likely to all be looking for jobs.

Lindsay Thompson was not going to let that happen. But, what was she going to do about it?

CHAPTER 4

Lindsay walked past the information desk and waved to the receptionist behind it. Alice had been there since Lindsay started working in the building. She knew about her children, her husband, and where and when they vacationed. She even knew they had a four year old golden retriever named Maddy that Alice said loved her more than her kids ever did. Her job didn't pay much more than minimum wage, but her family depended on that money.

She continued walking and glanced to the left at the Cafe Bar, the place of many enjoyable hours with friends and colleagues, talking about work, vacations, or the latest family saga. She engaged in conversation with the baristas, knowing about their college classes, romances, and sometimes heartbreaks.

Even the building held special memories. She loved this old restored warehouse that was considered chic these days. It had character, charm, and sometimes felt more like home than her own condo.

These were all constants she had become accustomed to and grown to love. Being anywhere else or losing it all was not an option.

She took the stairs and walked the long way around yearning to experience the creativity happening around her. There were architects working alone at their drafting boards, while others gathered around conference tables critiquing their designs. Some were scurrying, tablets in hand, and running to meetings with clients to discuss their requirements. The energy could be amazing. *How long would it last?*

CHAPTER 5

There were several examples of life changing before Lindsay could ever make it to her office. Her first encounter was at one of the senior executive's offices. She hesitated at the sound of loud voices booming behind Peter's office door. How could she possibly hear voices from behind a two inch thick, solid wooden walnut door? She paused.

"Tone it down, now. No one needs to hear this." The sound of Peter's voice trailing off. Peter Livingston was the Senior VP in charge of the Architectural Design Division, a position he assumed early in his career. He was a young and talented architect, highly regarded and continually sought after by their competitors. He had more than a little ego, but age and time had tempered him.

He was struggling just like everyone else after experiencing years of creating without concern for cash. Things were different now and he was the leader that had to figure out how to adjust and change the culture. Influencing these innovative architects to think about budget as much as their design work was going to be a tall order for creative minds.

The arguing voice was definitely Tom, with a sharp arrogance that was unmistakable and more than a little irritating. Another top notch talented architect that was stolen away from a competing firm. Unfortunately, it didn't take long to diagnose that he wasn't great with people and needed work on his interpersonal skills.

The door was slightly ajar and Lindsay couldn't help but hear Tom's continued rant over funding for their latest design project only to be interrupted by Peter's voice. "I am sorry. I understand how you feel. I'm having a tough time myself. But, you've got to scale it back. The design is too elaborate for the money."

"I took this job because you guys were cutting edge and now we're stifling and becoming mediocre. A baby panda could create these designs."

Starting to feel intrusive but leaning in even closer, Lindsay touched the wall to make sure she didn't fall in the doorway. She could see half of Peter's face and could hear his voice slowing and the volume increasing. "Tom, we talked about this last week. Didn't the Johnson Project mean anything to you? You're lucky to still have a job. I had to do some fast talking to defend you. I won't keep doing that."

Tom shifted into focus and she could see a scowl on his face and the coloring of a deep ruby bordeaux. Even the veins in his neck were bulging. "What do you mean, I'm lucky to have a job? I work hard for this firm. I could have worked for any firm, anywhere, and I chose here."

Peter put his hand up to stop Tom. "I'm not disputing that you work hard. Listen, we lost the Johnson contract because Claxton bid half the price. And, why was that?"

"They'll be sorry when they realize the design wasn't very good. They'll see."

"They may or may not. At least, they think it's good enough at this point. And, that's what matters most right now."

"Peter, come on. You know that cutting costs in design isn't the answer. It has to come from somewhere else. Otherwise, we'll be marginalized."

"If you have any ideas, I would love to hear them."

"I'll tell you our problem. We have too much overhead allocated to our rates. We might as well add the coffee barista to our pool. Everybody's talking about it. We're not competitive anymore," Tom stated flatly.

Peter raised his voice, "In this case, it was our over-designing and not providing the client what they wanted. Our arrogance. Thinking we know what they need more than they do. Clients want buildings that are functional and affordable, and still look pristine and spectacular. It's up to us to determine how to make that happen."

Lindsay had stood there long enough. Walking away, the last thing she heard was Peter saying, "Well, Tom, you need to figure it out if you want to stay with us. I think we better talk about this some other time."

CHAPTER 6

A crime. How did he get to this place? He didn't know where to begin or how to deal with it. This was completely out of his swim lane - a guy with strategic vision that could find a creative solution for just about anything, but not this. He knew exactly why. It had become personal, not a business transaction to be course corrected at a bad turn. This involved actual lives in danger, with devastating repercussions. People he loved.

He knew what he had to do. There was really only one thing. *Could he go through with it?* He had spent the entire sleeping hours rehearsing, coaching, and reminding himself of the mission. *Treat it like any other…* Then he would fall asleep and wake every couple of hours lying in sweat soaked sheets with his head throbbing like a beating heart pumping blood. Finally he rolled over and looked at his phone on the nightstand, deciding that 3:30 would have to do. The dizziness forced him to steady himself and he managed to shuffle off to the kitchen to make coffee. The pain in his head intensified, his brain reverberated against the side of his skull. He was certain it was attempting to escape. He threw back two pain relievers.

That had been the start of his day. This had to stop. *Could he actually go through with it?*

CHAPTER 7

Money stressors, high emotions, infighting, and Peter's uncharacteristic anger. Signs of eruption. The flares on full ignite mode.

Lindsay was turning the corner towards her office when she wished she had gone the other away. The longer walk would have even given her a few extra steps for the day. But no, she had to be efficient in her quest to return to her sanctuary, only to be interrupted by the least enjoyable person in the building. Jack Rolfe walked briskly in her direction, with not the slightest bit of emotion or even a head nod. *Oh great! That's all I need. Note to self, next time take the elevator.*

Without any small talk, Jack attacked, "Lindsay, have you guys finished reviewing the Stedman contract? I needed to close the deal, like yesterday."

"Hello Jack. I know we're looking at it, but my team is slammed right now. We're prioritizing some risk propositions. I'll check and get back to you."

"I would appreciate it. And, if you could speed it up, that would be great." Jack walked off as if he was in charge. He was the VP of Business Development but acted like he owned the place.

Don't mention it. I'll get right on it. Shaking her head, she continued a walk that felt like a journey all the way to her office.

Why did Jack bother her so much? She didn't know if it was his superior attitude or that he was aloof and didn't engage in conversation like normal colleagues. Just get to the point and move on was his style, and she didn't like his behavior, or care much for him.

Their last confrontation led to a meeting that should have been solved between the two of them rather than requiring the CEO to referee. Jack had sauntered into the conference room with his head held a little too high, dropping into one of the leather chairs on the opposite side of the table from Lindsay and her team. He gazed at his tablet without looking up, not speaking to anyone.

There had been back and forth discussions with the client's lawyers and it wasn't moving as quickly as anyone would have liked, especially Jack. He barked about legal reviews taking too long. Once again, he acted like the man in charge and it was insulting. Lindsay's face turned crimson but her response was deliberate, in a flat tone with no inflection. "We're having a difficult time coming to agreement on A&E liability requirements for the design effort. The client is squeamish and we're going back and forth to get the language right. We just can't accept more accountability and responsibility than we should."

Jack grimaced and looked at David. "We can't lose this client. I say, we let the language go. Accept what they want. When was the last time we were sued for a faulty design? We better start taking risk or we'll be irrelevant in the market."

She looked from Jack to David and back to Jack. Her tone was firm when she said, "Jack, this isn't a risk worth taking. I'm not signing off on it. One false move and we could bankrupt the firm."

Jack erupted, as he leaned back in his chair and waved his arms in the air. "Bankrupt the firm? Are you kidding me? We're going to bankrupt the firm if we don't change the way we approach these deals. You guys are way too conservative for today's market. You'll cause us to lose any competitive edge we have left."

David leaned in Jack's direction and folded his arms on the table. "Calm down and listen carefully. We've always paid attention to legal ramifications of our firm's actions. That is not going to change. We will continue to manage risk, and this is high risk. I'm good with radical and fresh, but not at the expense of the firm's liability."

Jack started to speak and David interrupted. "I've made up my mind. I don't want to talk about this anymore. Lindsay will let you know when the language is finalized. You can close the loop with the client then." He placed his palms on the table and stood, signaling the meeting was over.

Jack remained quiet until he reached the door. He turned, saying, "We're going to lose this client, and in this climate we can't afford it." He walked out leaving the others standing.

Knowing David all too well, Lindsay nodded for her team to leave the room. The second the door was shut, he focused his attention on her. "Are you sure we're doing the right thing with this contract language? Not being overly cautious or too conservative?"

Lindsay shook her head from side to side. "David, trust me on this. There are some screwy provisions the client wants to include. They don't want to accept responsibility for anything. I would never sign off on this type of liability. That's not taking risk, it's stupidity."

David's assistant walked to the door. Nodding at her to give him a minute, he responded quietly, "Okay. I'm counting on you to do the right thing. Keep me in the loop." He looked at his watch and swiftly exited.

And that was the end of it. The encounter felt like ages ago and working with Jack had only gotten worse. So, there were fights between her and Jack, Peter and Tom, and that was just for starters.

This was going to be a long day. What else could go wrong?

CHAPTER 8

Lindsay barely stepped through her office doorway before quickly removing her suit jacket and draping it over her right arm. She didn't break stride as she spoke to her assistant on the way to the inner sanctum of her office. She hung her jacket on the door and glanced at her desk cluttered with phone message slips and two contracts awaiting her approval. She frowned at the work before sitting in her oversized leather chair, opening one of the contract files.

Marcy peered in the doorway, "Well, hello to you too. Are you okay this morning?"

She looked up with a smile and said, "I'm sorry. Yeah, I'm fine. Just too much craziness going on."

"Anything I can do?"

Looking back down at the file, she asked, "Do you have several million dollars stashed that we can throw into the firm's coffers?"

"No offense, dear, but I would be on some tropical island sipping an umbrella drink if I did."

Lindsay laughed. "Yeah, me too."

"Don't forget that Tyler starts today. He should be here after 9:00. He has that employee indoctrination meeting now and then he'll be up."

Smiling big enough to brighten the room, her demeanor dramatically changed. Lindsay said, "Great. I can't wait to see him. I've missed him and I can really use his humor."

"I know. He came by to say hi this morning and he is as handsome as ever. If only he were ten years older."

"Simmer down. You're married." Lindsay continued to look at the contract file.

"A girl can dream, can't she?"

"It's probably not wise to dream about the new attorney that'll be working closely with me and you over the next, oh I don't know, several years."

"You're taking all the fun out of it." Marcy pursed her lips and teased her boss.

"Yeah, I've been told that before. And, since we're on the subject, his girlfriend might have a little something to say about that. But, I'll never tell you have a secret crush on him."

"News flash, they broke up. That little cutie is single now."

Lindsay dropped the papers and looked up. "Really, what happened? I can't believe it. They seemed so close."

"Broke up right after he interned with us over the Christmas holidays last year. He didn't say much other than, it was time. But, I'm sure he'll tell you. You know, he has a crush on you."

"Oh stop it. He does not."

"I'm fairly certain. And, you're not that much older than he is. Are you sure you want him working here, all those late nights, business dinners? Do I need to say more?"

"That's ridiculous. And, you need to stop watching soaps or reading novels or whatever it is that is filling your brain with nonsense. Now, I've got work to do."

"Something to think about." She smiled and walked back to her desk.

CHAPTER 9

He was still on the verge of becoming a criminal. No movement. No progress. No sleep.

A shower and coffee allowed him to be presentable like he belonged there. He looked and acted like everyone else, spoke to Alice at the reception desk and asked about Maddy, drank coffee with colleagues talking about the latest adventures of their kids, mentored junior staff hoping to become leaders, but now he was almost different. A person pushed.

Just like he rehearsed, he walked down the hall coaching himself all the way. *There was a good reason.* Pulling up a chair to the laptop, he logged in, fingers hovering over the keyboard, with sweaty palms and armpits. He could swear his trembling hands were cramping and the dizzying feeling was returning. He just couldn't do it. Placing his head in his hands, his body shook, and he wiped his eyes. There had to be another way.

CHAPTER 10

Peter poked his head in Lindsay's office doorway as if he was hesitant to enter. His voice was shaky when he asked, "Do you have a minute?"

Her first thought was fear until she looked up and saw his face. "Sure. Come on in, Peter." She motioned him to the couch and quickly walked from behind her desk, moving to a chair across from him.

"Lindsay, I need to talk about something."

There it was again. A split second when fear returned and flooded her mind until he reassured her with a smile and tilt of his head. He knew what she was thinking, but said nothing.

"What's on your mind?" she asked, crossing her legs and leaning slightly forward.

Lindsay and Peter had a connection, sometimes sharing more than any human should have to endure. A year earlier, Peter's son had unsuccessfully attempted to end his life, but the danger always lingered. He battled with severe depression and it was never far from Peter's mind. Not one day passed without worry.

At first, Peter didn't tell anyone but Lindsay. Hours spent behind her closed office door sharing tears and personal terror. This life-altering struggle, constant fear of what could still be, and the firm's future spinning out of control led to a bond that evolved into one safe enough to be vulnerable and talk about almost anything. But this day was about work.

"I'm having issues with my architects. I hate to even admit it. My best are acting like their designs are majestic creations for the Queen's Palace or an art gallery. And, funding restrictions are a personal attack."

Lindsay studied him for a second before confession time. "I was walking by your office and I heard the exchange between you and Tom. I have to admit, it was so loud that I stopped. I overheard part of what was said."

"Quite a moment. My guys want to design like money is no object. Tom and his team quoted a price for that admin building on 5th Street. Bottom line, it took three times as long, cost twice as much, and we had to bill the client the full amount. As you can imagine, that didn't go well. He is lucky to still be employed." Peter shook his head and sighed. He looked down at the floor and Lindsay could see lines forming on his forehead. She was certain they weren't there before.

"Peter, I think we're all faced with this challenge. I'm seeing the stress, the frustration everywhere. I'm not sure how it will end or if we're even equipped to handle this environment. We've never operated under these conditions, or the conflict we're starting to experience. I'm worried about our future."

He stared at Lindsay, hesitating, slow to bring up the next topic. He finally said, "Yeah, I don't know what to do about it. Speaking of conflict, I have to tell you what I heard. It involves you."

"What is it?"

"I wasn't sure whether I should talk about it or not, but you're my friend and you have a right to know."

"Please go on," she said in a measured tone.

"I was in a meeting with Bob Lowery and that new VP of Operations, Eleanor." He glanced around the room, letting out a deep breath before looking back at her. He said, "They were quick to bash your staff and the legal review process. They blamed lost work on what they called missed opportunities, saying we've lost our edge, and we're afraid of taking risks. I tried to diffuse to smart risk management, but Eleanor didn't want to hear any of it and shifted her focus to me. No telling what she is saying about the designers. She sure is making enemies quickly."

"So, let me get this right. You're saying she is bashing my Department for protecting this firm?" Lindsay felt the heat rise up her neck all the way to the top of her head.

Peter paused before telling her the rest, but Lindsay had the right to know. He said quietly, "And, specifically you."

Stunned, this was the first time she experienced an actual personal attack, or at least one she knew about. This certainly was a new operating environment. "I can't believe Bob went along with it. I know he is frustrated, but I expect a little more from him. He should have talked directly to me if he had an issue with my Department."

"It wasn't so much Bob. I had the feeling he just didn't want to go against Eleanor. They appeared to be chummy. Creepy. Anyway, his comments were fairly benign, but it was obvious he had concerns about speed." Peter glanced towards the door before looking back at Lindsay. He said, "Outside of Evil Eleanor, I think this is just a symptom of a bigger problem."

Lindsay sat back in her chair and smiled. "You did not just call her evil Eleanor."

"What?" With the mischievous grin of an innocent little boy, he continued, "I'm just playing, but she is a piece of work."

"And, you're just what I need today."

"Glad I could help since I am the bearer of the gossip. You gotta laugh about this stuff. But, it is too much negativity, change, too fast."

"You're right," she said, shaking her head. "It's a shame we're in this predicament, but we are where we are and we'll just have to adjust."

"There are too many of these smearing campaigns going on throughout our executive team, about each other. We didn't use to do that." He shook his head and looked towards the outer office. "Like you said the other day, we don't know how to deal with conflict. Heck, we've never had any."

"I know. I'm concerned too. I even spoke to David and he intends to take this on. His next move should be interesting." There was a moment of silence before she asked, "How is James doing?"

"Good today. We're still holding on to one day at a time." He walked towards the door and stopped, looked back at her and let out a deep breath. "One day at a time."

CHAPTER 11

A young man pristinely dressed in a Brooks Brothers suit and light blue tie highlighting deep sapphire eyes peeked his head in Lindsay's doorway. His dark hair was slightly flipped at the forehead and those eyes were shining like the high beams on a very fine automobile. "Hi Boss. Are you busy?"

"Tyler, come in." Lindsay smiled wide as she hurried from behind her desk. "Welcome back. I'm so happy to see you."

He grinned and walked to her. "It's good to see you. I've missed you."

"I have missed you. I've been looking forward to having you back with us. How was the orientation?" She continued without taking a breath, "Like you really needed it, but you know, it's part of the process. Please sit down."

He unbuttoned his jacket and waited for her to sit before taking the chair across from her. "Orientation was good. I knew most of what they were talking about, but I had the chance to meet the other new hires. I'm already having lunch with one of them. She wasn't a summer or Christmas hire, so this is really new for her."

"Her. Is she attractive?" Lindsay teased, with a familiarity she wouldn't use with anyone else.

"Now Boss, you know I'm not paying attention to that kind of thing. I hardly noticed. I'm here to work and launch my career into success," he said, lifting his head in an air of superiority. Then he grinned and said, "She is gorgeous."

"Uh huh. Now, that's the Tyler I remember. Glad you haven't lost your touch."

"I hope not. But, she is really nice too. An accountant starting in the Comptroller shop. I think I'll also ask this new guy in design engineering to join us. It's a little unnerving when you don't know anyone."

"Do these people have names?"

"Chelsea Egan and Bradley Thomas. They both have some strong credentials. We hit it off right away. I liked them immediately. Our new hire class is outstanding. I'm excited about it."

"Well, if they're anything like you, then we've done very well."

They spent the next half hour talking over coffee and catching up. Tyler had worked with them over Christmas and summer holidays for the past three years, and during the last one, he was offered a job predicated on passing the bar exam. When he received the results, he called Lindsay, and the HR Department contacted him to report to work.

Marcy knocked on the door and poked her head inside, "Lindsay, your calendar says David in fifteen minutes - no subject."

"Thanks Marcy. Will you take Tyler to his new office, please?" Lindsay stood and continued talking to him. "You'll work with Eric and your office is the one next to his. Your nameplate is already in place." She smiled and grabbed her jacket from behind the door. She turned to look at him and said, "And Tyler, I am so excited to have you here."

He turned his head sideways. He started to say something, but stopped and said, "I'm beyond thankful for this opportunity. Working with you is a dream come true for me."

"You've earned this job. Let me know if there is anything I can do to help you," she said as they walked out together. "Let's do lunch later this week. I want to hear how things are going."

CHAPTER 12

A partially collapsed building can ruin a day. As Lindsay walked in the direction of David's office, she thought about the infighting and some leaders having their own silos and self-interests, and caring about little outside of that. And, the latest news, a partially collapsed building on 2nd Street that a construction company blamed on their design. Even if they were on solid ground, court was risky and they didn't have the money to throw into a long, drawn out legal battle.

Enough was enough. Not wanting to fall into the drama queen trap, she cautioned her mind to slow down, but that only lasted a second. They were in deep trouble. *Calm down and breathe in, breathe out. Breathe in, breathe out. It's amazing what a few breaths will do. Now - drama aside. This will not happen and doors will not close if Lindsay Thompson has anything to do with it.*

The timing wasn't the best to work on transforming a culture, communication, or other emotional skills, but it didn't matter. They had to do something and the first step was David.

There was no one waiting outside of his inner office so she poked her head in, asking to enter. His slight smile and nod were permission enough.

She eased in the chair in front of his desk and let him know her lawyers were working on the collapsed building. "Tom and the team are standing by our design. Eric and I called the construction company's attorney and they are still saying it has to be our liability. We'll play it out in third party, maybe even court."

"Okay. Game on. Any other good news?"

She cleared her throat and said, "I'm hesitant to bring it up. I know it's not the best time to deal with it, but it can't wait."

He removed his reading glasses, rubbed his eyes, and sat back in his chair. She had his attention.

"David, we've got to do something about our culture. It's changing, even moving in the direction of toxic. Colleagues are starting to argue, blame, and talk about each other," Lindsay said. "We're not working together or collaborating the way we should."

"I'm listening," David said cautiously.

"Our financial problems are changing everything. Peter's designers aren't adjusting to the budget limitations we're imposing. Bob and Eleanor are starting to blame everybody else for anything and everything. Their new alliance is an interesting twist. I don't even want to know what's going on there." Lindsay said in mild disgust and rolled her eyes. She continued, "And now, there is internal fighting about our latest tragic event. A building collapses in what will likely become an expensive lawsuit."

She hesitated before saying more, "I'm not trying to be melodramatic here, but if we don't get our act in order, this behavior will destroy us."

"I know. I've seen it too. Money certainly has the power to change things. I was hoping we would adjust and settle in."

Lindsay leaned in and looked directly into David's eyes. "I adore this firm," she said, accompanied by a smile, "and most of the people in it." Then she hesitated, taking her eyes off David and staring out the window. Her mouth quivered and she took a deep breath and said in a low tone, "It's my life. I don't want to see anything happen to us. We have to do something before it's too late."

He started to comment about her life but changed his mind. Instead, he said, "It couldn't be a worse time, but I agree. As you like to say, hope is not a strategy. I have an idea. Do you have time to talk?"

"Sure. I'm free the rest of the day."

"Good, then let's get to it." He stepped from behind his desk and motioned her to his conference table. He poured them both a coffee and they sat down to work.

They spent the next hour formulating a plan to alter the degrading atmosphere. When they were done, David pushed back his chair and stretched his legs out in front of him. He said, "You know, it's comforting to focus on something we actually have some control over. I think this can work. Or I should say, it has to work."

Lindsay shook her head in agreement, but said, "This isn't going to be an easy fix. It's just the beginning."

"I know. But it is a start."

It all sounded good, but nothing could prepare them for what was ahead.

CHAPTER 13

It was practically dark when Lindsay headed back down the hall to where she spent most of her waking hours. She wandered around telling herself she was getting in a few extra steps and adjusted her eyes to the diminished lighting and sprinkling of illumination that looked like bathroom night lights. Offices dark, cubicles empty, almost everyone else had departed to be with their families. It was past any normal human being's dinner time when she reached her office.

The day had sucked the life out of her and she plopped in her chair, the leather swishing under the weight of her trim body. She frowned at the noise. There was nothing left to do about the collapsed building or fixing their problems except to wait on results. Not one of Lindsay's strengths.

Glancing at her phone, she knew she should have somewhere to go, something to do. This had become a habit.

She did what Lindsay did best, shifting her thoughts away from herself. It was easier that way and she had more important things to think about. Work needed her undivided attention.

She was struck by her most senior colleagues lack of basic interpersonal skills. It hadn't been all that noticeable until the game changed. *High powered executives acting like children, really?*

How far would they let it go? Would they allow the firm to bankrupt rather than take a hard look at reductions that might impact their Departments? Would they protect their own interests at the expense of the firm? Would they be authentic about a mutual purpose, the common goal(s)? Bottom line - could they put the firm's interests first?

Lindsay didn't like the answer she came up with and couldn't shake the feeling they were heading down a spiraling path. She was convinced they better learn how to improve their relationships and make the hard decisions together. They lacked teamwork, had ineffective communication skills, had a problem with trust, and the list continued. The stakes were high, and they were likely to have winners and losers.

The only thing for certain, they were not wasting any more time. Otherwise, they might as well turn off the lights and close the doors. They had a plan and they were putting it in motion. Soon. Very soon.

CHAPTER 14

Lindsay had fallen in love with the firm the first time she walked through the glass doors of the front entryway. Back then, the atmosphere brimmed with electricity, cutting edge creativity, and innovation.

A collection of design renderings of arenas, town centers, medical facilities, and malls no longer in business were displayed throughout the hallways and offices. They were proudly displayed with the firm's logo and design date imprinted on the bottom right corner. Basic designs, sexy designs, and those that resembled creations of art.

She would never forget that first meeting with David Thurmond, the CEO of the Company. Walking into his office, the first thing she noticed was his smile and spectacular white teeth. He was distinguished looking with slight graying hair and light brown eyes that sparkled behind the latest style in reading glasses.

Lindsay was nervous, thinking he wouldn't possibly hire someone so young for his top legal position. Even with an outstanding resume and interning under some of the finest law firms in the country, she was a long shot. But, she was not one to shy away from a challenge.

All that fear dissipated in the first five minutes together. They shared similar philosophies about leadership, business and success. David wasn't afraid of age or anything else. He called her the next day and she never looked back. Her amazing professional life more than compensated for the holes in her personal life. You can't have everything.

That first meeting was so long ago and things had changed. She didn't know when, but somewhere along the way it did. The electricity or energy or cutting edge was replaced by business challenges.

Hearing a slight audible rap on the door, Lindsay turned to find Tyler Hayes standing before her. "Hi Tyler. Come on in. How was your first day?"

"Incredible. I'm doing some research for Eric on this collapsed building fiasco. I just wanted to stop by and say thanks again for this opportunity. Lindsay, I never dreamed I would become part of your legal team."

"You've earned it. That's why being an outstanding intern is so important. We get to try you out before actually hiring you." Lindsay smiled at him.

"I know. You always told me that, but I didn't realize exactly what that meant, until now." He hesitated, leaving a second of silence between them. He continued, "It's getting late and I saw your light on so I thought I would stop by. Are you heading home soon?"

"Yeah, I was reminiscing about this place." Lindsay motioned for him to take a seat.

"If you don't mind my asking, what about it?"

"I was remembering the time David told me about the firm's history and his evolution to CEO. It had been a hugely successful Architect and Engineering Firm. His father started it some 50 years earlier with a college buddy, Michael Hollingsworth. The partnership was a winning team until Mr. Hollingsworth's accidental death."

"I've seen the huge portrait of him in the lobby. He must have been special because it looks more like a mural than a picture."

"It was a huge loss that affected their entire family. Mr. Hollingsworth devoted his life to the firm and that family. He never married and treated David like the son he would never have. Even back then, they had plans for David."

"It must be epic to walk into a successful career and not even have to worry about job hunting after college. Even though I thought I might get this one, it was still stressful. I have friends that can't get jobs."

"I'm not sure David would see it that way. It was a long road to get to where he is today. After Mr. Hollingsworth's death, David's father was consumed with work. He rationalized that he owed it to Hollingsworth and his family. To leave a legacy. He spent most of his time away from them and negotiating the next big deal, and then one day, his priorities shifted. He said he wanted to spend more time with them and needed a rest."

"Then, David became the CEO?"

"His father retired and relinquished the helm to David."

"One day his dad retires and he becomes the CEO. Wow, that's awesome."

"It didn't work like that. His father was not willing to give him anything. After graduation from college, he had to work in the mail room, marketing, sales, and finance until he finally worked his way up to CFO. His father made him remain in the CFO executive leadership position for years to gain experience." Lindsay smiled at Tyler before continuing, "Then, the magic happened. He decided David was ready. It was a day that made his father very proud, turning his life's work over to his son. He made David Thurmond the CEO of Thurmond & Hollingsworth."

"I'm sure it was hard work, but it sounds like a sweet deal."

"Yes, I guess you can say it's a sweet deal." They were quiet until Lindsay broke the silence between them. "Tyler, you don't need to work this late. You should be out having fun. Enjoying your life."

"I'm enjoying myself here. And, I don't have anywhere I have to be tonight. But, that's a story for another time. Thanks for telling me about the history of the firm."

"You're welcome. Now, get out of here. Go have some fun with friends."

"Are you okay?"

"I'm fine." She hesitated and said, "But thank you for asking."

"Yes ma'am. I'll see you tomorrow." Tyler picked up his briefcase and jacket and walked to the door. "Lindsay, I think I have a sweet deal, too. Thank you." He smiled and threw his jacket over his shoulder before walking out.

Lindsay smiled, nodded and watched Tyler leave. He was going to be a rising star, adding a little flair to the office. Over the summers and holidays, his work ethic, energy and passion had proven he was a perfect fit for them. He was exactly what they needed, and what she needed.

CHAPTER 15

It was the perfect time to commit a crime, if there was such a thing. Most offices were empty and there wasn't much traffic at that hour. He walked slowly to the computer screen. He had to make the withdrawal. He had resigned himself to the fact that he had to have the money. There was no alternative. This was much more than desperation. He took in a deep breath and let it out slowly while closing his eyes.

Yes, I can do it. He sat at the desk and entered numbers and letters to get into the financial system. He entered the transaction, the withdrawal, but could not bring himself to press the submit button. He stared at it and couldn't move. *What was he going to do? He had to do it.*

His heart was pounding and perspiration escaped through every pore in his body. The room was void of oxygen and he thought he was on the verge of fainting. He clumsily undid his tie and removed his jacket, letting it fall onto the floor.

He couldn't go through with it. There had to be another way. He pressed "logout" and stood up. He needed air. *Was this what a heart attack felt like?*

CHAPTER 16

Lindsay was alone with nothing but an incessant flow of thoughts when she heard a noise. Not a loud boom, but enough that it took her out of her head space. The first inclination was to go on an exploration, but she opted out, passing it off as building creaks, and her own paranoia.

Returning to her nostalgic journey, her mind went to David. A caring, dedicated leader that wanted people to enjoy work, find meaning, and experience accomplishment and success together. His life was about connection, relationship building, and communicating - critical attributes they all better find for the challenges ahead.

His presence in Lindsay's life took on many forms that included father figure, mentor, friend, or anything else she needed. A conversation early on in their relationship remained engrained in her memory. They had been alone in his office after everyone else left for the day, and she was doing something she rarely did, opening up and displaying vulnerability instead of her usual outward display of confidence.

David's response was exactly what she needed at one of those most exposed times. He told her she was firm and tough minded when the situation required unwavering strength, but there was another side. Gentle, capable of empathy and compassion, and being a caring and trusting friend. She could accomplish just about anything she set her mind to do. God, she needed to hear that, like an echo from her own father so many years earlier.

That conversation led to a question. Simple question really. An answer she hoped she already knew. "Some would say I'm too young and inexperienced to be your Chief General Counsel, but you took a chance on me. Why?"

"I just knew. We clicked and I saw your potential. I loved your style, your confidence, your intelligence. It felt right and I recognized you had talent that I wanted on our team."

Her relationship with David matured into trusted colleagues, and over time, she became one of the most influential of the executives on the team. She smiled at the endearing feelings of him having that level of confidence in her, in spite of the early office criticisms of not hiring someone with more experience. That all dissipated when they got to know her. They, too, were taken in by her capacity and capability. A powerfully striking woman with an aura of confidence, a commanding presence. They understood.

But it was his friendship…This one time, the most tragic moment in her life and he was there. Every day along that painful journey when she didn't believe in her ability to get on with it, he was there. The time her one true love had almost killed her.

Lindsay teared as she recalled the years with the man she was set to marry. The words from her loving partner burned into her soul. He told her she exuded sexy when she tossed back her head and ran her slender fingers through the front of her long blonde, silky hair. He adored that. And then there were her eyes. Her icy blues were intense and could burn a hole through any subject. Her deep gaze into his eyes made him feel he mattered, and that he was the most important thing to her. And, he was.

He said there was so much more to notice about her than her stunning, physical beauty. She had a presence, a charisma with quick wit, and a genuine likability. Everyone fell a little in love with her. That's what he said. *She didn't actually believe it, but she would give anything to hear him say it again.*

Remembering his face and those words caused a sick feeling in the pit of her stomach. *Why was she thinking about him so much on this day? She had been doing better. She had to stop.*

Taking off her reading glasses, she rubbed her damp eyes. She was tired, her head hurt, and her stomach ached. She looked at her watch and jumped, almost forgetting the date. Having to hustle to make it in time, she grabbed her purse and briefcase, and rushed out, slamming the door behind her.

Weaving in and out of traffic, she had a little over an hour to get home and do something with her hair and makeup, and maybe rationalize some reason to cancel. *For pity's sake, why did she let Patrick talk her into this?*

CHAPTER 17

Patrick Stephenson had a way of talking Lindsay into almost anything. Her closest confidante at work knew most of her secrets and every vulnerability trigger. His sensitivity and sensibility saved her more times than she could count, through the good and the bad.

He was the Comptroller and had been with the company longer than anyone except David. Approaching fifty without looking his age, whatever that means today, Patrick was tall and slender with silver gray hair, like a star in one of those gambling movies in Vegas. He was jokingly called the silver fox. While his look was conservative, he was far from it when it came to having fun. She smiled until she thought…

Back to the date. She met him at a dinner party hosted by Patrick and his wife, Stephanie. Ron was his name. His wife had died many years earlier and he never remarried, or dated much. He appeared nice enough, kind of cute. He had a paying job and that was always a plus.

They sort of hit it off. *Thanks to Patrick for too much pushing.* It was somewhere in between the main course, a little more wine than normal, or dessert and coffee that it happened. He asked her out for dinner and she reluctantly said yes. Now, it was time for the date and it was about the last thing she wanted to do. She needed a plan - early night, have dinner and say goodbye. Date over. Yes, that's how she would play it.

After fighting the traffic and speeding most of the way home, and cursing herself, she arrived at the front entrance of her condo, parked the car out front by the curb and took her time getting into the house. She would die for a nice bath, a glass of wine, salad, and an early turn in. Instead, it was a quick refresh of hair and makeup. She did a double take at her hair refusing to cooperate. Frowning in the mirror, she turned off the bathroom light. She wasn't trying to impress him anyway. *Less complicated that way.*

She got back in the car and applied lipstick before starting the engine. Hesitating before putting the car in drive, she groaned, *Patrick, you are a dead man.*

Lindsay agreed to meet Ron at "The Coastal Grille". There was no way she was letting him pick her up. It was a short drive, could be a quick dinner, and back home in an hour and a half. Of course, there was a glass of wine before dinner. Maybe two hours - tops. Maybe she shouldn't drink.

The restaurant, owned by one of her best friends, Sam, was a perfect place to meet up with a stranger. The interior was open, lively, and slightly noisy. It could drown out their talking, if it became too boring.

She arrived promptly at 7:00 and Ron was already there, waiting at the entrance. He smiled and greeted her before slightly touching her elbow to lead her into the restaurant. The touch bothered Lindsay.

They waited briefly before being called to their table. In a polite and gentlemanly manner, he held her chair for her. *That wasn't horrible, she thought.*

The minute her posterior touched down on the seat, the evening turned to disaster. For the next hour and a half, he talked nonstop about his deceased wife. Everything they ordered had a corresponding comment about her likes and dislikes. If they didn't discuss her, her life, dress, food, taste, then he talked about himself.

This was the last thing Lindsay needed after a grueling day at the office. The tedious one sided conversation added to her exhaustion and she could barely keep her eyes open. *What had she been thinking?*

By the time, he got around to asking her about herself, she was too exhausted and too disinterested to talk. She attempted to hide her lack of interest by saying she had an early day and needed to get home.

She insisted on splitting the bill. There would be no second date. *There shouldn't have been a first one.*

They walked out together and by the body language of her departure, she was certain he realized it hadn't gone well. She was out before they had a chance for any conversation. Before he could ask to call her, Lindsay was in her car and speeding off. *Patrick was going to hear about this. He was going to pay.*

CHAPTER 18

Lindsay woke the next day feeling annoyed and wasn't sure why. Actually, she knew exactly why. All the nonsense connected to dating and relationships was ridiculous. She was too busy for it. And, she liked living to her own schedule, eating when and what she wanted, executing television preferences with the remote solely in her possession, and no one offering unsolicited advice or telling her what to do. No need for compromise.

Focusing on work was the solution. She was better at that anyway. The office was the place she felt most useful and helpful to other people. The place she could actually make a difference in other's lives. *Yes, she would focus on work. Keep it simple.*

Vowing to ratchet up her level of workaholic behavior even more, she pulled into her parking space and checked her phone one more time before entering the building. Coffee would have to wait.

There was no way she would accept failure. Dropping her things off at her office, Lindsay headed to see David. The firm's survival would become her purpose.

She knocked lightly before entering through the open door. He was sitting at his conference table peering over handwritten notes from their last meeting when he looked up and motioned her over.

Smiling and removing his reading glasses, he asked, "How was your date?"

"Ugh. Don't ask," she groaned and frowned.

"What was wrong with this one?" he teased.

"For your information, he talked about his deceased wife the entire time. It was not me this time." She flopped in the chair next to him.

"Ooh, that's bad."

"Yes, it is. And, I don't want to talk about it. I am focusing on my work from now on." She held her head up high and opened her notepad and put on her glasses.

"Of course you are." He had a serious look on his face and started to say more, but sensed it was not a good idea. Studying her for a moment, he went on, "I did a lot of thinking about our last meeting. Let's talk about the possibilities."

Relieved, she leaned in closer and nodded in agreement. They exchanged ideas and spent the remainder of time searching for answers, nirvana, the silver bullet, the next great transformation, the exhaustive number of fads, and something more basic that could end up being so much more complex. One persistent day at a time, one day after another until...

They were definitely going on the offensive.

CHAPTER 19

Lindsay left David's office and practically ran into the door frame, walking and glancing down at her phone. Spotting a text from Patrick, she passed her office and kept going to the other end of the building.

They had corner offices at the opposite ends of the square. It wasn't a long hike or anything like that, but one would have to actually commit to take the time and effort to speak face to face. That would be a stretch for work environments that launch written words over neighboring cubicles and use all forms of social media for efficiency, responsiveness or the avoidance of contact, until they drive a wedge in actual connection. *Just crazy. Just wait.*

She spoke to Patrick's assistant, who motioned her in while picking up a ringing telephone. Lindsay and Patrick rarely waited to be announced to each other unless someone else was occupying space in their domain. They had that kind of familiarity and relationship.

"Do you want to go for coffee? I have a couple of things. And I need to hear about Andrew and basketball. I've been thinking about him lately."

"Sounds good. I want to hear about your date with Ron. You went out last night, didn't you?" Patrick inquired innocently while docking his phone into the charging apparatus.

"Ugh, it was awful. Let's just say, I feel like I know his dearly departed. He talked about her all night. Or, should I say two hours that felt like all night. Why didn't you tell me he is still living in the past?"

"I didn't know. He hasn't talked about her in my company. I don't even remember her name."

Lindsay rolled her eyes, "Sara. Her name was Sara. He is definitely not ready to date. I felt kind of sorry for him. Anyway, he is not my type, so it worked out fine. Now, can we go for coffee and forget about Ron, please?"

He smiled and she knew what he was thinking, but threw her hand up before he could pepper her with comments. He shook his head and stepped out of his office to hand Nancy a document and let her know he was leaving. While they discussed an upcoming schedule change, Lindsay glanced around his office for the hundredth time.

It had a masculine flavor with pictures of pristine golf courses across the country. His bookshelves were lined with photos of his wife and son on a golf course, at the beach, or posing for a professional photographer. Lindsay couldn't stop herself from wondering how that would feel. Who was she kidding? *God, she was all over the map.*

CHAPTER 20

The lobby was a perfect example of craftsmanship connecting to art, possessing deliberate and precise nuances, and a penetrating light flowing from floor to ceiling windows on all sides. Lindsay looked up at the skylights letting in the natural illumination and prisms of color bursting across the top of the renovated warehouse Thurmond & Hollingsworth had created.

The Cafe Bar occupied a third of the space, to left of the main entrance. Lindsay loved the feel, the dark wood, recessed ceiling lights sprinkled with a few teardrops dangling, and the cozy decor displaying small round tables and other pieces of furniture arranged in conversation areas. Her favorite spot was sitting by the fireplace in one of the two overstuffed chairs to the right and left, rarely free during the fall and winter months.

The appearance was not unlike most coffee shops, but this one had special purpose for her. The place she shared real conversations about life and work with the people she cared about. Being coffee junkies, she and Patrick used it as their gathering haven to talk about life events, and good, not so good, and personal things.

Her order was a simple black coffee they poured while she paid. Patrick had to wait until the barista shouted out, "caramel macchiato, skinny with whip creme" to this grown middle-aged businessman. Lindsay smiled as Patrick grabbed the cup.

"What? I'm comfortable with my manhood. In fact, my wife finds it kind of …"

"Oh God, please." She held up her hand. Lindsay adored him.

They met shortly after her graduation from law school, introduced by a mutual colleague at a party. There was an instant affection between them, but they didn't see each other again until years later when they began working together.

Their relationship had blossomed into a personal one almost from the start. She became close to his family and acted as a godmother to his son, Andrew. She spent many nights and weekends during the basketball season with Patrick and Stephanie cheering on their superstar and his team at the local university games.

Lindsay placed her coffee cup on the table, and watched and waited for Patrick to add something else to his drink at the bar. Before he could sit all the way down, she started talking. "I'm afraid JJ Smith is going under before they finish the sub work on the building on 10th Street." She gazed down and tapped her perfectly gel polished fingernails against the side of her cup. "We have got to stop partnering with these guys we haven't worked with before. No relationship, just low price killing us," she said, shaking her head.

"I agree, but I don't know what else to do. With the competitive playing field and our financial situation the way it is, it makes sense."

"I know. I know. I'm just venting. I didn't say I have a better solution." She looked up. "Patrick, from your perspective, how bad is it?"

"It's not great. I mean we won't close our doors tomorrow, but we could down the road if we don't make some changes. Everyone needs to understand this is serious." Patrick shifted uncomfortably in his chair before continuing, "What's the deal with this Executive Board meeting later this afternoon? Do you know anything about these changes David is talking about?"

"He doesn't like what he's seeing. All the infighting, blame being thrown around, and overall bad behavior. It was easier when we had money. Tightening the belt brings out the worst in people. He's even worried about us getting through the budget process with the stakes this high. So, he's hiring a consultant, a facilitator to work with us and work through our budget planning meeting."

"You've got to be kidding. Well, that's a waste of time and money." Patrick shook his head in disbelief. "We're executives. I think we know how to get along."

"Well, you would think, but we're not acting like it. You should hear the accusations being thrown around," Lindsay barely took a breath before continuing, "And, frankly I agree with him and helped him with the planning."

"You can't be serious, Lindsay." Patrick leaned back in his chair and looked around the room. Leaning in, he asked in a low tone, "So, what's this consultant going to do for us?"

"The normal consultant stuff that we can't do in-house. Analysis and recommendations, coaching and relationship building work, and he'll facilitate us through the budget strategy session. But, the main focus here is saving the firm."

"That must be why David's assistant called to set aside some money. I didn't think much about it. It wasn't that much, but is this really necessary? Now?"

"He was very clear that it isn't some touchy feely scheme. The guy he hired has quite a reputation."

Patrick rolled his eyes. "Who is he?"

She shrugged, "I don't know much about him, but I guess we'll know soon enough."

"I don't know about this. I think we should address our financial issues more quickly, and direct some immediate action rather than wasting time on changing culture and learning how to get along."

"Oh, I think this is exactly what we need. David isn't playing around. He will set expectations and demand change in behavior. We don't have much time to evolve. He wants change now."

"I hope it works," Patrick said with an apprehensive tone in his voice.

"It has to." Lindsay was already standing and pushing her used napkin down the rim of the paper cup. "Are you finished? I've got a meeting in a few minutes."

"I'll walk you to your office, I need to stop by and see Peter."

After Patrick left her, she started to question the way ahead. What if she and David had been wrong? Could they work together, communicate, handle difficult emotions, and save the firm?

CHAPTER 21

What did all this mean? It meant turning to the highly regarded Adam Bennington, a consultant to work on the human side of this executive team. He was hired to review their health, conduct an executive workshop focusing on tools for building and maintaining relationships, and facilitate their upcoming budget reduction strategy session to shape their future.

David met Adam prior to hiring him for this project. He read a business article about Adam's work turning around a local semi-professional basketball team with too many egos. While impressive, he wasn't ready to admit his executives needed teamwork training. After all, they were highly experienced, educated, intelligent professionals. How could they not know how to act? To get along? To be civil? Well, just look at our executive and legislative branches of the Government and you'll have your answer, he chuckled, sadly.

He was meandering through the local author section of an independent bookstore one afternoon and discovered a book written by Adam. The book was in the leadership section, but focused on people, connections, interactions, and changing lives.

An hour and a cup of coffee passed and David was still reading the book. He believed in the "softer" skills and focusing on the emotional aspects. He considered it paying attention to the most precious resource. He shared Adam's perspective that the ability to relate to people in a genuine, vulnerable way separates the good from the great. By then, he was thinking about his team.

David purchased the book after reading a third of it. He returned home to a quiet house, relieved that he could keep on reading. Grabbing a snack and a drink, he headed to the family room, with book in hand. He turned on a table lamp and sat in his favorite chair, grabbing his reading glasses and opening the book to the next chapter.

The relationship and emotionally minded focus was captivating. As he read on, he could picture some of the members of his executive team. Some good, and some not so good at the author's principles. He made notes in the margins, dog eared pages, and kept reading.

The author's approach was radically different than the traditional leadership books David read over the years. And, he had read many. The others were about learning through models, algorithms and principles. All good, just different, and times called for even more different.

Adam used a novel application as a method of learning. He told a fictional story with a mystery plot and characters to teach basic non-fiction principles associated with interpersonal skills and personal enrichment, as well as organizational behavior and development.

David reflected on the book's message after turning the last page. The principles were not designed to be complex, but they were crucial skills. Getting back to the basics - blocking and tackling. They could make the difference between being a success or failure in different walks of life, including relationships, communication, and personal health and growth. It was an intriguing style of training, and perhaps an interesting method for learning and retention.

He stared at the inside back flap, reading about the author. His wife, Alexandra walked into the room and sat down next to him. He didn't even notice until she spoke.

Puzzled, she inquired, "What have you been so engrossed in this afternoon? Must be a great read."

David smiled. "It is. I just finished a fascinating book. A very simple and fun approach to learning, with little effort, but valuable teaching on human behavior."

He handed the book to Alexandra. She flipped through the pages and understood his interest. She said, "Maybe I should read it. From just glancing through the pages, it looks like these principles can be applied to everyday life, not just business."

"That's right. As I read it with a focus on work, I found myself thinking about some of it's application to you and me. The communication and trust stuff is really good."

She smirked, "Are you saying we have communication and trust issues?"

He laughed and shook his head. "Not at all. I think we can all improve in those areas, even if we're already good at it. And, we're really good at it."

She smiled and put her arms around his neck and kissed him gently, and then more passionately. "Good answer," she replied as she grabbed his hand and led him to their bedroom.

CHAPTER 22

Adam Bennington was preparing for the first day of work with his new client, Thurmond & Hollingsworth. He spent most of the prior week and weekend digesting details and background on the firm and preparing for the workshop training.

He had a number of phone calls and meetings with David over the past few weeks to learn everything he could about the firm, the people, and their culture. He could already envision it. These senior executives and obviously educated colleagues would start out as non-believers, being underwhelmed by the simple, basic concepts until it hit them square in the face, and they needed it. We all need it sometimes.

They would evolve. View these concepts with a renewed sense of respect and even accept the level of complication because of one extraordinary element. And, it would be THE essential ingredient to success. The human relationship. That was always a fulfilling "aha" moment he enjoyed experiencing with groups. Watching them get it and watching their egos deflate. Then, the real surrender and learning would commence.

Adam's initial relationship with the CEO began when David first wrote to let him know how much he enjoyed the book. They traded emails and thoughts back and forth for a time before finally meeting at one of Adam's talks.

He remembered the exact gathering. He was speaking to a group of executives at a local conference about the ever increasing importance of connection and relationship building to amp up success and lead to fulfillment, both professional and personal.

When it was over, David walked up to the front of the room and introduced himself. Adam immediately recognized the name and extended his hand. "I'm so glad you could make it."

"Thank you for sending me the information. I've been hoping for an opportunity to meet you. And you already know I really admire your work. In fact, my wife and I both read your book and could not put it down. Super insightful."

"Excellent, two believers. I'm happy you both enjoyed it. We're proud of the book and the research our team put into it. What was your favorite part?"

David laughed and said, "It changed the way my wife and I relate to each other. The section on communication is outstanding. Your concepts are straightforward, but take into account the complexities attached to dealing with relationships, with people. Nothing is easy with people. We all have varying backgrounds, experiences and baggage."

"That's it. The human relationships. Dealing with people and their emotions, their baggage, their history, and on and on. That's what makes it challenging."

"You certainly have a believer in me. I successfully tried your principles on a couple of my colleagues at work," David continued, "I have a challenging manager that I can't seem to relate to. I used the communication model to guide us through a conflict just the other day. It turned out that once we started listening to learn from each other, we realized we had both misinterpreted the situation."

Adam nodded in agreement. "That's often the problem. We conduct a lot of research in this area, and I'm astounded at the number of conflict cases that are directly related to misunderstandings or incorrect perceptions."

They continued to talk until David asked, "May I have a few minutes of your time? I'm afraid my firm is in trouble and I would really like your thoughts on what you would do in a situation I'm dealing with. I mean, if it's not imposing too much?"

Adam looked at his watch. "I'll tell you what. I need to make a quick call and then I'm free. Would you be interested in meeting me in the hotel bar for a drink or a cup of coffee? We can talk there."

David called his wife to let her know he would be late. He entered the bar before Adam and scanned the room for an open table. It was the start of drink specials and appetizers resulting in a room buzzing with chatter. There was a two person table in the middle of the room. He seated himself and ordered a beer.

* * * * * * * * * *

When Adam arrived and ordered a drink, David began the conversation with a background on the firm. They had been very successful with little worry about the budget until the past couple of years. Things were changing. At first, it wasn't a big deal. But, as time went on, the budget challenges increased. This year, they were in trouble.

Adam asked, "Have you thought about what it will take to get you through this? Do you have a plan?"

"I have a plan and it is two years too late," David answered with a sigh and a frown. He picked up his beer and drained it.

"So, if time is critical, what does that mean for you guys?"

"It means I have very senior people that lived in a culture of money and little conflict. Now that money is a problem, everyone is stressed, short tempered, pointing fingers and blaming each other. We don't know how to react or communicate in an emotional or high risk environment. And, my fear is that it's almost too late to change."

"You said you have a plan? If it's really too late, will it work?"

"It has to work or we'll be shutting our doors. The plan is to place the fate of my firm in the hands of the executive team to work together and construct a realistic budget reduction strategy. But, I don't seem to be getting through to them and they don't comprehend the magnitude of the problem. This is serious and they are still thinking about their own interests over the firm."

Adam signaled the bartender and said, "Why don't you tell me more about your budget reduction strategy and some of the challenges you're facing with the environment. Maybe I can help."

They ordered two more beers and talked for the next hour, and every day after for a week. Together they devised a different plan. One that involved Adam.

CHAPTER 23

David left the meeting with Adam feeling optimistic about their chances for the first time in awhile. He was convinced this was their last opportunity and it had to work. He got in his car and called Lindsay to tell her about their conversation.

There was excitement, a passion in his voice. "Lindsay, I don't think I'm being naive about this. We've got to deal with the human behavior aspects of our relationships if we want to stick around. I know it will be a challenge, but I think it just might work. No, it will work."

"I agree." She decided to listen, rather than talk. She had been trying to tell him this for some time. She asked, "So, what exactly are you thinking?"

David's inflection increased with excitement, "Doing the work on ourselves and persuading our executive team to have the selfless capacity to put the company's interests first. The survival of the firm over Departments." He paused and there was silence on the other end of the line, "As basic as it is, I think that's the key."

"You mean, act as leaders for this firm rather than just department heads for a change?" she said in a sarcastic, playful tone on the other end of the phone.

David laughed as he was turning into his neighborhood. "Yes, that's exactly what I mean. And, I've enabled this behavior and it's time to hold people responsible and accountable."

Lindsay was pacing the floor of her condo, still holding onto a contract document she was reading. Realizing it was still in her hands, she dropped it on a side table and walked to the window. She responded in a quiet tone, "You haven't really had to before. We could afford to be on autopilot until now. I wouldn't beat myself up over it." Lindsay continued, "David, what you're saying is all a good start. You know I've been an advocate for this all along." Lindsay didn't say everything she was thinking.

"But what, Lindsay?" he paused, "I hear 'a but.'"

"No, I just want to be cautious. I'm trying to be realistic about our challenges. It's going to be a tough road. I hope we have the mental capacity for it."

"I know. But, I don't think our behavior is based on any ill intent. It's the normal reaction when things become challenging. Human nature."

"I hope you're right."

"It will work. We'll make it work," David declared emphatically. He drove his car into the garage and hit the power button on the dashboard. He sat for a moment.

"Yes David, we will make it work." He didn't have to convince her. She had started a similar conversation when the toxic behavior first surfaced.

They hung up the phone and she thought about their conversation. She hadn't said much about it and didn't want to be negative, but she was apprehensive about the team's intentions. She had advocated for this, but there were still concerns. There was a nagging feeling there might be more. There were a couple of the newer executives that were overly ambitious. A couple that she didn't know very well, but she didn't have a good feeling about them. Her intuition was rarely wrong. Lindsay hoped she was wrong this time. Was there more?

CHAPTER 24

(Executive Training - Goals, Connection and Caring - Easy Part, Until It's Not)

Adam walked into the building that first day knowing things were about to change. He had been hired to help this firm in trouble and he had done this enough to know it would prove to be an interesting look deep into the lives of these people.

The atmosphere was buzzing with executives running around, tying up loose ends on tasks and projects prior to the meeting. David's direction was mandatory attendance unless there was an emergency akin to the building burning down. What were the chances of anything crazy like that? *Oh, you have no idea.*

David's assistant was in the conference room placing water pitchers and glasses on the table while the caterers finished the set up of breakfast and assorted snacks. As the team members walked in, the aromas of fresh bagels, pastries, and coffee permeated the air. It was like walking into a local bakery at opening time.

They were gathering around the food and talking when David asked them to take their seats. "We're here to take control of our future. Right now, two of our strongest competitors are strategizing behind closed doors on how to take us down. Heck, they may be teaming up for all we know. Examining our weaknesses, vulnerabilities, and yes, even our strengths. Let me pose a couple of questions to you - rhetorical for the moment. What are we going to do about it? What are we made of? That's what we'll decide over the next few days.

"Our relationships are going to be challenged. I'm not being melodramatic when I tell you that if we don't take action, make major fiscal decisions for the good of the firm as opposed to just looking out for our Departments, we'll find ourselves without jobs to go to."

Lindsay scanned the room for reactions. She knew the hard part was about to begin. The real test. She eyed Patrick and he nodded. She turned her attention back to her Boss and his messaging.

"I'm confident we can do this, be successful, if we draw on our collective experience, strength, and brain power. Our first step is to focus on us and a framework to operate within. There will be highly emotional conversations, and we need to improve how we navigate through them. That's where Mr. Adam Bennington comes in.

"Adam comes to us with an outstanding reputation for turning organizations around. He has worked with a multitude of corporate firms not unlike us, as well as sports teams, government agencies and medical facilities. He'll target our teamwork skills, our communication process, and overall building and maintaining trusting relationships.

"I'll let him tell you more about the way ahead. I think you'll find this journey both professionally and personally life altering."

Lindsay suddenly felt a pang of nerves, second thoughts. Could a consultant, no matter how highly regarded, really help turn this around? She had played heavily in influencing David to do this and she hoped it wasn't a mistake. Too late now. She had to own it.

She sized up the man that stood before her. She didn't think he looked like the stereotype of a consultant or facilitator. He didn't wear glasses and he didn't look all that academic. He was tall, slender and had the trim build of an athlete. A cute athlete.

* * * * * * * * *

Adam thanked David, as he shook his hand and walked to the head of the table. Lindsay watched his steady, confident walk but looked away when his eyes glanced in what she thought was her direction.

The consultant briefly supplemented David's introduction of purpose but didn't waste any more time. "Let's talk about teams for a few minutes. The concept usually makes people roll their eyes because it seems so basic. One of the most overused and incorrectly used words out there. We think we know how to be a team and we'll say we're teams, but those are just words. Some of us simply aren't good at it or we underestimate the value. No matter how hard we try we can't get there.

"Think about successful athletic teams. They're successful because they've figured it out. It's more because of their abilities together, not their individual talents. Simply put, they care about each other/the relationship, find a way to maximize their collective strengths, compensate for weaknesses, are accountable and responsible to one another, and they know how to capitalize on their work together." He managed to say it all without taking a breath.

"Sounds easy, doesn't it?" he said with a chuckle, along with a few laughs and shaking heads around the room.

Without waiting for a response, he continued, "Working together seems commonsense, even intuitively obvious. Unfortunately, people don't apply their understanding or discipline to what they already know. At the conclusion of our time together, you will possess the tools to manage and maintain your relationships, as well as have the ability to cultivate new ones."

Adam walked around the room and had all eyes on him. Attentiveness was certainly a good sign after more than a few minutes of talking about teams.

"How many of you have played team sports? Let me see a show of hands," Adam said as he threw his hand in the air.

A few hands went up. He nodded to the striking blonde located to his right. He shouldn't, but he noticed her beauty and thought she looked a little young for this room, and him. He did quick math that put her at late twenties, early thirties, or maybe she just aged really well. *Interesting.* He asked her, "Were you part of a winning team?"

"Mostly winning," she said somewhat nonchalant.

He smiled, "Tell us about it."

"I used to play basketball. We won a couple of state basketball championships in high school," she said proudly.

"I would call that successful," he nodded before continuing, "What made you winners?"

Lindsay turned her head upward, contemplating the answer. She said, "From the early days of practice, we set individual and team goals. Our common goal was to win a state championship. And, we worked well together. Even as young as we were, we developed a mutual respect and made the investment in the relationship. We trusted each other."

"Did you work well together all the time?"

"No. There were times when it was hard. Times when conflict and egos got in the way. But we had a great coach and we believed in her system. In those experiences, we managed to talk through things, resolve the conflict, get back to the goal, and trust each other again. I guess another goal was tied to caring about each other, our bond."

Adam shook his head and smiled. "Yeah. I couldn't have said it better." He continued, "People working together to achieve a common goal. Much of what we talk about over the next few days will circle back to that. We won't spend a lot of time on the mechanics of goal setting, but we'll talk more in terms of how it links to relationships.

He walked to the flip chart and wrote, "Establish a Common Goal." He placed the marker back in its' place and turned back to face them. "We'll talk about stakes, how to shift from focusing only on your own desires to include the desires of those around you. Being interested in them and collective contributions to the overall goal.

"Asking yourself - what do you have to contribute for yourself and for the benefit of the others? Expand your thoughts about contribution to mean helping each other. Shift to a form of thinking outside of yourself. What are their challenges? What are they up against? Learn to become interested in their success too. Don't settle for personal goals being pursued at the detriment of the team. And, everyone has to agree to accept responsibility and accountability.

"Companies make a fatal mistake in goal setting when they do it in a vacuum with various departments acting as individualized components doing their own thing with their own interests. When that happens, executives don't see themselves as having responsibility for goals outside of their area and they don't accept responsibility for success of the big picture. In your case, the firm's survival - you have to focus on the same priorities and demand placing a higher priority on the firm than you do your departments. It's the only way.

"How do you provide rapid response/delivery to your clients in a reasonable timeframe and at the appropriate quality and cost? Oh, and don't forget this part, while following the rules and laws, and still being judicious with your firm's financial situation. If you can come up with a goal that fosters that behavior you'll do more than just survive."

Adam paused and scanned the room. Could they shift to selfless acts to win? Did they have it in them? It was going to be a wild ride. He turned back to the flip chart. "First, let's talk about the basics of connection and creating common ground. Here is how it works:"

FLIP CHART 1:

FOUNDATIONAL BASICS AND LEARNING PHASE: ESTABLISHING COMMON GROUND, CONNECTION, AND GOAL SETTING; FOCUSING ON THE SAME PRIORITIES

- *Learn to Care. Search for commonality in the other person(s) - find something that resembles yourself within them.*

- *Let them know you care. Explore who they are, what they care about, what's important to them. Be willing to see their point of view and challenges.*

- *Who am I? Share yourself. What is important to you, what do you want, and why do you want it?*

- *Accept an obligation to each other. Responsibility to help each other achieve their goals. Ask yourself if you're hindering or helping?*

- *Collective contribution to the overall goal. Everyone accepts responsibility and accountability. Give each other an opportunity to be part of the solution. Ask yourself - What can I contribute for the benefit of others and what is my contribution to the overall goal?*

- *Be bold. Be vulnerable and admit your mistakes and weaknesses. What's holding you back?*

The room was silent for a moment. Adam glanced around and could sense it was time for lunch. That was not a problem because he would certainly capture their interest by the afternoon. The interaction would get real as the day unfolded. "Let's break for lunch. I'll leave you with a couple of questions to think about. Do you think you're a good team? Given your other challenges, does it matter?"

"I can answer that now." Patrick spoke up. His words were direct and without hesitation. He said, "I think we're a good enough team. We have our issues like everyone else, but I think we do okay. I'm more concerned with our financial condition right now."

David looked at him, but didn't say anything. Patrick hesitated before continuing, "I'm not sure we can afford the luxury of focusing primarily on our relationship and teamwork ability at this point. We have bigger problems. I think most importantly, we need to rely on everyone to do their part, look for opportunities to reduce costs and increase revenues, and do it with a real sense of urgency."

Adam responded, "Patrick, you bring up a great point. When we return, we'll look at why this is exactly the time to worry about your team. I would offer that you can't afford not to work on the dynamics of the relationship. Stay with me and I think you may change your mind."

Adjourning for lunch led participants back to their respective offices without another thought. They all had too many things on their plates and didn't have time or energy to worry about their relationships. They were good enough. There were emails, voicemails, and clients to serve.

CHAPTER 25

Lindsay and Patrick quickly checked in with their offices before meeting at the front of the building and walking to a nearby bistro. The sidewalks were cluttered with the noon crowd and they had to sidestep, stop and maneuver around the masses of people. They could barely hold a conversation while walking and that was fine with Lindsay. It gave her more time to think about what to say to him.

The restaurant was one of their favorite lunch spots, famous for a variety of organics, salads, and homemade dressings. Seated at their usual table and orders placed, Lindsay didn't waste any time. "So, your words back there were spoken like a true Comptroller, but you really don't think we need to work on our relationship? You were fairly obvious you weren't into it this morning."

"It's not that. I'm more worried about focusing on our future. I feel like time is ticking. We better come up with solutions. At this point, I am definitely all about the numbers. I don't think we have time to build on our relationships." He paused before continuing, "I'm not sure it's makes all that much of a difference anyway."

She thought about his statement and looked at him, but didn't speak or argue, sensing he was in no mood to be persuaded. She was surprised they weren't on the same page. That was unusual.

They had been close for as long as she could remember. She respected him as a colleague and friend. They had shared life's ups and downs and she couldn't imagine the workplace or an existence without him.

Their conversation quickly turned to one of their favorite subjects, basketball and Patrick's son, the star point guard for the local university that fans fondly called the 'U'. As a rising senior, his life was falling into place, and this charming and talented young man had a plan. After graduation, he was set to become an Assistant Coach for the school and marry his long-time girlfriend.

Lindsay loved this time with Patrick. They talked and laughed for close to an hour before she glanced at her watch and gasped at the time. Standing and grabbing her purse, she said, "I've got to get out of here. I have a couple of things to check on before the afternoon session."

They paid their checks and proceeded back to the office. Patrick teased, "I guess the afternoon will be fun filled. Getting in touch with our feelings."

She smiled up at him and refrained from comment. Lindsay always felt better when she spent time with Patrick. It was their relationship and the sense of being really cared about by someone you work with. He had her back. It made differing opinions easier to address. It's not like they never disagreed, but they viewed conflict between them as an opportunity to learn the other viewpoint. She could talk to him and she trusted him probably more than anyone in her life. It made work better, fresh and more meaningful.

She was still thinking about their relationship when they neared the entrance to the building. She smiled, stopped and looked at him. "You know, it wouldn't be any fun around here without you. Not to mention, all this time, I don't know what I would have done. About him. You have helped me through some really tough times. Thank you for always being there for me."

He was a little taken aback by the serious turn in the conversation. He didn't know what to say and his face turned a slight shade of red. He simply replied, "You're welcome and thank you. You've always been there for me too."

As she started walking away from Patrick, she hesitated, called out his name, and looked back. He paused and turned, with his hands in his pockets. She said, "This is why relationship building is important. Don't underestimate the power." She smiled and walked away.

He returned the smile without saying a word. Maybe she was right.

CHAPTER 26

Lindsay approached Peter's office door but didn't walk into the darkened room. She hesitated, thinking about leaving him a note when Tom's voice from a cubicle away was a couple of octaves too loud. There were no other voices so he must have been on the telephone, or worse, talking to himself.

She walked towards his cubicle, planning to speak to him until hearing his next words. She stopped abruptly and didn't make a sound.

"I don't care. After what they've done to me. They brought me here, talking about all the great things we could accomplish and then basically tell me to stifle my creativity. I know. I know. Look, it's too risky to talk about it here. Later, yes, later. I've got to go."

He went silent. She assumed he was listening to the person on the other end of the line. His voice emerged again in a low tone that Lindsay could barely make out, but she was fairly certain she heard what he was saying. It went something like, "We'll talk about the when and how later. Call me at home where I can talk. Sounds good." He hung up.

Lindsay started to say something, but decided against it. She should relay the conversation to Peter for him to handle. *What was he up to?*

CHAPTER 27

It was lunchtime again and the office was vacant enough for a crime. He kept finding those perfect moments, but couldn't do it.

His mind shifted back to a time when he was a young adult and wouldn't allow his twin buddies to take booze from their parent's liquor cabinet. It was dishonest. They called him a dork and rolled their eyes, but at least they put it back.

And then there was the time he intervened, persuaded, and restrained a star college football player from going into the bedroom of an alcohol-induced cheerleader. Everyone else turned away.

The adult was no different. He sat at the dying bed of a friend's friend that he only met a couple of times, but they had no one. He wasn't afraid to cry at sappy movies, and not so sappy movies.

He didn't cheat, lie, or break rules. His friends referred to him as the voice of reason. They sought his advice and considered him a moral compass. Look at him now.

Peering left and then right, he stepped over to one of the cubicles, far away from home. He sat down in front of the computer screen. He looked around once again. *Was anyone working on this floor? No wonder productivity was in the toilet.*

He pecked away at the keyboard, entering some initial numbers and letters, leading him from screen shot to screen shot. He finally reached the final transaction page. He bypassed a few approval requirements.

He hesitated. Couldn't do it. Still searching, but finding no other alternatives. He breathed in, let out a deep breath and pressed a few more buttons.

CHAPTER 28

When Lindsay stepped through the conference room door, her eyes scanned the table looking for Peter. Not seeing him, she made a mental note to tell him what she overheard. Additional signs of toxic behavior, or more sinister?

Her mood quickly shifted as her eyes met Adam's. They smiled at one another and she felt a rush of heat, and hoped her reaction wasn't obvious. Surprised, she sat down and thought, *he is handsome.*

Adam smiled after he returned to the flip chart. *She is easy on the eyes.*

He admonished himself for the second time to focus. *What is going on here?* He continued making a couple of notes before turning around. Everyone had taken their seats and were checking their tablets. The evolution of the information age. It seemed like yesterday when Blackberries were attached to everyone's hands.

Adam continued the afternoon conversation about goals and relationships. "You should be getting the picture by now. Find a way to care about each other, or at least be considerate, and you might find you can actually like one another. It's so much more exhilarating and fulfilling to work in that kind of environment. I'm not sure if it's the information age or the fast pace we're all operating under, but we've drifted away from basic caring into picking sides and that's it. You're either on my side or the other. No common ground. You're not even viewed as a real person any longer. You're the enemy and I'm not listening. Period."

Adam introduced his next concept. The finished product was reduced to a one page Flip Chart:

FLIP CHART 2:

BUILDING A SYSTEMS APPROACH TO GOAL SETTING WITH FOLLOW-THROUGH

– *What do you want/need?*

– *What do I want/need?*

– *What do we all want/need (applicable to a team)?*

– *Separate the wants (nice to have) from the needs (must have).*

– *What can I do to help you through your challenges?*

– *What can you do to help me through my challenges?*

– *Establish an Action Plan with a solution*

– *Measure results - Did the Action Plan achieve the objectives? Did we help each other and walk away satisfied? What is the temperature and biggest strength/weakness of the relationship at this moment? Did we learn anything? What could we become together and where do we go from here?*

– *Performance Appraisal - Add a performance element - How did I contribute to the goal(s)? How did I help us succeed or not?*

Adam ended the day with a discussion that left him feeling uneasy. When he asked about problem signs for a relationship or a team, someone said trust, and continued with "you have to believe you can trust each other. And, that will lead to supporting one another. Leaning on each other. That's the value of trust."

He observed more than a couple of heads turn downward at the table in front of them. He could have sworn faces turned red. *Were they uncomfortable, ashamed or hiding something? Or, was it nothing?* The next few days would tell the story.

Adam scanned the room, checked the wall clock and said, "We're at a good stopping point. We'll get back together two days from now at 9:00AM.

That's when the real fun begins. You'll do a little soul searching. It will get raw. It may even change you.

Adam walked to the flip chart but didn't write anything. Instead, he turned back around and scanned the room. "I'll leave you with a question to ponder over the next couple of days - do you want to be a team that throws each other under the bus for sport, or do you want to help each other miss that bus and actually accomplish something? Think about it. Good night. I'll see you in two days."

CHAPTER 29

Lindsay responded to a couple of critical emails, signed off on a contract review and looked at a mountain of pink slips for catchup calls. She shook her head and said out loud, "Uh, not today." Grabbing her briefcase and jacket, she flipped the light switch.

It was her turn to cook dinner for the weekly get together with Sam. Her abilities might not be in the same caliber as Sam, but Lindsay could hold her own in the kitchen. This was a night to forget about the firm, the people in it, and enjoy the company of a special friend.

After a quick trip to the grocery store, Lindsay's next challenge was navigating her house key into the hole without dropping the bags that were flopping around in her arms. *Being a runner, wouldn't two trips to the car make more sense? Not to mention clocking in a few extra steps for the day.*

Successfully entering her condo with no casualties, she placed the groceries on the kitchen counter and grabbed a favorite blend of Cabernet Sauvignon, Merlot, Cabernet Franc and Petit Verdot from the wine refrigerator. Opening the bottle and leaving it to breathe, Lindsay took a quick shower and changed into jeans and a tee.

Feeling more relaxed and comfortable, she returned to the kitchen and poured herself a glass of wine and started working on the salad and marinating the steaks. It wasn't long before the doorbell sounded.

Lindsay greeted Sam with a hug and led her into the kitchen, motioning towards a bar stool. "Have a seat and I'll get you a glass of wine." It was time for cocktail hour and catching up.

Samantha was one of her oldest and dearest friends dating back to their twenties and growing up together. Lindsay was always interested in the law and Sam interested in food and catering, spending too many years working for other people and other companies, until she could afford to go out on her own.

Then it happened, seven years earlier. She was the owner of a very successful, trendy tapas bistro, The Coastal Grille. The restaurant was one of Lindsay's favorite dining spots. Located downtown near her office, Lindsay and her colleagues were frequent regulars for dinner or drinks after a late evening at the office. The food was excellent, the atmosphere cozy, but the service was impeccable.

It was packed almost every night with a blend of both young and middle aged professionals. Sam had an ability to transform waitstaff into business focused, young talent like few other leaders Lindsay had known throughout her career. She had an open and direct approach to leading people.

Even in totally different businesses, they shared the philosophy that interpersonal leadership skills were critical in any type of work. It was all about building the talent of people, and the relationships.

On this night, Sam wanted to hear more about Lindsay's situation at work. How they were managing their organizational health and internal communications issues, given their fight for survival. She couldn't get that saying out of her head that desperate times call for desperate measures.

Sam tilted her head upward and breathed in as she sipped the wine. She was working entirely too many hours and feeling the strain of being a restauranteur. Some might consider working with college age students and letting them be responsible for the restaurant's customer service scorecard high risk, but she disagreed and found it rewarding. She employed an interesting approach to culture that trained them to be a business team, to work together. It didn't matter that the employees were from different generations or in different types of work. Teamwork is teamwork.

"Why is it so hard?" Sam asked, swirling wine around in her glass and eyeing the legs. "Even though we have been talking about teams forever, I still find people aren't very good at it. It seems so simple."

"I know, right? It's basic stuff. I think we're not good at putting it all together - thinking in terms of common goals, communicating through issues, or managing relationships with trust," Lindsay poured Sam more wine before continuing, "The hard part is when you mix all of that with behavior and emotions. It sounds good but harder in practice. People are complicated."

Sam laughed, "Yeah, that's the truth. Also, I think there is a certain amount of common sense. It really is about the basic principles of doing what you know is right. The challenge is consolidating all of that into some organized system or culture or whatever you want to call it."

Lindsay shook her head. "I like what you're saying about putting it together in an organized system. There is too much leadership thinking that emphasizes taking care of your own people at all costs. That isn't the right focus for a leadership team. You have to strike a balance between your Department, other Departments, and the good of the entire company - everyone has to be connected to the overall common goal."

Sam said, "People really underestimate that power. I read this case study in graduate school about conflict intolerance, but I was more struck by the lack of teamwork that crippled the company. They were at a crossroads about some product direction in the marketplace and the senior leaders only recommended options to benefit their departments. It stymied progress, resulted in no action, and that inability to work together led to lost customers, lost opportunity in a viable market, hundreds of lost jobs, and a plummet of the stock price. It eventually resulted in the destruction of a company that should have thrived. Analysts later blamed their demise on the inability to operate with any unified strategic vision and common goal. Simple stuff that can lead to success or destroy you."

"That's one of the reasons we're doing this workshop. The business has become so competitive. We're losing our market share. We haven't found ourselves in this place before, and are virtually untested when times are challenging and conflict is a real possibility," she hesitated before continuing, "David started seeing some behaviors he didn't like and doesn't think we can afford to ignore it. We have to build better relationships and our culture of teamwork. For the first time, we're worried about survival and that's why we are putting so much emphasis on it."

Sam offered, "At least you are being proactive before it's too late. I commend David for making this investment in the company, especially at this time. And, I have a feeling you may have had a little something to do with this idea. Did you?" She smirked.

"I might have shared my thoughts when David and I first started talking about our problems," Lindsay said with a coy smile.

After dinner, they went to the couch to enjoy decaf and more conversation. It all started out innocent enough since they both had zero romance in their lives. Until Sam broached the subject of the past.

"Linds, I've been wanting to ask and didn't know how to approach it, so I'll just say it. How are you really doing?"

"I'm fine, why?"

"Well, we haven't talked about him in a long time."

Lindsay stared at her for a second without saying a word. She put her coffee mug down on the end table on her side and let out a sigh before turning to face Sam. She started to speak, stopped, and said, "There are times when I feel really good, like life is getting better. I'm back in control. But, it only lasts for a second or two until I think of him. I get that sick feeling in the pit of my stomach again. He was the love of my life and then he died."

"Oh sweetheart. I've wanted to talk about this for so long and was afraid it was too painful. I've been worried about you, but you seem a little different now."

"You know what I do? I have to stay aware - stop the careless and dangerous thoughts the minute they emerge and I prevent myself from slipping further down that deep, dark hole. I sometimes wonder when it will end and then I tell myself that I'm trying, but that's not good enough and I need to try harder. That's what I do."

Sam nodded her head but didn't say anything.

"Want to know what I thought about the other day?"

"What?"

"I probably bought that car because of the color blue, like the Caspian Sea. It was a place that holds both wonderful and so deeply sad memories for me. But, I will never forget the vacations we spent on those captivating shores."

Sam looked down at the floor and continued to let Lindsay talk.

"God, I still can't bring myself to think or say his name, still. That was such a different time in my life. Our time together on that private beach by the Caspian Sea."

"I remember. You talked about living there."

"Yes, we did. We shared a passion for the beach, salt water, sand between our toes, and seafood, any seafood. We were going to live on that beach one day."

Sam recognized the start of a glassy look in Lindsay's eyes and said, "I never told you, but I secretly worried that you would move to that beach. Leave me. I told myself that I would go too. But, I wanted you happy."

"You never told me that."

"I know. I was embarrassed. It seemed so silly at the time."

"It's not silly. You're my best friend and I would have taken you. He would have wanted that too." Lindsay wiped tears from her eyes. She smiled at Sam, "I remember the last time. We were running on the sand, fishing in the surf, and lounging in chairs reading the latest bestselling novels. Well, he was reading a novel, I was reading some autobiography or nonfiction business or leadership thing that I don't even remember."

"He loved you so much. Don't shut out the thoughts of him. Hold on to the memories."

Lindsay didn't speak right away. She stared at the wall across the room before turning back to look at Sam. "That was so long ago. He is gone, they're fading, and the only thing remaining is the pain that I have worked so hard to force away. I don't have time to think about it now. Or him."

Sam put down her coffee cup and pulled Lindsay into her arms and held her. She whispered, "Just make sure you've grieved. You have to grieve. I worry about that."

"I'm good."

"I know. I can tell."

They sat in silence for a couple of minutes. The only noise in the room was the clock in the corner ticking away.

"Wow, that was heavy," Sam said, attempting to stifle the sniffle. What was she thinking? Lindsay did not need that.

"What made us go there?"

"Me. I'm sorry. I just worry about you."

"Don't. I am definitely getting it together."

"Okay. I believe you. But, if you need me…"

"I know. And I love you for it."

"It's after 9:00. I have got to go. An early day tomorrow," Sam said as she was getting up from the sofa.

"Oh, I wish you could stay longer."

"Me too. But, it's a school night for both of us," She said in a tone her mom would use.

Lindsay walked her out. When she was back in the house, she had an odd feeling wash over her. The room didn't feel as cozy as it did when Sam was there. She shrugged and put it out of her mind.

She went to bed thinking about the firm and the second day with the facilitator. She fell asleep wondering how they were going to build a solid relationship with this group of executives. It would be challenging, but it might also be fun, if they succeed. And, the facilitator was charming. *God, I need a good therapist. Or maybe, I'm making the turn. I'm definitely making the turn.*

CHAPTER 30

Lindsay got out of bed early the next morning to make time for a run and an opportunity to clear her head of all the swirling thoughts about life's predicaments. After three miles, she returned home feeling exhilarated and in the right mindset to tackle the day.

A shower, a fresh perspective, and a breakfast smoothie that involved vegetable nutrition you don't have to taste lightened her mood. It was the perfect vitamin fortified "to go" concoction for the commute.

The annoyance and delays of the drive didn't even bother her that morning. *How was Adam going to help them build a better relationship? What kind of magic did he have in store for them?* She smiled.

His assessment was spot on. Connection, relationships, major decisions aligned with common interests associated with the firm's survival. She hoped it would work, especially since their livelihood depended on it. She would take this on as her personal responsibility to be selfless and influence the future of this firm. *What else did she have to do?*

* * * * * * * * * *

Lindsay grabbed a coffee and walked down the hall, hoping to get a moment with Peter. The atmosphere in his area was somehow different, almost too quiet. People walking with purpose from cubicles to printers and from conference rooms back to office areas. No smiles or chatter. Just long faces. It felt like it was devoid of energy. *Oh Lindsay, stop it. You're being dramatic.*

As she was approaching Peter's door, Tom walked towards her, or actually by her. Along the way, he said without stopping, "Peter's not in his office. He said he had an appointment this morning." He kept walking, carrying his smug tone with him.

She couldn't help but think he had to be guilty of something. If nothing else, his attitude was bad. She made another mental note to let Peter know what she overheard on his end of the phone call the other day.

Opening the exit door and taking the stairs, she couldn't shake the feeling the walls were crashing in on this normally resilient firm. A collapsed building, budget crisis, bad attitudes, and their battle against a running clock. What was wrong with these people?

Even David, normally steady had become edgy, tense, and different. It had to be more than the pressure. She knew him as well as anyone and recently he wasn't behaving like himself. His temper was quick, he was much more emotional than usual, and there was a nervous energy that didn't use to be there. She didn't know how to articulate it, other than it was not David. She could see it in his eyes.

CHAPTER 31

Lindsay barely sat down at her desk when the phone rang. She looked at the display and quickly picked it up. "I was just thinking about you," She said, leaving out the part about why.

"I need to see you right away," he said in a low tone, and abruptly hung up the phone.

"Okay. I'll be right there," she frowned and said to an empty line. *What on earth is up with him?*

As soon as Lindsay entered his doorway, she stopped. David looked up from behind his desk. His face was drained of color and his eyes were dark, the bags more prevalent and he looked like he hadn't slept. He flung his glasses on a stack of papers and rubbed his eyes.

Motioning for her to sit on a nearby couch, he walked from behind his desk and shut the door. He sat down across from her and put his elbows on his knees as he leaned in and paused a few seconds that seemed like minutes. He pulled the knot out of his tie.

His silence and his look frightened her. A million things ran through her mind during that brief moment.

His voice was low when he said, "We have a problem. I should say another problem, an even bigger one."

"What's going on, David?"

"Someone has been embezzling funds from the company."

Had she heard him right? The shock was visible on her face. She paused before speaking softly, "That can't be." She continued without waiting for an answer, "How do you know?"

"I discovered it by accident. The bank attempted to call Patrick and since he wasn't available, they contacted me. We thought one of our analysts made a data entry error on a financial upload to the bank. Since anything over a million dollars requires senior level approval, this action was flagged. The bank called. I said I would check it out. Usually I'd give it to one of Patrick's senior analysts, but I decided to take a look. I didn't want to bother them with something I thought could be cleared up with a quick fix. I was wrong."

David let out a sigh and rubbed his hands across his face. "I looked at some of the financial data history and it didn't add up. The entries before this one were for $10,000 and $25,000 and this one was for $1,000,000. I still didn't suspect anyone embezzling money, but I was curious since the entries were made without the financial analyst being identified. I accessed the electronic contract files and discovered we were dealing with a corporation that doesn't exist. That's when I figured it out."

"I cannot believe this," Lindsay said, shaking her head. She looked down at the carpet, and then back at David. She asked, "Have you told Patrick yet?"

He spoke firmly, "No, and I'm not going to. This has to stay between us. I'm telling you as my Legal Counsel. I want to keep him out of it, especially if it involves one of his employees. We have to start a formal investigation immediately." He looked down at the floor, rubbed his hands through his hair and stood up, walking towards the window. "Not that there is a good time, but this is the last thing we need right now. Trying to deal with a collapsing building, our firm on the edge and now someone amongst us is embezzling funds. I just can't believe it."

Lindsay sat silently, trying to process what she was hearing. It didn't make any sense. *Who would do this? Why would they do this? That's a stupid question - they did it for the money.*

David continued, "I wish we weren't in the middle of this budget planning session, but we are, and it is what it is. Bad timing and we just can't catch a break here." He turned back to look at Lindsay and his expression changed, a hard look of determination spread across his face. "I'm not letting whoever is behind this get away with it. They will NOT control what happens here."

Lindsay didn't know what to say. She let out a deep breath before asking, "What did you do when you discovered the dummy corporation?"

"Nothing. I just figured it out. I haven't talked to anyone, but you. We need to come up with our strategy, our legal course of action."

Lindsay paused thoughtfully before answering, "We have some options." She sighed and stood up, walking over to David. She looked him directly in the eyes before asking quietly, "David, is there any possible chance you could be wrong?"

David shook his head, looking down, "I wish I was, but there is no way I'm wrong about this."

"Then we have some decisions to make. Do you want to hire a forensic accountant, have our CPA conduct an investigation, or have us do it?" Without giving him time to think, Lindsay said, "Before you decide, my recommendation is an outside source. I think we should stay out of it."

"I agree. Let's have our CPA conduct the investigation. People won't be suspicious or alarmed with him around. It'll look like he's performing a routine audit."

"Obviously, my advice is to keep this confidential." Lindsay hesitated before continuing, "But, David, don't you think we should tell Patrick? We may need him."

David said emphatically, shaking his head, "No, I want this strictly between you, me and our CPA at this point. I think Patrick is better off not knowing. This will get ugly and he needs to be on the outside of this investigation. There will be a workforce that needs to be put back together after all of this. He needs to be the leader that restores trust in his Department. Pick up the pieces at the end."

"I'm not sure that's a good idea. He has a right to know about his Department."

"Lindsay, I appreciate your opinion, but no. I've made up my mind."

She started to object, but knew that look on David's face. He was not up for a discussion. "Okay. Then, our next step is to get with Mark and come up with an investigation strategy. I'll call him tonight and hopefully he can begin tomorrow. I'll head back to my office and research some options. Let you know what I find out."

David was looking out the window as she walked to the door. He turned towards her and looked exhausted. "Lindsay, thank you. Let's meet back in my office tomorrow morning. Don't stay too late tonight. This may be a long ride and there is nothing we can do about it until we meet with Mark."

She looked at him and didn't have to say anything. They were both thinking, could anything else go wrong? They had no idea.

CHAPTER 32

Lindsay went back to her office in a fog, not noticing the people she passed in the hallway. She moved with determination and focus without speaking to anyone.

So much for a relaxing night at home with a glass of wine and a hot bath. This was going to be painful, and she wasn't even sure where to begin.

The office was quiet. Too quiet. She looked around and thought about all the late evenings spent in this room over the years. Not once had she faced anything as hurtful and personal as this. She gave her soul to this firm and treated it like it was her own. Yes, it was personal.

She picked up the phone and called Mark Sarranato, hoping he might still be in his office. He answered on the second ring and Lindsay skipped the pleasantries, telling him the reason for the call. They had to start a possible embezzlement investigation and she asked him to meet her and David the following morning.

Lindsay explained a few of the details. "It started with a call David received from the Bank. There was a large accounts payable that required his or Patrick's signature and verification before proceeding. Since he used to be the CFO, he can maneuver the system as well as anyone and decided to handle it himself. As it turned out, there was a data entry error including an extra zero, but he didn't know it at the time, and that wasn't all that was wrong.

"He discovered there were a few unexplained accounting transactions of varying amounts to a single company over the last few weeks, unusual account payable transactions. The vast majority were made to one company, ZZ Corporation. And guess what? It doesn't exist."

Lindsay paused to breathe and give Mark a second to catch up. She could hear the fast scribbling on a notepad on the other end of the phone. She continued, "It appears to be a dummy corporation that was set up to embezzle money from us. Another interesting fact involved the transactions. They could not be traced to anyone in the Comptroller Department. There was no audit trail."

Mark dropped his pen and stopped writing, thinking about what he heard. "We need to start investigating this right away. I have a breakfast meeting scheduled tomorrow morning, but I can change it. Will 8:00 tomorrow work?"

"That would be great. You know, Mark, I haven't the foggiest idea how to come up with a process for investigating embezzlement. This is new to us and we've never had to worry about anything like this before."

"I'll help you get through it. We'll figure out what, and who we're dealing with."

"Thank you. I appreciate you rearranging your schedule to help us. You know we wouldn't ask this of you, if it wasn't serious."

"No problem. Don't worry about it. We'll get to the bottom of it. You should go home and get some rest. We may have some late nights ahead. See you in the morning," he answered as they said goodnight.

She hung up the phone slowly, not realizing how right he was. She looked at her watch, knowing there was nothing else to do. She turned out the light. It had been an exhausting day.

CHAPTER 33

Lindsay's plan was to take the long way around before exiting the building. She had to rekindle that feel of walking down the hall where all the action happened, where the energy was usually electric.

That didn't happen. The cubicles and offices were mostly dark except for one light in the distance that was Peter's office. She bypassed the exit door and kept on walking to the end of the corridor.

She started to approach but heard voices speaking in a low tone. Lindsay stopped herself, not wanting to interrupt. Turning to go in the opposite direction, there was an exchange that halted her progress. The voices were from Peter and Tom.

"We need to pull this back a notch. We can't afford any unnecessary inquiries. We are too close."

Tom reassured him, "Listen Boss, don't worry. Not to toot my own horn, but you know I'm a computer genius. I have it under control."

"Keep your voice down. We're taking a big risk here. We could lose everything. And, I don't know about you, but I have a family and I need the money. We can't afford anyone getting suspicious," Peter said in a quiet tone that was barely audible from Lindsay's angle.

"I know, I know. Trust me on this," Tom spoke softly and said something Lindsay couldn't hear. She leaned in and started to move closer but heard footsteps from inside the room heading in her direction. She almost sprinted for the other end of the hallway.

Lindsay walked to the car, replaying what she heard. Could Peter and Tom be involved in the embezzling of funds? There was no way, especially not Peter, not a chance. There had to be a logical explanation. She was just being paranoid.

She had to think about it and figure out if it was even worth mentioning to David. He might not say it, but he would wonder if she was going off the deep end and being ridiculous. And she had never been a fan of gossip and certainly didn't want to be the one leading it. This was silly. Peter wouldn't do anything like that.

As she turned the key in the ignition, she slammed her hand on the steering wheel and let out a deep breath, dreading what was ahead for all of them. The investigation would get ugly, feel personal and people would get hurt. *Who did this to us?*

CHAPTER 34

God, I hate this. What am I doing? Who am I? He admonished himself and abruptly ended the inner dialogue. There was no purpose for the conversation. He was too far in to turn back now.

He waited in a parking lot across the street until the building was almost empty. The waiting felt like forever, but he could get in and out unnoticed at this hour. The best time to successfully hack into a financial system without any onlookers.

As if he wasn't feeling bad enough, he saw Lindsay leave the building and get into her car. She walked rapidly with such confidence and determination. He got caught up in thoughts of her and actually smiled, until he remembered his mission.

He leaned back on the headrest and wiped his eyes. He said out loud, "I have got to get this over with." He opened the car door and headed for the building.

He walked slowly, peering around corners like he shouldn't be there. In fact, he shouldn't, not to do what he was about to do. At least he knew his nerve endings were working. His brow was beaded with sweat, his stomach had butterflies that made him feel like he might faint, and there was the now familiar feeling of his heart thumping out of his chest.

He attempted to steady himself by taking deep in and out breaths. He needed a minute so he walked around the darkened spaces, mostly cubicles. He gazed at family photos, coffee mugs, and various calendars. *They wouldn't be affected by this. It would be fine. It wasn't the end of the world.*

None of that really mattered anyway. He had to go forward. There was no turning back.

He possessed the necessary skills to make this work. In fact, he could hack into any computer and no one would ever figure it out. He would find his arrogance amusing under any other circumstance.

It's not the end of the world. Come on. The internal dialogue wouldn't stop. He had to sit down and do it. Get it over with quickly. *Stop wasting time.*

His heartbeat increased again and he was feeling unsteady on his feet. His chest hurt and the nausea wouldn't go away. With sweaty palms and shaky hands, his fingers touched the keyboard. One stroke led to two and before long, the transaction was complete.

He let out a deep breath and stared at the screen. It was over. He did it.

He quickly stood up from the computer. Certainly not feeling satisfied, but relieved. The hallway was dark as he quickly moved towards an exit stairwell.

Before opening the door, he stopped. One stop first. A bathroom break. *You have got to be kidding. I can't even wait until I get out of here. Nope, there is no way.*

He sighed and quietly pushed open the bathroom door. Flipping on the light, he noticed the floor was wet. The janitor. A quick heat flushed over him. *Please tell me the janitor didn't see me. That would not be good.*

He used the bathroom and washed his hands, but refused to look in the mirror. Quickly turning to leave, he slipped on the wet floor, but caught his balance. Breathing deeply, he opened the door and left through the stairwell.

CHAPTER 35

Mark arrived at Lindsay's office shortly before 8:00 the next morning. He stood in the doorway admiring her concentration as she was flipping pages in what looked like a comprehensive contract document. "Watching you work that hard is a thing of magic," he said, smiling and standing there with his coat in one hand and a briefcase in the other.

"You say it like it's rare," She said, as she glanced up. Her face brightened as she stood and walked towards him, pointing to the couch. "Please, come in. You can put your things down over there."

"Lindsay, it's great to see you." He shook her hand and held on a little longer than normal. "I wish it was under different circumstances. I know this must be awful for you."

She nodded and said, "It's not one of my better days or weeks, that's for sure."

"Well, you're hiding it well. You look magnificent."

"Thanks. You're looking good yourself, mister." Another smile and a look at her watch. "We're due in David's office any minute."

They walked and talked comfortably on the way to David's office suite. Mark and Lindsay had known each other for a long time, developing a good working relationship over the years. He had proven to be invaluable in his role as the Company's CPA, saving them from financial mistakes more than once. Back then, it didn't matter as much as it did now.

For Lindsay, her fondness for Mark had become more than just his professional capability. She liked him personally. Early on, they discovered they shared many similar interests. They were runners, viewed vacations as beautiful beaches with a good beach read, were connoisseurs of exquisite foods, and shared an interest in fine French and Italian wines. They were both foodies and liked to talk about their most recent adventures with new wines and restaurants.

They occasionally shared a drink that turned into a meal after a meeting that ran too long into the evening. They enjoyed each other's company, but neither of them had ever crossed the line or even hinted at it.

Not that he wasn't handsome. He was tall and trim with an athlete's build. He had beautiful light hazel eyes and curly jet black hair. He was definitely easy on the sight. Lindsay imagined she could have been interested in him, but didn't have an explanation for why not, other than their working relationship. It made a good excuse anyway, like so many of the others. There was always some reason.

CHAPTER 36

When Lindsay and Mark entered David's outer office, they could see him slowly pacing back and forth in front of the windows behind his desk. Lindsay startled him by asking if they could come in, muttering something about his assistant not being at her desk. He frowned and walked quickly towards them, extending his hand to Mark before gesturing to seats on the couch.

David closed the door and without wasting any time, he said, "Mark, thank you for dropping everything and jumping on this. I'm sure I don't have to tell you how damaging this is to our firm."

"I'll do what I can. We'll get to the bottom of it."

David shook his head and said, "We have to. For many reasons." He let out a deep breath that could probably be heard in the other room. "So, let's get down to it. Where do we go from here?"

Mark said, "I'll start with analyzing some of your transaction processes and conduct a deep dive into the financial records and system." He looked at Lindsay. "And, I'll need a list of employees having access to the firm's financial information."

"I can get you the list today," Lindsay said.

"Great. That's perfect." Mark continued talking about the way ahead. There was an aura of calm, but subtle authority about him. It would have been comforting under any other circumstances. He spoke without hesitation, "After my initial look, I may have to interview employees. I'm hoping we don't have to go that far, but if we do, I'll need Lindsay's assistance on the legalities of interrogation and confidentiality requirements."

Lindsay nodded in agreement. She looked from David to Mark and said, "I'm leading the investigation on David's behalf. I'll be the point of contact for anything you need. Please keep me abreast of any issues that come up."

"I'll do it. Let's get started."

They finalized their plans for updates and walked down the hall in silence until they entered Lindsay's suite of offices. Mark picked up his things from her couch and said, "Don't worry, I won't be moving in permanently." He smiled and studied her for a second. "Let's wrap this up quickly, and I'll take you to this new Italian restaurant I discovered. They have some of the best Italian wines you have ever tasted."

"You're on. I'll hold you to it." She walked him across the hall into the conference room, his new home until it was over. It was the only response Lindsay had the energy to manage as she walked back to her home away from home.

CHAPTER 37

It was early morning on the second day of the workshop when Lindsay arrived at the conference room ahead of everyone, except Adam. She was a little early, but had stopped by to see one of her colleagues and didn't have time to return to her office and get anything done before the session. Or, that was what she told herself.

Adam was in the room setting up when she walked in. He acknowledged her and added his appreciation for her participation on the first day. "Your comments were spot on about the importance of the work we're doing," he paused before continuing, "I have a question for you. Do you think this group has what it takes to build a better team, better relationships?"

"We don't have an option. This is about our future and the only way to survive is to determine how we can work together to stay competitive. Or, we will no longer be here," she shrugged.

"Well said. So, do you think you can do it?"

"Yes, I do."

He shook his head in agreement. "Maybe I should have you facilitate the session." He finished getting ready for the start of the day, but smiled to himself as he continued. After witnessing Lindsay's action during their first day together, he sensed she was passionate, perceptive and intelligent. He liked her style. Adam was pleased that she shared his feelings about the importance of this work. He hoped the others would feel the same way. He now had an ally, he thought as the other executives started filing in.

They had a few minutes to grab breakfast and coffee before the start. Lindsay spoke to a couple of her colleagues. Trying to be nonchalant, she managed a few glances at Adam. She found him intriguing. She reminded herself not to stare.

Her attempt at not gawking was assisted by Patrick's entrance into the room. He saw her and immediately walked over to where she was standing.

"Here we are for day two," he said with more dread than enthusiasm.

"Oh, come on. It's not that bad." Lindsay frowned at him, refilling her coffee cup.

"I know, but I can't get my mind off of the pile of work on my desk. This isn't a good time for me," he paused, deciding whether or not to say more. With a sigh and an already tired look on his face so early in the morning, Patrick continued, "Ugh, I've got a lot going on right now. Stephanie has some health issues we just found out about. I need to be out of the office for a couple of days soon."

Lindsay put her cup down and faced him. She abruptly asked, "What health issues? You didn't mention anything yesterday." She stared at him with an alarmed look on her face.

Patrick's face turned red and he looked embarrassed before responding, "Just got the results. Some female issues. I don't think it's too serious."

"I'm sorry to hear that. Is there anything I can do to help?" Lindsay asked.

He spoke a little too quickly, almost dismissive. "No, thank you. We've got it under control." He looked down and poured creme in his cup, glancing around for the sugar that was right in front of him.

Locking her eyes on his, Lindsay handed him the sugar and said, "Let me know if I can help. You know I'll do what I can for either of you." She started to say more, but the expression on Patrick's face stopped her. She assumed it wasn't a topic he was comfortable discussing, even with her. It was a difficult conversation for a man to have with any woman other than his wife. She backed off, and decided she would take her cues from him. She wouldn't push.

CHAPTER 38

Adam asked everyone to take their seats. His eyes shifted to Lindsay walking to her chair, picking up the water pitcher and pouring the clear liquid with perfectly manicured, long and slender fingers. He took in the faint scent of perfume as she sat down in her designated seat that just happened to be on his right side.

He walked around the conference table with coffee in hand, patiently waiting for people to settle in. "I want to thank all of you for allowing me to interview you over the last couple of days. Your willingness to be open has given me a good read on where we need to go." He glanced around the room, catching himself lingering a little too long in Lindsay's direction.

They spent the next couple of hours talking about their strengths and weaknesses. Nothing too earth shattering, but a little more interesting when they approached the issue of trust.

When one of the board members indicated it as a strength, Adam caught a glimpse of Lindsay and David exchanging a glance. Of course, neither Adam nor David could see what was going on inside Lindsay's brain - *embezzling funds, collapsed building and everyone for themselves, and what about Tom, and God please, not Peter. Have I missed anything?*

Adam asked, "Everyone agree that you trust each other?"

There was some hesitation, and a couple of shrugs, but most heads nodded up and down. He continued, "Have you been in the position to test it before?"

David looked around the room to see if anyone else would offer their opinion. After what felt like a long silence, he reluctantly said, "Not like the challenges we're getting ready to face. Potential winners and losers. We'll certainly get the opportunity to test it."

Adam contemplated his next move, but decided it wasn't the most appropriate time to address the problem that had become clear to him over the last couple of days. He continued, "Hold on to that thought. We'll put it in the parking lot and come back to it. Any other comments before we move on?"

"I would like to say something." David took a second to scan the room and make eye contact with every single person at the table. "This is a bright group of people with diverse skills. If we can merge our talents, and work on our connection, strengthening our relationship, we'll not only get through this, but accomplish some remarkable things. That is why we're doing this. And, that's what keeps me going."

"Anyone else?"

"I agree with David - we do this together. If college and pro athletes can play to their collective strengths and win championships, then we can do it, too." Lindsay said with a hint of enthusiasm in her voice. "Today, it's more important than ever."

Adam couldn't help but notice, and admire Lindsay's style. Her passion kept knocking him in the head. He sensed it was genuine, straight forward, and not hokey. His gaze definitely lingered a little longer than it should have. "This is a good stopping point for a break. Let's take fifteen."

CHAPTER 39

As people filed out of the room, Adam was looking down at his tablet and pounding away on the keyboard. He didn't seem to notice Lindsay until she walked past him and reached the door. He smiled to himself and redirected his attention to the work in front of him.

There was nothing groundbreaking about the last couple of hours. This group had shared the same responses he heard from teams more often than he could count. In these controlled learning environments, you hear things like they get along, respect and trust one another, and avoid confrontation and conflict.

Based on his detective work and observations over the last couple of days, he suspected there was something much more going on here, and it bothered him. Maybe paranoia, but there was even a vibe in the room.

He had a nagging feeling conflict was happening, but only behind closed doors. And, he wasn't ready to accept trust. They may have said they trusted each other in the good times, but what about the bad? Just how bad was it?

CHAPTER 40

Lindsay glanced quickly at Adam on her way out. He appeared deep in thought with his head buried in his phone. She caught herself feeling slightly disappointed that he didn't seem to notice her walk by. *Better get that in check - school girl is not a good look for a grown woman.*

She made a left turn out the doorway and headed towards Peter's office. There was no sign of him anywhere. His light was off and his desk was clean so she would have to settle for leaving a note. She couldn't find anything to write on, not even a piece of paper. It looked and felt like it hadn't been occupied in a while. *Where was he? What was up? What was wrong?* She stopped herself. *He would have texted.*

She reluctantly ripped a piece of paper from her notepad, something she didn't like to do since it threw off the page count. She frowned, *obsessive compulsive much?* As she was finishing the note, she looked up and found Tom staring at her. Or glaring at her. It was a bit off-putting since he had been acting so strange the last few days. Distant and strange.

"How are you, Lindsay?" Tom asked in a voice that actually sounded like he was interested in the answer.

Signing her name to the note and looking up, she responded, "I'm good. I'm on a break and thought I would leave a note for Peter. I need to talk to him. Do you know where he is?"

Tom shrugged, "No, I haven't seen him much lately. He's been in and out. Sorry I can't help you." He didn't miss a beat and asked, "How is the executive training going? It is training, isn't it?"

She started to mumble something about it going well so far but being too soon to tell. Instead, she seized the opportunity. "It's actually more than training. We have a consultant working with us, and facilitating our upcoming budget meetings. It's no secret we're going to have to change our behavior given our funding challenges. It's impacting all of us. Not easy. How do you feel about it?"

He shrugged and replied, "I think it's been a struggle for everyone. I'm having a hard time myself. I came here thinking we were on the upswing. We have the reputation of cutting edge designs and our funding profile is going to change that. It's a struggle."

"I understand. Hopefully, we can strike a balance, Tom. I think we're all trying to figure out how to stay competitive, cutting edge as you say, and remain viable."

"Yeah. I guess you're right. It's still hard," he said emotionless, and locked eyes on her.

"I know. Hang in there. It's more important than ever to keep the lines of communication open. Talk to Peter, and keep talking to him. Be open about how you feel. We're all in this together," Lindsay said.

"Thank you. I'll keep that in mind. I appreciate it." His smile appeared genuine.

They exchanged goodbyes and she walked back to the conference room. *Tom was a mystery. He would do something disappointing and then he would seem like a good guy. Was she wrong about him? Had she misunderstood the conversation she overheard earlier?*

CHAPTER 41

On Lindsay's way back to the conference room, she approached David's office. She slowed, until she heard the noise. His door was closed, and there was another example of loud voices behind mahogany. She elected not to knock and kept moving. It was obviously not a good time. *Where was his assistant? And, what was up with this firm? What was in the drinking water these days?*

She stopped by the kitchen and grabbed a green tea. As she walked across the threshold, she almost bumped into David. "Oh, I'm so sorry. I should watch where I'm going," she said while laughing.

"No problem. I wasn't paying attention either," he muttered. No smiles and no laughter.

He looked up from the floor, stepped aside, and waited for her. She noticed his face was red and void of any sign of emotion. They walked together in silence until she spoke.

She suspected all the real life drama was getting to him. He was a resilient guy, but this was challenging for anyone to handle. She asked quietly, "Are you okay? You look really tense."

"I'm fine."

"David, hang in there. I know you have a lot on your plate right now, do you want to talk about anything?"

"I can't now. Maybe later," he whispered, looking down at his feet.

"Well, I'm here if you need me."

"Thanks."

They walked the rest of the way without either of them saying a word. When Lindsay entered the conference room, she scanned the table to find that both Peter and Patrick were absent. She frowned and thought so much for mandatory attendance. Just before Adam resumed the session, Patrick rushed in. Still no Peter.

CHAPTER 42

There was laughter and joking as they all filed back into the room and took their seats. Adam wondered how long that would last. He didn't waste any time. "During the earlier part of the day, you guys mentioned that you avoid confrontation and conflict. Let's camp on that observation for awhile. What do you think about it?"

Lindsay spoke up, "I think it's problematic that we avoid tackling conflict. It sounds like we may be afraid to confront real issues when they come up. I think we better learn to be up front and tackle our challenges head on. Learn to work through them."

"Thank you, Lindsay. Anybody else?" Adam was working hard to hide his interest.

For a moment, the room was silent as if everyone was afraid to speak. David nodded agreement with Lindsay, but kept quiet, wanting to hear what the others had to say.

Jack broke the silence, "I think Lindsay is right. We're not as effective as we can be. Sometimes we settle for the 'it is what it is' mentality or 'pick your battles' mentality and we might say it doesn't matter, but it does. We have to start tackling the hard issues that lead to results. It hasn't been a big deal so far because we haven't had high stakes on the line. Things have changed and we keep hearing there may be winners and losers, but I don't think we should just settle for that."

Lindsay attempted to hide her shock that she and Jack might actually agree on something. That he almost seemed human. *Can't be. Probably a momentary lapse.*

"Your comments are spot on, Jack and Lindsay. We'll spend some time exploring and navigating through conflict over the next few days," Adam said.

And much more, Adam thought. It was perfect timing for the discussion about the real key for them.

* * * * * * * * * *

Adam walked around the conference table to get to the Flipchart, scanning the room as he moved around. There was a brief moment of silence and he stole a look at Lindsay before continuing. Their eyes met briefly and exchanged smiles. She was attentive and engaging as usual. He was definitely intrigued.

Getting his head back in the game, he said, "You guys made some really good points about your team. Based on our analysis, there are three areas we'll focus on with our remaining time together." He turned to the flip chart and scribbled notes, speaking out loud as he was doing it: "Three things - building and maintaining valuable relationships, learning a more effective way to communicate, and building and retaining trust."

He placed the marker in the tray and turned back to the group. "If you follow this fairly simple advice, you'll make all the difference in your professional relationships. And, when we get to the Budget Reduction Strategy, you'll see how interesting things can get in the heat of the moment."

Adam checked his watch and picked up his coffee cup. "You already know this, but these tools and behaviors we're talking about will work in both your personal and professional relationships. It's simply about being human - but, let's take a minute and discuss a situational difference. If things fail in a relationship, you're likely to have the option to leave, but not so much in business. So let's camp on personal for a minute. Let's say you think it's worth it and you don't want to leave. So, what do you do next?"

Scanning the room, Adam observed some interesting physical responses. There were a few heads turning down, some looking away, others staring off in contemplation, and only a couple with their attention focused squarely on him. There was a lot of personal stuff going on in the air they were breathing. At least, they knew how to feel and that would give Adam something to work with since the next exercise might momentarily suck the life out of them.

His eyes met David's, but only for a second. David turned away, thinking about Bob. He shouldn't have allowed him to miss this part. He was one of his VP's that was usually upbeat and positive, but not lately. Affairs will do that to you. Especially one involving someone else in the office, or so the rumor said. What if the rumors were wrong, or what if they were right? David wasn't so sure, but he couldn't ignore it any longer, had to figure out how to approach it, quit procrastinating, and get on with it. He caught himself drifting off in thought and missed part of what Adam was saying, but he caught the most important part.

"You have to know your emotional triggers and pay attention to them during the interaction. Learn to express your opinion and be willing to be vulnerable, listen to understand the other viewpoint regardless of how hard that might be in the moment, respectfully disagree when you don't see eye to eye, and discuss things openly without feeling fear of conflict. Use it as an opportunity to learn, deepen understanding and maybe even lead to greater connection. You stop seeing conflict as a bad thing to avoid at all cost."

Adam continued, "The real key here is taking the personal attack out of it, and reiterating you're both working for the same thing, the common goal. It reminds everyone of what is important. If you take nothing else away from today's conversation, take this away: When things get challenging, go back to the common goal. And if you need to revisit, revise or tweak the common goal, do it. It's basic and simple, but very powerful."

* * * * * * * * * *

Adam paused and gazed around the room suspecting that people were evaluating their own lives, their own work environments. Their own issues.

"It isn't easy dealing with human emotions. It takes a lot of energy and soul searching to do what we'll be doing together. You'll be amazed at the depth of exploration over the next few days." Adam looked around the room before asking, "We discovered a couple of interesting things about your team. What are they?"

Lindsay answered, "The major discovery surrounded conflict resolution. We have historically shied away from addressing conflict outwardly. Until now, we didn't consider avoidance as a bad thing."

Adam responded, "Good point. I think you'll agree it's something to work on. And, you'll have many opportunities, very soon."

David chimed in, "The other area involved the power of building and maintaining a relationship and looking at each other as much more than people that work at the same place. Seeing this as a valued relationship. I'm going to continue harping on this. Care about each other and feel responsible to help each other. Build a 'we're in this together' system that includes "What can I do to help? And, when things go south, we'll revisit the common goal(s) together. We'll have an action plan and measure success."

Adam smiled, "Exactly. I couldn't have said it better. Excellent place to end for the day and we'll reconvene tomorrow morning for a fascinating and thought provoking exercise. I think you'll find it intriguing, challenging, even gut wrenching. You don't want to miss it. Good night." Adam smiled and began shoving papers in his briefcase. He failed to mention the next session would have them getting to know each other in a way they had never even considered. They were about to enter raw, naked and vulnerable territory.

CHAPTER 43

The room was empty except for David and Lindsay lingering behind, talking. Adam hesitated slightly before walking over to them. "David, you had good insight on this. Getting your team thinking about the relationship and culture in a different way will definitely help you navigate through the challenges you're facing."

David smiled and responded, "I would like to take full credit, but Lindsay was a big part of this. We were talking about our challenges and she strongly urged me to consider a consultant and my only role was selecting you. She has amazing intuition where people are concerned, and I know when to listen."

"I can see that. Her participation has been spot on. She nailed the discussion about conflict and she made a couple of other very interesting observations." Adam looked at her, "Have you had much formal human behavior or organizational development training?" Adam asked.

"Not really. Just the normal executive leadership stuff, but I'm intrigued by human behavior and any kind of business study. I've always been interested in how people think, how businesses operate, and how cultures are built."

"You give me a call if you ever want to do some work with me," Adam offered.

"Oh great, I hire you and now you want to steal my highly esteemed Legal Counsel," David kidded.

She threw her head back and laughed, "I think I'll hang out with the two of you more often. You're good for my ego."

They continued talking when David's assistant walked to the door and interrupted. There was a crisis that required his attention. Lindsay watched his face turn to fear as they walked out together. Outwardly showing his emotions was definitely not his style, until now. *Earlier fears nagged at her - financial crisis, collapsed building, embezzlement. What else could possibly go wrong?*

Lindsay momentarily stared at the doorway after David left the room. She and Adam remained standing without saying anything for what appeared to be forever. It was a little awkward until Adam asked, "What made you interested in the human behavior elements of business?"

"I don't really know. Growing up, I always knew I was going to be a lawyer. It's all I ever thought about and it was the only thing I wanted to do. It wasn't until I gained corporate experience that I became intrigued by the notion that success is directly tied to relationships, probably more than technical skill set. The differentiator. It's the human side of business relationships that build culture and make teams and organizations great."

A colleague came to the door and called out her name. She gave Adam a smile and said she better go. He returned the smile, saying he would see her the next day. He attempted to hide his disappointment. He was more than a little surprised by his reaction. He found her interesting and wanted more time.

He gave an "oh well" shrug and picked up his briefcase and left for the day. There was a spring in his step. He wasn't sure why, but he was definitely in a good mood. Actually, he did know why. It had something to do with the beautiful blonde executive.

CHAPTER 44

Lindsay was not overly happy about the interruption, but it was just as well. She didn't need any distractions anyway.

She walked down the hallway with her colleague talking about a problem they thought might have an easy fix. As it turned out, nothing was easy anymore. They stopped at his office doorway, agreed they had to include a couple of the others, and he volunteered to set up a meeting invite.

Irritated by the lack of progress on just about everything, she turned and walked in the other direction. She was thinking back to Patrick's comments about the need for urgency and had been a little surprised by his reaction. He was usually interested and engaged when it came to people and relationships. She smiled at the thought of teasing him about getting grouchy in his old age.

Needing a caffeine fix, she went for coffee before returning to her office. She was still thinking about Patrick as she entered the Cafe Bar. The relationships mattered, his presence in her personal and work life mattered, and none of it would be as fulfilling without him. They talked about almost anything. Sports, fun, good times, sad times, frightening moments, even tragedy.

CHAPTER 45

The Cafe Bar was the place Patrick told Lindsay about his son losing one of his best friends while hiking down Lassiter Mountain. A tragic accident. Patrick would mention it occasionally, but hadn't talked about it in awhile. He never told her all the details, but enough that she could relive the scene in her own mind.

At the end of his first year in college, Andrew and two of his buddies were on a weekend hiking trip in the western part of the state. They drove up on a Friday night and spent the evening setting up camp, grilling burgers and telling stories.

They woke early the next morning to spend the day on the mountain. It was considered a moderate to strenuous hike, with wildlife, a stream and a couple of waterfalls. With cameras and backpacks, they headed out.

The weather was mild and the sun shone bright. They took pictures, horsed around more than they should have, and ate lunch on a ledge over-looking a crystal blue waterfall. After close to seven hours on the trails, they were exhausted. With sunburned faces, they returned to the campsite for dinner and an early turn in. The sun had done a number on their energy and they weren't interested in anything but their sleeping bags.

They planned to get up early the next day and make a big breakfast, tear down the camp site, and hike one more time before driving home. The weather forecast predicted rain for late in the afternoon, but they would be well on their way home by then.

Sunday morning arrived and it was another stunningly beautiful day, with the sun shining and the sky a royal blue. They made their way up the mountain and surveyed the intoxicating views one last time. There were few hikers on the trail, so it was quiet and peaceful and they could take their time, stopping and gazing.

They brought out their lunches and ate at the top of the peak, feeling the let down of their much anticipated weekend coming to an end. They sat in silence and devoured their sandwiches as young boys do. Towards the end of lunch, Andrew tilted his head towards the sky and thought he smelled rain but there wasn't a cloud in the sky. They soaked in the sun a little longer before gathering their gear for the two hour hike down.

About halfway through, the sky started changing to a light gray color. A couple of clouds rolled in and the temperature decreased slightly. Rain was definitely in the distance.

With about thirty minutes or so to go, the weather changed dramatically. The sky turned black and the wind swirled in a circular motion. Tree branches began swaying back and forth, rain was misting, and the temperature dropped so much that it was almost cold.

The rain grew harder, coming down in pelts, and the wind picked up even more speed. The precipitation caused the rocks to become slippery so quickly that it was increasingly more difficult to navigate the way down.

The sudden change quieted the boys. They focused their attention on the trail and the rocks. They picked up speed more than they should have.

Patrick had recalled his son mentioning he was a little unnerved by the circumstances and something didn't feel right. At the time, he blamed it on the uncooperative weather.

Andrew was usually a skillful hiker and had climbed some of the most difficult mountains in the state. Being an athlete, he had the stability and upper body strength to lift himself up and over most tall boulders with little effort. Ricky and Chad were skilled hikers, but not as agile as Andrew. Knowing that, Andrew stayed close, but led the way. The trail was near the edge of the mountain, but free of brush and rock, making it easier. Ordinarily, it wouldn't have been a problem. The weather made it more treacherous and them more cautious.

Everything after that turned out to be a blur. Since Andrew was in front, he didn't see what happened next, but Ricky did.

Ricky said they were going along and following behind Andrew without a problem. On one turn, Chad grabbed on to a boulder slightly above his head and attempted to lift himself up. Half the way above the massive rock, his arm gave way. He started dropping to his feet like he had done a hundred times before, but this time the landing was slippery and his ankle turned hard. He slipped, trying to grab for anything to hold on to, but there was nothing there. Ricky realized what was happening and lunged for him but he couldn't reach him.

Chad screamed and Andrew stopped and turned. He ran to them, but was too late. His last image of Chad was watching helplessly as he was falling and flailing in mid-air, screaming for his life. The noise grew distant quickly, but it also felt like they were operating in slow motion.

The next thing they heard was the far away sound of Chad's body hitting the ground. They saw him, but heard nothing. He didn't respond when they called out his name.

Andrew and Ricky tried to get down the side of the mountain as fast as their legs would carry them. The rain and wind curtailed, but the surfaces remained a slippery mess. They scrambled from rock to rock, but could not find an escape route. Andrew grabbed his cellphone from his backpack and prayed for reception. He was relieved when his phone displayed two bars and it held on long enough to make the 911 call.

They reached the bottom a couple of minutes behind the EMT and recovery team. They were busy hovering over Chad when the boys found their way. One of the officers saw the boys running towards them and put up his hands and grabbed them, stopping them from getting any closer.

Andrew stared without moving or saying a word. He wanted to let him know he wasn't alone, but he was directed to stand back. His eyes were glassy, tears streaked his cheeks, and he felt faint, but he gathered enough strength to drop to the ground and say a prayer.

Not long after that, they stopped attending to Chad. There was nothing left to do. He suffered severe trauma to the head, falling more than 3000 feet. They pronounced him dead and turned their attention to the surviving boys.

Andrew couldn't remember the last time he had cried so hard or so much. His stomach became queasy and he started to lose consciousness when one of the EMT workers put his arms around him to keep him from falling. He guided Andrew to the back of the truck to sit where both boys were given water and wrapped in blankets.

Later Ricky recalled that he couldn't escape the image of the terror in Chad's face. He couldn't get the vision out of his head and couldn't stop wondering if he could have done something more. And, Andrew said he would never shake the image of the shock and fear as Chad tumbled down the side of the mountain.

The police ruled the tragedy a terrible accident that resulted in a kid being deprived of a future and being taken from his family.

Patrick had talked from time to time about the devastation Chad's parents had experienced. Their son tragically killed on a hike, doing what the boys loved, and doing what they had done many times before. Parents shouldn't have to go through something like that. Nothing was comparable to the loss of a child.

Patrick and Stephanie attempted many times to reach out to comfort Chad's parents. After all, they were neighbors and friends that had vacationed and socialized together over the years. The pain proved to be too much of a reminder. The contact became infrequent and the friendship dwindled. On the rare occasion Chad's parents actually returned their calls, the small talk was void of tone and emotionless.

Patrick wondered how Chad's parents kept going. Chad's father once told him they get through it by putting one foot in front of the other every single day. One day turns into two, two turns into three, and you're still going on. They would never forget and never stop grieving, only learn to accept it, to continue because they had other children that needed them.

That day changed the lives of so many. It was a day that all of them wished they could do over.

CHAPTER 46

For Andrew and Ricky, losing Chad would be one of the toughest struggles in their young lives. Watching their friend die and not able to do anything to stop it.

Chad had been Andrew's best friend. They attended school together from kindergarten all the way through high school, and had always planned to go to college together.

Ricky didn't enter their lives until the start of their junior year in high school. He was the new boy in town and Chad was the first to meet him in a class. Because Ricky didn't know anyone, Chad occasionally invited him to hang out with them. It was the kind of human being he was, not wanting anyone to feel alone. The three spent more and more time together and grew to be good friends. Over time, they became inseparable.

"Ms. Thompson, your coffee is ready," shouted the Cafe Bar employee as she placed it on the counter. Lindsay looked up with a stunned look on her face. She had almost forgotten where she was and what she was doing.

Every time she thought about it, she got a sick feeling in the pit of her stomach. The level of detail she remembered was a bit perplexing. There were times she couldn't recall what happened yesterday, yet she remembered Patrick's account, recalling the details, almost vividly.

She suspected her recall was due largely to witnessing the impact it had on Andrew. She cared deeply for this young man that was evolving into a decent and compassionate replica of his father.

His father. *What was going on with him? How bad was Stephanie's health?* She vowed to check in and provide support like he had done for her all these years, and that time. A man she could really count on.

CHAPTER 47

Lindsay returned to her office and sat at the computer screen and read the same lines over and over. Not making any progress, her mind kept wandering back to the workshop session, and the facilitator.

She wanted to concentrate, to focus, but she just didn't have it in her. Feeling like she was on a caffeine buzz or something, her thoughts were running around in circles. For the first time in a long time, she might actually feel happy, or feel something.

After several failed attempts, she shut down the computer. She grabbed her things, turned off the office lights and walked to her car.

The early evening sun was warm enough to drive with the top down. Increasing the volume on the radio, singing loud and driving fast, her car purred for a couple of miles until she hit the rush hour congestion. For once, not even the slow moving traffic bothered her. She looked forward to staying in with a nice glass of wine, a chopped salad with her famous marinated tuna, a hot bath, and no work. *Or maybe stop for salmon? No, tuna, let's not go crazy with this euphoria.*

She looked at the car's clock as she was parking her car. On the road for fifty three minutes and it didn't even seem that long.

She changed into shorts and a tee and fired up the grill. With a glass of wine she measured to be exactly five ounces, she placed a couple of tuna steaks on the grill. Lightly searing the fish would only take a couple of minutes and the salad was already prepared.

It wasn't long before she sat in front of the television and ate while watching the news. She quickly became preoccupied and opened her computer, searching the internet for Harvard Business Review articles on communication and relationships. She was getting immersed in the fascinating study of human behavior when her mind drifted to Adam as she read a story about organizational health and social psychology. Looking forward to the next day's session, there might be an opportunity to discuss her night's study, with him.

After a couple of hours reading, she made herself retreat to the master bathroom. She lit candles surrounding the tub, turned on the jets, and went to the kitchen to top off her wine. Allowing herself three more ounces while lounging in the warm, bubbly water, she kept telling herself the wine was good for her heart and it was her peace and serenity time. She should have been tired, but was surprisingly rejuvenated. Studying behavior was fascinating.

Or, Lindsay had a crazy thought. *Could Adam have anything to do with it?* He certainly was handsome. She was attracted to a tall and slender frame, but usually preferred blonde, blue eyed men. His dark hair and eyes were almost perfect. She had noticed that a five o'clock shadow emerged late in the day and he had a cute little sheepish grin when he was being charming and quick witted.

Getting into bed, she was still thinking about him. There was no wedding ring and he didn't talk about a wife or children. She would definitely have to find out more. He appeared to be almost too perfect.

There must be something wrong with him, she thought, following her usual line of sarcasm about romance. He was probably a serial killer. She turned off the light and went to bed.

CHAPTER 48

Lindsay woke the next morning still energized, not worried about the work on her desk, her laptop, or her phone. She was thinking about the day ahead and the upcoming workshop.

On the drive in, she dialed Patrick's number to ask him to join her for a drink at the coffee bar. He answered his private line, sounding tired or half asleep with a flat, "Hello."

"Hi there. Do you want to meet for coffee? I am pulling in the lot now."

"I can't. I have a couple of calls to make before the workshop. I'm sorry," Patrick replied.

"No problem. Just thought I would check. Maybe we can catch up for lunch later." She ended the call as she parked the car.

She grabbed her briefcase and closed the door when she saw Adam getting out of his vehicle. Her pulse quickened and she didn't know whether to look the other way or directly at him. They were obviously headed in the same direction. She nonchalantly quickened her step.

"Hello Adam. How are you today?" She smiled.

"Hi Lindsay. I'm good, but a little slow moving this morning. I worked way past my bedtime last night and I'm in need of a very robust coffee."

"I'm heading to the Cafe Bar. You're welcome to join me." She crossed her fingers for a yes.

He looked at his watch and said, "I would like that. I have a few minutes before I need to get the room prepped."

A little awkwardly, they walked and talked about the weather and other idle chatter. In the Cafe Bar, they placed their order and looked around the crowded room for a table. The only one left was a small circular, cozy one in the corner by the fireplace. They both looked at each other with only a slight hesitation before walking to it. She feared he could read her mind, thinking it was a little intimate for strangers, but at the same time, secretly experiencing a twinge of excitement.

They barely sat down when their orders were called. Adam excused himself and walked to the counter to get their coffees. It was a forgotten feeling, having a man wait on her again. She surprised herself and smiled, feeling her face starting to flush.

He returned to the table with their drinks and a couple of napkins. The more they talked, the more comfortable they became. There was a quick familiarity developing between them. On a couple of occasions, they leaned in close to hear each other over the noise and their knees touched. It was a little unnerving, but at the same time, exhilarating. There was definitely chemistry.

Lindsay couldn't fight it. She was interested, intrigued and wanted to know more about him. This curiosity was beyond anything she had felt for a very long time. She wanted to know how he got to this place, and he was willing to share his story.

He told her how he became involved in the study of business, humans and behavior. He had been a college athlete and was always interested in the dynamics between people, their interactions, and how successful team cultures were built. He knew when he graduated from college he was more interested in people, than in profits and losses in business. But he didn't have any practical experience so going out on his own would have to wait. He worked for a consulting firm and someone else way too long, before getting the nerve to take the plunge and go out on his own. He did, and wondered why he hadn't done it sooner.

He looked down at his watch to discover he was almost late. He hesitated and said as he was in the process of standing, "This has been great, but I better get to the room and set up for today. Will you walk with me?" he asked.

"I would love to, but there is something I need to do before today's meeting. I enjoyed having coffee with you. We should do it again. And, I would like to hear more about your business. I find it fascinating."

"I would like that. We'll talk later." It was more of a statement than a question.

"Yes, we will," she said with a confident smile.

With that, Adam may have hesitated too long as he gazed at her before indicating he would see her in the conference room. Lindsay watched him walk away. He was definitely charming. She admonished herself. *Why didn't she just ask him to dinner?* She was almost certain she sensed a spark between them. She hated missed opportunities.

CHAPTER 49

Lindsay stepped back up to the coffee bar and ordered a drink for Patrick. His voice on the phone had sounded like he could use a pick me up. She couldn't even count the times he had done that for her over the years of late nights at work or back-to-back meetings.

She walked down the hall without seeing anyone. Adam was still on her mind. *Ugh, not good. God, she was all over the map. Make up your mind.*

With coffee in hand, she nodded at Patrick's assistant and peaked in his office door. He was on the phone and looked startled at the sight of her and said to the caller, "I'll get back to you."

Standing in the doorway, she felt like she was interrupting. Almost a bother. It was a strange feeling given the history between them.

"I hope I'm not interrupting. You sounded a bit tired earlier. I thought you might be able to use a cup of coffee," she said, handing him the cup.

His face changed and there was the Patrick smile she knew so well. "Aw, you're my hero. Thank you for the coffee. I'm okay. I have a lot going on right now, but this is just what I needed." He took a long sip, leaned back in his chair, and closed his eyes before motioning for her to sit. He said, "I'm finished with my calls. Have a seat so we can catch up."

They discussed a couple of work issues. Not too exciting and nothing about sports or a great wine or dinner they prepared the night before.

She sensed he wanted to talk about something, but he didn't say anything. She asked, "How about lunch today?"

"I'm sorry. I can't today. This workshop has put me so far behind. I can't wait until this is over and we can get back to work."

"Why do you feel that way? I still believe it's exactly what we need. Help prepare us for what we're about to face. It may actually enhance our relationships and allow us to focus on the firm above our departments and ourselves."

Patrick smiled and teased, "Or, perhaps you like Adam."

"What? I don't know what you are talking about," she shrugged, lifting her head into the air.

"You can't fool me, Lindsay. I see how you hang on to his every word. You like him."

Even if it was at her expense, it felt good being playful with him. She started to defend herself, but was saved by the phone. Patrick's assistant hesitated in the doorway and said softly, "The doctor is returning your call. He is on your private line."

"I better take it," he looked at Lindsay before picking up, "I'll see you in the Board Room in a few minutes? And, on second thought, let's do lunch. We'll need a break," he said, as he swiveled in his chair to grab the phone from the receiver.

"Lunch it is. I'll leave you to your call," she said, already standing and walking to the door. He was still on her mind as she walked down the hall to her office. He was definitely off his game and seemed more than just a little worried. Lunch would be the perfect opportunity. An invitation to open up about what was bothering him.

CHAPTER 50

Lindsay had only fifteen minutes to spare. She looked at the pink message slips on her desk and decided they could wait and so could her emails.

Even with all the turmoil swirling around them, she was excited about the day, the possibilities, and her heightened interest in the subject matter. The last few days had stirred a passion in her. Maybe she discovered a couple of passions worth exploring. She smiled, knowing she would have to parking lot that for later.

On the way to the Board Room, she saw David talking to Jack. He was probably discussing some new business development venture. *Ugh Jack. So annoying.*

Jack had been swept away from another firm to head up their Business Development Department about a year earlier. He was one of the few outsiders hired directly into a senior position. She had to admit his outstanding credentials set him apart and made him the only feasible solution, but he came with an air of arrogance and distance that Lindsay found unnerving. She tried to build a rapport, but there was no reciprocity. He was aloof and didn't appear to be interested in a relationship with her, or any other colleagues.

He found out about the VP position from a past connection with Patrick that she didn't understand. They couldn't be more different. When they were canvassing for the right fit, Patrick recommended Jack. He said he was a great guy.

They worked together years earlier, when they were younger and without families. They were close buddies going to sporting events, restaurants, and clubs. He had beamed the first time he talked about him. Said he was looking forward to working together again and Jack was interested in rekindling their friendship. Couldn't wait. Until Jack was in the job.

Once he joined the firm, he didn't associate much with Patrick or any of his new colleagues. It was surprising how he treated Patrick, a guy that was supposed to be an old friend. Lindsay asked him about it and he shrugged and simply said, "Jack has changed a lot. I can't say I know him anymore."

Jack was an odd guy. He was friendly on some occasions and even acted like he wanted to be part of the team. The next time, nothing. Not the slightest interest in a connection. Lindsay couldn't figure him out, but there was definitely something about him. She intended to keep her eye on him. Yes, he was strange, or worse.

And, then there was the relationship between David and Jack. He had been instantly taken with Jack, and knowing David, Lindsay didn't understand that either. He was usually a good judge of character, but this time? There was definitely something off.

When David saw Lindsay heading in their direction, he stopped and they waited for her. They spoke and made small talk before David asked, "What do you think about the workshop?"

She paused for a moment, "I believe it's exactly what we need. I don't think everyone bought in initially, but we are making progress and starting to get into it." She looked in Jack's direction before asking, "What do you think, Jack?"

"I'm pleasantly surprised. I'm not usually into this soft skill stuff, but I'm warming up to it. If today is anything like Adam said it would be, I'm looking forward to the mechanical twist that involves tools and models. I can relate to that," he said, with a slight smile.

Shocking. I'm sure you can, she thought. She replied, "It should be interesting."

David nodded and looked at his watch. He said, "We better get in there. It's almost time to start."

CHAPTER 51

(Executive Training - Exercise 1)

The three of them entered the conference room together. They were the last ones in. Everyone else was seated and looking at their various electronic devices. Adam was at the head of the table, scribbling notes on the flip chart. He glanced at his watch and turned to face his audience. "Let's dive in and start with an exercise that is one of my favorites. We'll have an opportunity to connect on a more personal level. Find out some interesting things about each other.

"We'll start by pairing up and sharing with each other what a typical day looks like. Partner A will talk for five minutes and Partner B will be an active listener, no words are to be uttered unless it's to get clarification or more information. Not even anything like, 'I do that too' or 'I know how that feels' or shifting conversation to them. Then, we will switch places and Partner B will share their story."

They didn't realize Adam had studied this group and made some intentional pairings. It was definitely not random. He started with Patrick and David. When he got around to Lindsay, she thought she would faint when Adam placed her with Jack. *Really? Anyone on earth but him.*

When all the other pairings were set, the partners moved their chairs to face one another. As Adam expected, the conversations started off slowly.

Jack looked as thrilled as Lindsay about the prospect of spending any more time together than they absolutely had to. They faced one another and the timer began. Jack talked first and it wasn't all that interesting or extraordinary. Lindsay had zero interest and just wanted to get through it. *Blah, blah, blah.*

He said the majority of his time was spent supporting his managers. He let them manage, but stayed engaged to see what he could do to support them or make their lives easier. Lindsay raised an eyebrow, surprised that he even cared about the relationships with his staff.

Adam was walking around the room, observing the conversations. He stopped to listen to Jack describe his day. He asked, "Let's step back. How does your day begin before you get to the office?"

Jack hesitated and shifted uncomfortably in his chair. He paused for a moment before speaking. He finally said, "My day begins when I get up at 5:30. I bring my wife coffee in bed. We sit and talk until we finish our first cup. By 6:30, I've showered and am in the car. I drive by my mother's apartment to make her breakfast and spend a little time with her."

"Do you mind saying a little more about your mother?"

"Well, my father died a long time ago and my mom lives alone. Until recently she had been doing quite well. Over the last year, her health has really deteriorated and we've been caring for her. She probably shouldn't live alone any longer. My wife and I are trying to decide what arrangements to make for her. It's going to be a difficult conversation when we move her out of her home. She continues to tell us she is not moving."

Lindsay's listening perked up as he talked about his mother. She was surprised, even a bit shocked. She hadn't known, and couldn't imagine the difficulty of being the primary caretaker of his mother. He probably had a full day before he even made it to the office. Maybe that explained some of his disinterest in building relationships at work. He had all he could handle at home and there wasn't room for anyone or anything else.

Her mind wandered for a second to the implications of perceptions and assumptions. She had been making judgements about Jack that were perhaps unfair. No one was immune to some type of personal struggle, even those that seem to have it all. That's just life.

Adam looked at Lindsay and smiled. He thought he knew what she was thinking. This was her first "aha moment" of empathy for her colleague. He walked away still smiling.

Jack continued describing his day and some of its challenges. But this time Lindsay was listening a little more closely. She would occasionally throw in a comment like, "I had no idea. What you go through every day. How do you do it?" or "Tell me more about that." When his time was up, she thought about the hardships he faced on a daily basis. *Maybe he wasn't so bad.*

The surprise showed on Lindsay's face. She had a few struggles like all of us, but nothing as difficult as caring for an elderly parent everyday. Hearing about Jack's daily activities made her a little more empathetic to his life challenges. He didn't complain or try to be a martyr and she didn't make a habit of feeling sorry for herself or sympathy for people that wallowed in their problems. *Hmmm - Jack might have some redeeming qualities after all.*

She glanced up and saw Adam looking at her. Their eyes met and without a word, their expressions showed they were thinking the same thing. She may have been too quick to jump to negative conclusions about Jack. Maybe a little too hard core at times, she was beginning to think about her need for more compassion, and the importance of empathy for all relationships, not just those you're close to.

CHAPTER 52

Next, it was Lindsay's turn. She began by describing her day and was embarrassed to share something so trivial after Jack's story. Sure, her life wasn't perfect, but avoidance had always worked for her. She coped by pushing undesirable thoughts out of her mind. Not thinking about them when they crept in. *Why make them real?*

Adam paused and asked a question that shocked Lindsay, "You've talked about your passion for work. Is there anything in your life you find challenging?"

She looked surprised, diverting her focus from Jack to Adam. She wasn't expecting the question and wasn't quite sure how to respond. She blushed and paused too long. *Busted.*

Adam couldn't help but notice the dramatic shift on her face. The minute he realized what he had done, he was sorry for making her feel uncomfortable. *Why did it have to be her?* He continued, "I apologize if I put you on the spot. I wish there was another way, but this level of sharing is critical here." He left out the part about this being just the beginning. The next exercise will suck the air out of their lungs, filled with too much personal, raw vulnerability, and finding their own measure on the empathy meter.

Recovering quickly with a faint smile and low tone, she said, "That's okay. I understand. Give me a moment." *Ugh, he wants something a little more personal. I don't do personal.*

Adam replied, reciprocating the low tone, "Take your time." Without waiting for a response, he continued moving around the room to observe the other participants in action. He hoped he hadn't offended her.

Lindsay sighed. *Here goes.* She held her breath and said, "Work is good. It always has been. It's the personal life I'm not so good at. Can't have everything right?" She let out a nervous laugh, buying time for courage and the right words. *Oh, the hell with it.* "Frankly, I suck at commitment. I guess I'm afraid of it, but afraid of being alone too. That's why I throw myself into my work. That way I can avoid dealing with it."

Jack didn't know how to respond, what to say. She really went from benign to deep in a nanosecond. He was caught off guard and out of his comfort zone on this exercise. He wasn't comfortable with the personal connection of the conversation. He didn't even know what questions to ask, so he stayed silent.

Lindsay didn't offer up anything else or say any more other than plead for Jack to keep this between them. She smiled and said it was personal and she didn't like to share her shortcomings.

Jack was relieved to drop the topic. He grunted, "I'm with you on that one. This whole thing makes me a little uncomfortable." He assured her it was between them and hesitated before saying, "It's nice to know that Lindsay Thompson isn't perfect."

She chuckled nervously and smiled at him. He actually smiled back. Two smiles in the same day. She might even believe him. That he wouldn't tell anyone. She couldn't explain it, but maybe she was wrong about Jack? Maybe she should think differently about him and just maybe they could attempt to build a relationship or something that resembled amicability. Interesting how bonds develop. *No way, not with Jack.*

CHAPTER 53

Adam continued walking around the room and stopped at David and Patrick. During David's five minutes, he shared a constant fear that he might not be able to live up to his father's legacy. The firm his father built from the ground up. What if he couldn't maintain his father's competitive edge? What if he couldn't live up to the expectations of his children? What about all these people he would let down if he failed? They had put their heart and soul into making the company what it had become. Many of them had participated in the success his father had built. They deserved the success. They were like family, too.

Patrick put up the palm of his hand and interrupted. He said, "David, I have to stop you for a minute. I think you're putting way too much pressure on yourself. You are worthy of achieving your father's success and more. You're not going to fail. Look at what you have provided for all of us," Patrick's voice cracked as he paused and couldn't speak any further. Fortunately, for Patrick, he was forced to stop.

Adam witnessed this exchange occurring and gently motioned with his hand for Patrick to let David continue. He didn't want to jeopardize the powerful message they would soon figure out.

David talked about the rest of his day as being typical of most CEO's. Most of his work was based on furthering the strategic vision for the firm. To lead. He wanted to inspire others to create the work they could love and be passionate and energetic about. He was a strong believer the number one ingredient to success was hiring the right people into the right jobs and letting them run. He would be there to support them.

Patrick was nodding his head as David talked. He knew these things about David. He certainly did walk the talk. He was a leader and a good man.

Why hadn't Patrick shared the challenges going on in his life? He trusted David and Lindsay. He thought they would help, but it didn't change the feelings of being alone. Those things in life that are beyond your control and you have to do the best you can. Sometimes there aren't any good solutions. He paused only for a second before realizing he was hearing David tell him it was his turn.

CHAPTER 54

Patrick assumed the spotlight and talked about the typical day in the life of a Comptroller. He saw his leadership role as supporting his managers and being the financial advisor. He had an experienced staff of accountants and the normal pressures of running the Department. Keeping the firm out of trouble, which had become increasingly more difficult recently.

He reflected on his work relationships. Enjoying the morning coffees and business meetings with Lindsay. His interactions and interest in assisting others through their fiscal challenges. It made him see his job as one of making a difference for his colleagues as well as the firm.

He didn't share his next thoughts because he couldn't. They wouldn't understand. He started to remember how he used to feel, getting up every morning jazzed about taking on new challenges and solving complex financial obstacles at work. He was disturbed by the fact he had lost interest and become a little more cynical and distant along the way. *What happened to him?* He knew the answer. He just couldn't tell them.

But, his face brightened when he talked about his life after work. He was describing the family he adored, spending time with his wife, and catching up with his son on those occasions they could get together. How much they enjoyed their son's sporting events and the simple things like having dinner together. His chin quivered slightly as he talked about them. He abruptly stopped and said, "That's about it for my normal day."

The change in Patrick's demeanor was noticeable and even a bit startling to David. He watched an array of emotions ranging from disengaged, to passionate about what he was accomplishing, to a look that resembled hopelessness. It wasn't like Patrick, who was usually predictable and balanced with a passion and energy that now competed with sadness. There were slight changes over the last few weeks, moments when he seemed so far away talking about his life that it was almost as if he was watching it through a window rather than living it. Patrick had always been so positive and engaging, until now.

At the same time, Patrick was thinking about David and what he had said. David talked about how much he cared about the people he worked with. They were more than just colleagues, they were family. He would do anything he could for them. Patrick forced a smile, knowing he was one of those people. David's words meant something to him. He should talk to ... He was interrupted by Adam's voice.

CHAPTER 55

"Time is up. Let's get back together and discuss what happened." Adam asked, "How did you feel as you shared your experiences with one another?"

No one spoke so Lindsay jumped in. "It was a little unnerving at first. I certainly altered my perspective, looking through life from another person's lens." She paused and looked at Jack before saying, "I had no idea how much you have on your plate. I admire what you're doing."

Jack's face turned slightly red and he nodded a thank you. He said he had a confession of his own. He hadn't realized she was so easy to talk to, a good listener, until now.

But, he couldn't bring himself to say out loud that he hadn't taken the opportunity to get to know her and that maybe he should consider working on it. He might be missing out. As they talked, he looked around the room and realized these were decent people. Until now, he felt like an outsider. That's how he had wanted it. No connections, no hurt. He had been there before and it almost destroyed him, but... *Was it worth the price?* He had to think about that.

Patrick smiled at Jack's comments. He knew what Jack meant about Lindsay. He had been Lindsay's closest colleague for a long time and depended on her for friendship, advice and loyalty. She was certainly steady and consistent.

Several others shared their perspectives and what they had learned about each other. The universal response was a sense of better understanding. Adam witnessed them starting to evolve and experience empathy. He continued, "What do you think happened during this exercise?"

Surprisingly, Jack was the first to speak. He said, "The environment really changes when you start talking about hardships, our similarities. Being human," he hesitated before continuing, "and I hate to say it, but being a little vulnerable. And that's scary. I'm really good at fighting that emotion." He chuckled.

"I agree with Jack. Also, it wasn't just about work. I started wanting to see Jack as a person, not just someone I work with, and," she teased, "fight with."

Heads nodded in agreement and Lindsay and Jack's observations represented consensus for the room. Adam brought round one to closure by summarizing the key points. He said, "As you start to really see each other as people with feelings, you can experience more understanding, and if you're lucky, an evolving closeness. We're going for empathy - change your narrative to look at our similarities instead of our differences. Be mindful, pay attention, catch yourself when you immediately go to differences and shift back to thinking about similarities. You'll be shocked at the results. This is a giant first step in the building of a relationship and new team culture."

He looked around the room as it grew quiet. He said, "Let's take twenty. When you return from the break, we'll get back in our pairs and step it up a notch. You might want to bring tissues for round two."

CHAPTER 56

Lindsay had just enough time to run to Eric's office and get a status on the collapsed building. When she got there, she discovered that Eric was at an off-site meeting, leaving Tyler at his conference table pouring through some files. She paused in the doorway admiring his focus. He was deep in a file and had his tablet open, checking out what looked like US Code. He was so engrossed that he didn't notice her leaning against the door with her arms crossed.

Still admiring from the doorway, she said, "That's impressive. Multi-tasking with such focus." She smiled and walked in the room and sat next to him.

Tyler flashed those youthful white teeth and pushed back from the table. He said, "I love this stuff. Do you think I'm becoming a nerd?"

"No, I think you picked the right career and like what you do. "Keep it up. It will pay off." She leaned in close and asked to see what he was working on. "Aw, the collapsed building. That's what I was coming to see Eric about. How's it going?"

"We're still researching some loose ends, but we're feeling confident we're on solid ground. And, Tom's help has been amazing. He is such a sharp guy when it comes to the design business."

"He is definitely talented. Let's set up a meeting to brief me on where you are. Touch base with Eric and you guys get back to me."

"Will do. We'll check your calendar and see what works for you."

"Excellent. Tyler, I'm glad you're here. You're doing outstanding work already. Is there anything I can do for you?"

He started to speak and hesitated, looking down at his hands folded in front of him. He spoke, talking so fast he couldn't have been taking any breaths. "I know you're really busy, and probably don't have time, and you have more important things, and you're the big boss and all, but," he paused, with a sigh and a 'here goes' kind of look, "would you consider being my mentor? If you're too busy, I totally get it and I apologize if this is out of line."

She sat back with her arms across her chest and was amused at his incessant jabbering, from a normally confident to overconfident young man. She smiled and studied him for a moment before responding. "You know Tyler, I saw great potential and that's why I hired you. I was very fortunate when I came to this firm to have a great mentor, David. I would love to be your mentor."

"Really? Aw, that's awesome." He started to jump up and give her a hug and stopped himself. Instead, he relaxed and simply said, "Thank you so much."

Lindsay stood to leave, still amused by the uncharacteristic meekness in Tyler's tone. She couldn't help but think that confidence slips away from all of us at one time or another. She said, "Let Eric know and get on my calendar for our first mentoring session. Let's do it later this week or next."

"Yes ma'am. Thank you again. I'm excited about it."

"Me too." She smiled and left the room.

CHAPTER 57

(Executive Training - Exercise 2)

Lindsay barely had time to stop by the ladies room before returning, but she did it anyway, thinking that waiting would be a really bad decision. When she finally met up with the others, she rushed in, out of breath, and was the last one to take a seat. She and Adam exchanged glances and she mouthed "sorry" and he nodded.

"This time, we're getting a little more personal," Adam smiled as a he scanned the room. He raised his hand and slanted his head slightly to the side as he silenced a couple of moans. "I know, this makes you a little uncomfortable, but, as some would fondly say, you'll thank me in the morning." He smirked and laughed along with some of the others.

"Get back in your same pairs and each of you take five minutes to describe one of the most difficult challenges you've ever experienced. I don't want to be pushy but make it count. Let's get started."

CHAPTER 58

Patrick had a couple of thoughts, winced and knew immediately what he was going to talk about. His best friend from college.

Phil Sutton was the basketball coach of the local university, their alma mater. One night after a particularly difficult loss, Phil and his assistants went out after the game. They ran into fans at a local bar and the coach hung around until early morning hours when the bartender finally told the remaining stragglers to go home. It wasn't the first time he closed down the bar.

Phil said he thought about calling his wife, but decided against it. She would be furious or wouldn't even care. They had drifted apart into a lonely existence over the last couple of years. She rarely even attended his games any longer.

He admitted he thought about the tall slender brunette he met at the same bar a few nights earlier. He had seen her a couple of times, but hadn't thought about her again until that night. He had never cheated on his wife. It was time to go home.

He walked out to his car, still thinking about the brunette. He tried to push her out of his mind, but she lingered a little longer than she should have. He shook his head and sighed, as he fished keys out of his pants pocket. He had enough troubles without thinking about some woman that was probably way too young for him anyway.

He put the key in the ignition and started the car. He drove slowly out of the parking lot, doing well until he failed to see the stop sign he had passed a hundred times before. He realized it after it was behind him and he muttered about the sky being black and hard to see. Until he saw flashing lights in his rear view mirror.

He groaned and pulled over, fumbling in his wallet for his license. He would have to talk his way out of this one, once again. The police officer would recognize him and give him a break. After all, he was a local celebrity. He had been there before.

But, this time was different. There was no pass from this police officer that was interested in safety, not celebrity. Phil was arrested for Driving Under the Influence. The next day, it was splattered all over the newspapers, radio and television. It was the hottest local scandal of the week. As if that wasn't bad enough, his wife left him and the university fired him for violating the terms of his contract. Being arrested for drinking and driving was an automatic fireable offense.

Patrick wasn't as surprised as he should have been. Phil's increased drinking concerned him and they had talked about it more times than he could count. He still wished he had done more for him before letting it get to that point.

It cost his buddy everything. His wife, career, and a big part of himself. He and his wife had struggled with his drinking before. When they first moved back to the area to take his dream job, he had it under control. They seemed happy and excited about the basketball program.

It had been a chance to have a fresh start. He spent more time with his wife and worked hard to include her, make her feel like an integral part of the program. She accepted the role as team mom for these young men and Phil seemed to dedicate his energy and devotion to making his team a success. It was an especially exciting time for them and even meant more since he had been a former star basketball player at that school. It was a big part of who he was.

That night and many nights leading up to it, he let the school down. But most importantly, he let himself and his wife down. He let the drinking ruin his marriage and end his career. It wasn't just one night of drinking, but a way of life and an addiction.

Patrick talked about the close relationship he and Stephanie had with Phil. When everything fell apart, they let him move in with them temporarily. He had no where to go and nothing left.

Initially, the hardest part was watching him hurt every day, losing a sense of himself, his identity. He could no longer hide behind his alcoholism. They tried to be there for him, spending too many late nights talking and pleading for him to get professional help, but he kept telling them he wanted to kick it on his own, saying he could do it.

It all came crashing down when they returned home one night to find him and several empty beer cans and a whiskey bottle, sitting in front of the television set and watching some show that had been rerunning for years. They weren't supposed to be home until much later, enough time to destroy the evidence. He had no place to hide.

Disappointment was an understatement. They came to the realization there was nothing they could do for him. He wasn't willing to help himself. It was one of the most difficult things they had ever done, but they told him to check himself into a rehabilitation program or he would have to leave their home.

Patrick ended the story with how it made him feel. "I failed one of my very best friends. I watched him self-destruct and did nothing about it. I should have urged and assisted him to get help a long time before, rather than feed into his habit. Heck, I went out after the games with him occasionally. I didn't realize how bad his drinking had become. I let him down," He said, shaking his head and speaking softly.

He stared at the floor for a second before his voice picked up and he continued, "But, there is a happy ending. The challenge for him has been life altering. We urged and pushed until he went into rehab. He put in the work, finished the program and is trying to get his life back together. Unfortunately, he and his wife are divorced, but he is working on his career. He works as an assistant coach at a mid-major university out of state. He's making progress. We stay in contact and try to see each other as often as possible. He sometimes spends the Christmas holidays with us. After all, he is like family."

David said quietly, "That's quite a story. You're certainly loyal and compassionate. I don't know if I could have been that patient. I wish I had a friend like you."

Patrick responded, uneasily and with hesitation, "You do. But, thank you for saying it." He thought to himself that David was giving him more credit than he deserved.

CHAPTER 59

Adam walked around the room, listening to gripping accounts, people reacting to each other as ordinary people with different life struggles. He thought to himself, we all have some prison garment that has the ability to paralyze us, if we let it. One of his former clients said it best, "We all have a thing."

There was something a little different about this group, the dynamics or whatever was going on here. He didn't know what, but he would figure it out. They would all figure it out.

He walked over to observe Patrick and David. Patrick saw him approach and uncomfortably shifted the emphasis to David, asking him to tell his story. Adam smiled briefly and continued moving around to observe the others.

David's story was about career disappointment. Well, not really disappointment but... he had always dreamed of being a physician except his father wouldn't support it, demanding he follow in his footsteps and become an architect. If he wanted to go to med school, he would pay for it himself. He would be on his own.

His father said he had built the company and spent his blood, sweat and tears to make it what it was for his son. He had worked hard for David to take over the firm. It wasn't a choice. He guilted him into believing it was his duty to carry on the family business. So David did what was necessary and his biggest challenge was following a career path different from his true passion.

He said his relationship with his father was complicated. He was a good man, but a patriarch, controlling and opinionated. His dad's love and acceptance was everything to him throughout his childhood and into most of his adult life. So, he took the only path he could.

David closed with, "So, this has become my passion. I have a company and I work with phenomenal people that challenge me every day. I wake up in the morning and enjoy going to the office. Spending time with you.

"I love having coffee with Lindsay while plotting how to keep us out of trouble. Discussing profits and losses with Patrick. Walking down the hallways and stopping at cubicles to say hello. Stopping in the threshold of Peter's conference room with my coffee cup in hand. Observing Peter and one of his architects standing over the latest design, pointing out changes that would make it perfect. I can almost see and feel the energy flowing through the room. And, there is so much more. So many wonderful people. I'm a very lucky man."

David's mood shifted as he continued. There was fear in his voice. He said, "My biggest nightmare is that I can't lead us through this. That we can't keep the legacy alive during these competitive times. I keep having this vision of watching the work slowly dwindle, the energy and passion depleted, good people leaving for other jobs, and me having to make the call - to call it quits. Having to make the final decision that our firm can't survive, and people have to pack up their boxes." He hesitated and let out a deep breath, struggling to keep it together, his voice trembling before speaking softly, "I turn off the lights and close the doors for the last time." He looked up and said, "God, I can't believe I'm telling you this, but that's it. My challenge and the challenge we all face."

Patrick didn't know what to say. He wanted to make him feel better, reassure him, but he couldn't. Instead, he said, "We'll work through this, together. We have to do it and we can." Patrick believed they would. He knew the financials and kept an eye on the numbers. He was watching them even more than anyone knew. They would not fail.

Patrick asked the question before he realized it left his lips. "Do you think it was a mistake? Are you sorry you didn't become a doctor?"

He smiled faintly, "I don't think it was a mistake, but I sometimes wonder what it would have been like to be a doctor. Look, I'm grateful for the opportunities and the good fortune I've had throughout my life. I'm grateful to my father for all he has done for me."

CHAPTER 60

Adam eased closer to Lindsay when it was her turn to tell her story. He didn't want to be obvious, but he had to know more about her. It hit him like a punch to his face, and he wasn't prepared for that.

She hesitated before beginning, hoping Jack couldn't sense the fear bouncing around inside her head. Once it was said, she could never go back. She wasn't sure she wanted, scratch that, she wasn't sure she could describe something this tragic. This personal. It still was.

It felt like all eyes were on her and no one was talking. She knew it wasn't true, but that was how it felt. She couldn't think of the words, wasn't sure she would, until something happened within her and she made a decision. To be committed to this group of people, to do her part, to let them into her deeply personal being. If she didn't, she was nothing more than a hypocrite. If she was going to build a more meaningful relationship with these colleagues, it was the only way.

She drew in and let out a deep breath. *Here goes.* She was going to tell Jack what happened several years earlier. It involved a weekend she spent with her fiancee at a lovely inn on the river in a tiny southern town in Virginia. It was late Sunday evening and they were driving back to DC for the workweek.

They were mostly driving on narrow, curvy two lane roads. They were laughing and enjoying each other's company, as they always did. He used to tell her to laugh often, it was good for the soul. Oh, did they ever laugh.

Not too much traffic. They heard a faint siren in the distance. They didn't pay much attention, until it became louder and closer.

He said he couldn't stand these two lane roads. They made him nervous. His first inclination was always to look for a place to pull over for a car to pass, if necessary. He looked to both sides and didn't see a shoulder, only a wooded area and what looked like a deep ditch.

As the siren grew louder, he made a comment that he wouldn't be able to pull over on this narrow little road. He wasn't sure if the siren was behind or in front of them until it came closer. Then he saw it was coming from the other direction.

He slowed below the normal 45 MPH speed limit to make the sharp turn he could see in front of them. His stomach felt like he was plunging down the tracks of a roller coaster as the car flew by and the noise went with it.

He glanced over at Lindsay and back at the road, letting out a sigh. They drove in silence while he focused on the road. Few cars passed. He was starting to relax when another car appeared, moving towards them in the opposite direction. As they approached one another, no big deal. And then, at the last second, it was coming right at them, moving into their lane. Lindsay screamed, and her fiancee's hand gripped the wheel tighter, steering hand over hand, trying to get the car off the road to avoid a collision.

"There were screeching tires, lights blazing from every direction like a kaleidoscope, and the feeling of spinning, spinning, spinning, and then a loud boom as they catapulted into what was later described as a very thick oak tree. Then there was silence.

It happened so fast that Lindsay was fuzzy on the details. She remembered the sound and feel of hitting the tree in front of them, and the air bag causing a jolt that felt like an explosion in her chest. The pain was excruciating, searing even, but if it hadn't been for the air bag, well, it was the air bag.

Everything was quiet and she slowly opened her eyes, squinting for clarity until it came to her. She turned her head sideways and glanced at her fiancee. It didn't compute at first that his air bag had failed to open.

She would never forget the vision of what had been his handsome face, transformed into one that was barely recognizable. He was lying limp and bloody against the steering wheel, with what was left of his profile turned in her direction. She even thought he was smiling at her, but that couldn't be.

She described how she screamed at the top of her lungs and tentatively touched his shoulder and gently tried to shake him, then more urgent pushing. She begged him to say something. Anything. He wouldn't respond.

The driver of the other car limped towards them, until he abruptly stopped at the driver's side. He dropped his head and looked back up, already knowing. But, he had to try. When there was no response, she knew. She could see it in the young man's face, but she wasn't ready to give up. "Do something, do something," she pleaded. He went to her and pulled her close, leading her away from the vehicle.

Once the ambulance arrived, the emergency team looked, addressed him, but there was no use. He was pronounced dead shortly thereafter.

It was the most horrible thing she had ever experienced. She lost the man she was about to marry, and he lost his life at way too young of an age. And, the college student driving the other car had such promise until that day. She didn't know until later that he had crossed over into their lane because of his own negligence, texting while driving. He couldn't take it back, if only... he, too, was devastated. Three lives changed forever.

Lindsay finished by looking down at her feet and speaking softly, "As you can imagine, it was the most traumatic thing I've ever experienced. I lost the love of my life and I still haven't been able to get over it. I suppose I never will." She gazed up at Jack, with a slight smile, no tears, and said, "Now you know why I am OCD when it comes to work. It's my life."

What she thought, but didn't say was that she was scared. Scared of loving and losing. She could not bear to experience that kind of loss again. She had learned to live alone, to accept her single life. It was easier that way. In fact, she had actually begun to enjoy it. Make peace with it. Until the last couple of days.

Jack was silent. Adam didn't move. His eyes were damp and he was standing next to Lindsay. He wanted to reach out, but didn't, shouldn't. That would be inappropriate.

Adam looked at Jack and could tell he was contemplating how to respond. There was definitely empathy in Jack's eyes, maybe even an understanding, maybe starting to see her in a different way. Jack didn't know what to say, other than, "I'm so, so sorry."

"Thank you. Me too, but I've learned to live with it." She actually attempted another smile.

One of Lindsay's colleagues sitting to her right overheard the part about losing her fiancee. He couldn't hear everything, but he heard enough. He instantly knew. It explained the story behind the great Lindsay Thompson. Yes, we all have a thing.

CHAPTER 61

Jack was set to recall some benign challenge as his contribution, but Lindsay had changed all that. Could he really be thinking about sharing the worst thing he'd ever experienced? Why did Lindsay have to mess everything up?

Actually, he thought he might admire her for talking about something as life altering and painful as the loss she experienced. If she was willing to work on a relationship with him and prove her commitment to them, then he needed to step up and do the same.

He, too, held his breath and let it out before starting the story. There was a lot of that going on in the room.

Years earlier, he was sitting in his office talking to his colleague and good friend, Steven Lewis when he received the call. He cupped his hand over the phone and gestured that he needed to take it. Steven excused himself and walked to his office, adjacent to Jack's.

They had just returned from lunch and were planning to review some sales data before their weekly meeting. Steven didn't think much about the intrusion at the time since there were always interruptions in their type of work. He certainly didn't realize how this call would impact his life.

It was from Steven's brother and he was calling for Jack, not Steven. His voice was more sobs than words as he tried to tell Jack that something horrible had happened. Steven's little boy had been napping during the afternoon when the nanny checked in on him, as she always did at that time, to find something was terribly wrong with his coloring. When she stepped closer, she discovered he wasn't breathing. She became frantic, touching and pressing lightly on his little bare skin. She said she was careful not to hurt him, but she had to be sure.

She dialed 911, already knowing it was too late. He had stopped breathing in his sleep, Sudden Infant Death Syndrome, a death in infants that still remains hard to explain. There was nothing she or anyone else could have done.

Details of many life experiences grow sketchy over time, but not one like this. Jack remembered exactly where he was and how he felt. It was one of those select memories that affect you so much that every detail remains engrained in your brain. He remembered being numb, hazy, and feeling a gut wrenching pang of sympathy for his friend. How would Steven survive it? He realized he had stopped listening to his brother's words on the phone. Feeling dazed and lightheaded, he asked quietly, "What can I do to help? I will do anything."

"Can you drive him to the hospital? I hate to put you in this position but I don't know what else to do. Would you tell him his son has been taken to the hospital and you don't know any details? If you have to, tell him he is having breathing problems. I know we are asking too much, but… and, thank you is all I know to say."

Jack didn't have to think about it. "I will handle it. We'll see you in ten minutes." Without another word he hung up the phone and sat for a moment with his head in his hands. He had to get himself together first, before talking to his colleague, his friend.

As Jack was telling the story to Lindsay, she noticed he had tears in his eyes and his voice was cracking. He paused several times. He wasn't the only emotional one. Lindsay was shedding tears of her own.

Adam walked over to check in. As he approached, he witnessed Jack was struggling, taking his time and regaining his composure. He let them proceed without interruption.

Jack continued with the story. He walked by Steven's office and looked in to see a guy that's world was about to crumble, but he didn't stop. He kept walking. He went to the bathroom, splashed water on his face, and dried it with a paper towel that felt like sandpaper. Looking in the mirror, he hesitated long enough to breathe deeply and get his thoughts together. He told himself, come on. You can do this. You have to do this. He walked back to the office. "Steve, I just received a call from your brother. We need to go to the hospital buddy. Your son has been taken there. He isn't feeling well. I'll drive you. Let's go."

Steven's face went from confusion to fear and then horror. There was no color left, but his voice was steady when he asked, "What's happened? What is wrong? How is he?"

"I don't have any details except he is experiencing some breathing issues. We need to get to the hospital. Let's go." He gently touched Steve's arm to guide him to the door. He thought, please no more questions. It was not for him to tell.

Jack told Lindsay how hard it was to lead him out of the building, knowing what he was leading him to. It broke his heart.

He momentarily stopped talking and looked towards the windows on the far end of the conference room and let out a deep breath before continuing. The drive to the hospital was another one of those things he would never forget. He said, "Steven didn't say much on the ride and I didn't either. I was rushing to the hospital, yet dreading to get there. My stomach was weak and my heart ached for what he would go through. What his family would go through. This was just the beginning of an eternal, cruel nightmare."

He looked down and continued, "The rest of the day felt really grey and it was one of the darkest I'll ever remember. I parked the car at the emergency entrance. We walked down the hall to the room I was instructed to meet them. When he saw his wife's face and the way his brother was holding onto her, he knew. Her face said it all. He shook his head saying no, no and began sobbing. His wife nodded. I put my arm around him to steady him, to regain his balance before going to his wife.

"I stayed with them for most of the day. I teetered on whether to be there for support or give them their privacy. I'm not good at knowing what to do or say in these tragic situations," Jack said as he was shaking his head.

Lindsay reached out and touched his hand. She said quietly, "You were perfect."

Jack didn't realize he must have raised his voice an octave too loud because everyone was listening. Adam looked around the room and observed the group, experiencing the pain of Jack's friend and probably even thinking about their own children.

Jack's description of the event was so real and focused that it was like he was reliving the experience. He was openly vulnerable in front of his colleagues for the first time and said, "I don't know how Steven has continued to go on, but he has. Even for me, it took a long time to come to terms with it. I held his son in my arms when he was born. It broke my heart to watch him go through the grieving process and take everything he had to put one foot in front of the other every day. I think the experience hardened me. I didn't realize it until now, but I secretly vowed not to get too close to anyone at work again. It can be so painful."

Jack looked at his colleagues before continuing, "Over the last couple of days and sharing experiences with you, I realized something about myself. What I've been missing. You really do get what you give."

Lindsay thought for a moment before responding. She said, "Thank you for sharing that side of you. The compassion. The empathy. I understand now."

CHAPTER 62

There weren't many dry eyes in the room and there was silence until Adam addressed the group. He hesitated to use this tragedy as a teaching point, but he didn't have much of a choice.

Adam walked over to Jack and spoke in a low tone. He said, "Jack, let me apologize for listening in on your private conversation with Lindsay. I can't even imagine the pain," his voice trailed off. Adam whispered something to Jack and he nodded. Then, he spoke to Lindsay and she nodded.

Adam turned to Lindsay. "When Jack finished, you made a couple of comments to him, describing your feelings. If you don't mind, will you share them with the group?"

"I think I have a better understanding of who Jack is and why he comes across as aloof sometimes. I get it now. I'm actually starting to admire him," she looked over at him and smiled, "He is growing on me." There were a few other smiles in the room.

"Thank you, Lindsay. Anyone else?"

Patrick piled on, "I agree with Lindsay. I didn't think Jack was interested in developing relationships with us. He was distant and it appeared he wanted it that way. I had no idea what was behind the feelings."

Another team member, who was normally hesitant to participate said, "It's interesting how our perceptions about people can be wrong. I didn't know Jack was such a caring person. This has been an eye opener for me. Made me want to see him in a different light."

Adam asked Jack, "What do you think about all of this?"

"I haven't been honest with myself. I didn't realize how much I miss this type of relationship with colleagues. You can't live in fear of getting too close and losing people. I guess I need to remind myself to live rather than exist. The best way to do that is through building rich friendships and relationships. I'm going to work on it."

Lindsay gazed down at the floor. She hoped no one noticed. Jack's words struck a chord with her. It was almost a deep, sharp pain. Maybe she should pay attention to Jack's realization in her own personal life.

Adam looked around the room and noticed most of the team members were sitting quietly with their heads staring at the table in front of them. He asked, "What happened here today?"

They spent the next few minutes talking about the experiences they had just shared. Another normally quiet participant spoke up. "We saw each other as real people, and looked through their eyes, at their struggles and vulnerabilities. All of us have them."

Adam nodded in agreement. "We've talked about this before, but it's really critical and requires nurturing. One of the most life altering ways to build a relationship is to start seeing each other more clearly as human beings, with good intentions. Get off the self-indulgent mentality. As you said, see life through the other person's perspective, their challenges and burdens. You have to make that part of your thinking process. You already know all of this, but it's my job to bring it out and put it right smack in front of your face, so you'll think about it in the future. Make it a habit. I can say the words, but today you experienced it. So much more powerful. You saw for yourself, the result is greater understanding, empathy, compassion, and hopefully caring about each other."

He looked around the room, hoping he wasn't getting too preachy with senior leaders who already knew these things. But like the rest of the world, they can get caught up in being human with baggage of their own. No one gets to be immune from that, he smiled to himself. He continued, "This is just the beginning, the first step in building the foundation for your relationships. Tomorrow we'll transition to building on our communication skills and critical elements of healthy relationships."

Adam was encouraged by what he had witnessed and the value in this personal interaction. He said, "Tomorrow will be another eye opening experience. We'll take what we learned today and build on it."

He looked at his watch. "It's time to call it a day. I'll let you get back to it. You guys did great work. I'm looking forward to tomorrow. Have a good night."

Adam stuffed papers in his briefcase, feeling a little uneasy or unsettled or something he wasn't sure about. What he didn't share or bring up during the exercise was Lindsay's tragic story that he overheard. He had lingering thoughts of Lindsay losing her fiancee. He probably shouldn't have listened so closely to the intimate conversation between Jack and Lindsay, but he couldn't stop himself. He wanted to know so much more. How long ago? How long were they together? What was he like? How did she get through it? Has she dated? Does she date? What, how, when - so many questions.

CHAPTER 63

David walked to the head of the table to speak with Adam. Shaking his head, he said, "Today was powerful. There was a time when I wasn't sure I was going to survive, but I actually experienced the value, even as we were going through it. We're starting to make progress. I know it's a journey, but we'll get there. I'm beginning to see some real possibilities for this team."

David noticed Lindsay moving towards the door and stopped her, wanting to engage her in the conversation. "Lindsay, what do you think about today?" David asked.

This immediately grabbed Adam's complete attention. He stopped and looked directly at her, hoping for a kind of response, rapport, alignment or something. He wanted something.

She looked up from her tablet and stopped walking. "It was difficult. I am kind of amazed by what transpired. Progress. Hopefully change. Like Adam said, we started looking at each other as people with good intentions first, all of us having challenges and complications. We shared some brutal moments in our lives and displayed some real empathy. It wasn't easy."

There was a brief silence between them before she said, "Putting this into action is what I'm most concerned about. It is still a very fresh moment. I've seen this type of reaction in retreats before. People get together and they bond and it feels transformative. Then, life takes over and everyone goes back to their old way of doing things. We'll have to work hard on maintaining our relationship so this doesn't happen. I worry about whether or not we can sustain this behavior when the stakes are high and conflict arises."

Adam nodded and replied, "I get your concern. It's work. Like any other relationship. It will be a process and you have to be committed to making it your culture. The next few days will be crucial in continuing to build a relationship that can be maintained in the long haul. Once the foundation is firmly in place, you'll have a better chance of withstanding the tests in highly charged situations. Sure, you'll make some mistakes. But, it'll be the responsibility of all of you to pay attention to the culture. You'll have to become accountable to one another. We'll talk about how you do that. "

Lindsay contemplated for a moment, "How do you do that?"

"Good question. We'll figure it out over the next few days."

"How about a sneak preview," she teased.

"Well, okay. Here goes. You'll have to work hard to build a relationship worth maintaining, communicate through the good and bad times, and demand the kind of trust that will sustain the relationship. And, you'll make a commitment to be accountable to the team. That's my sneak preview for you." He smiled.

Adam and Lindsay were lost in conversation, back and forth, and passionately discussing what transpired over the last couple of days. David thought he noticed a spark between them. Could that be? He smiled at the thought. Adam was a charming guy and seemed to have his act together. He might be a good match for her. As for Lindsay…He was probably getting a little ahead of himself, but he liked the possibilities.

They realized at about the same time that David wasn't saying anything, and they both turned to look at him. "I agree with both of you. It will be up to this team to maintain and nurture what we're building. Spending this time together and getting to know each other differently has already had a positive impact, and we're just getting started. We'll keep an eye on the ball and make sure we continue with the progress we're making."

Lindsay added to David's words, "You'll know we have arrived when each of us accepts the responsibility and accountability. When we're accountable to each other, we'll be a winning team. I like it."

"Ah yes. That is staying power." Adam smiled. "I think both of you are doing an exceptional job of leading the direction."

With that, David looked at his phone and excused himself like he had an emergency. He smirked as we walked out of the room thinking this might be an opportunity.

A moment passed, Adam looked down at his shoes and gazed back at Lindsay. "Would you care to join me for a drink? We could talk some more about this."

She started to say yes, when her phone buzzed out of control. She glanced down and saw Patrick's number on the screen. She looked back at Adam and put one finger in the air and whispered, "Excuse me for a sec. I have to take this." She stepped a few feet away and answered, "Hi there. What's up?"

On the other end of the line, his voice was edgy, urgent even. He said, "I need to talk to you. Do you have a few minutes?"

She knew him well enough to get that something was wrong. She had to meet him. She asked, "Now?"

"Yes, now. I have something to talk to you about. Can you make it?"

"I'll meet you at the Cafe Bar in five." She hung up the phone, frowned, and hoped Adam would understand. "Something has come up. I'm sorry. Can I have a raincheck on that drink?"

"No problem. Another time," Adam said, trying not to sound disappointed.

"Thank you. I would like that." She paused and gazed at him long enough to let him know there would be a raincheck. She did not know what to say so she didn't say anything. She didn't want to leave, but her head shifted back to Patrick. "I better go. I will see you tomorrow."

CHAPTER 64

Lindsay walked through the door of the Cafe Bar to see Patrick sitting alone at their favorite table. His head was looking down and his fingers were tapping the tabletop.

"I'll buy. You bought the other day. Do you want your usual?" she asked.

"Just a tall black coffee, please. Thank you."

"Really? Nothing fancy. Just black coffee?"

"Yeah. That would be great." He was in no mood for teasing.

She came back with two tall black coffees and two napkins. Before sitting down, she announced they were trying a new blend, a lighter roast. "I thought it might be better for us this late in the day. Won't play as much havoc on our tummies," she smiled and chatted nervously as she sat down.

There was silence for a few seconds, other than, "Thank you for the coffee." Then Patrick began. "I have to go out of town briefly and I need you to cover for me, especially at the introduction meeting with the audit team that's looking at our timecard system. It shouldn't be a big deal since they're just beginning their preliminary work. I'll be back by the time they actually get heavy into the onsite stuff." He turned the coffee cup clockwise in his hands and stared down at the table. He continued, "I'll miss some of the workshop and a couple of other meetings coming up. Can you represent me on the principal only exec meetings? I wouldn't ask this unless I absolutely had to."

"Sure I will. It must be a big deal if you're missing the auditors. What did David say about it?"

"He understood. This just came up. I think I mentioned Stephanie's health the other day. I don't want to go into it, but Stephanie is having some medical tests out of town. I want to be with her."

"Of course, I'll be happy to cover for you. Don't worry about the office." She waited for him to say something until she realized he wasn't going to. She didn't want to be intrusive, but they were important to her. "I didn't know about the tests. Is it serious?"

"No, I don't think it's anything to worry about, but we don't want to take any chances. I would rather not talk about it until we know more, if you don't mind."

"No problem. I don't intend to pry, but if you need to talk any time, day or night, I'm here for you. You know that. And don't worry, we'll handle the office."

"Thanks. If anything comes up during the audit or they have any questions, give me a call. I can be reached by phone."

"Hopefully we can handle it without bothering you. You take care of Stephanie. And, tell her I'm thinking about her."

"Thank you. I will." Patrick loved Lindsay. She was one of his best friends, and certainly his best friend at work. He wanted to tell her everything. Every little detail, but he couldn't. He usually trusted her with his life, but this was asking too much. He couldn't put her in that position. *Why his family? Why did this have to happen to them? He would just have to deal with it.*

It seemed like minutes rather than seconds before the conversation moved on to other topics. Lindsay did most of the talking. She shared her feelings about how much she was learning and enjoying the last few days. She thought the executive team had responded well to Adam and the work. She was even intrigued by the idea of consulting on human and organizational behavior. The human psychology of it all was fascinating to her.

She talked incessantly without realizing she wasn't letting Patrick say a word, speaking passionately about the work and saying she thought they were all getting to know each other in a different way. They were building something and Adam was doing a phenomenal job guiding them.

As she spoke about Adam, Patrick noticed a spark, and she used the word phenomenal. He didn't know if he had ever heard her use the word before. Normally, she wasn't easily impressed. He smiled and teased, "What do you think of Adam?"

Her face flushed, "I think Adam is good at what he does. Why do you ask?"

"All this time, I thought you were pushing the relationship building stuff and trying to get me to buy into it. Now, I get it. You're interested in Adam, aren't you?"

Blushing, but trying to remain matter of fact, she replied, "That's ridiculous. You're reading way too much into this. Of course, I like Adam and I think he is exactly what we need."

"And? You aren't answering the question."

She continued, slightly defensive. "And nothing. I'm surprised you aren't as jazzed as I am about making us a better executive team. One of the things I love about you is your empathetic and caring nature. Not to mention, with your involvement in your son's basketball career I know you're familiar with the dynamic. You've experienced team relationships that work really well and not so well over the years."

She tried to change the subject, "And speaking of, how is Andrew doing? Now that he is a senior, how is he feeling about it all?"

"He doesn't talk much about it. I know he has worked hard over the summer, so we'll see." He looked at his watch and told her he had to go. They discarded their empty cups as they exited.

Lindsay was still thinking about Patrick and Stephanie when she stepped inside her office. What he had said. Or what he didn't say. He usually talked to her about things, anything.

She knew him well enough to know he was concerned about Stephanie's health. His eyes looked tired and he was different.

CHAPTER 65

Lindsay was tapping away on her keyboard when the phone rang. Glancing over and seeing it register Samantha caused her to pick up without a second ring. She knew these calls. Invitations for delicious food to satisfy ignored hunger pangs and the yearning in her palate for something far better than average sustenance to simply keep her going.

"Helloooo," she said in her deepest voice. "I hope this call is about food."

"Hi there. You are correct. I've decided I need the night off and was wondering if you can join me at the restaurant for an early dinner?" asked Sam.

"I would love to. What time are you thinking?"

"Can you meet me, say 6:30?"

"Sounds great. Count me in." Lindsay hung up the phone. She had enough time to make it to her condo, take a quick shower, and change into something a little more casual, if she left immediately. She grabbed her things, turned out the lights, and locked the door.

Waiting for the elevator, she watched the floor numbers light up above her while her mind drifted back to Patrick. It was unusual that he didn't discuss Stephanie's health with her, even if it was a female issue. They usually talked about everything, even personal things. She wouldn't push. Patrick would talk when he was ready. The next thing she knew, the elevator dinged.

When Lindsay stepped out into the fresh air, she looked up and let the sun take over her face. She put the top down, pressed the power key and stepped hard on the accelerator, gunning the car onto the highway. Freedom.

She thought of Adam. She was thinking about that raincheck. If he didn't ask her out in the next couple of days, she might ask him. Why not?

She wasn't prone to being bold and asking a man out, but he was too intriguing. She felt different in his presence. She was alive and invigorated, even a little passionate about the work he was doing, and maybe even him. He was interesting, not to mention handsome. And yes, very sexy. She would definitely step out of her comfort zone or whatever this was. It might be worth it.

The commute took longer than she had anticipated but she could still make 6:30 if she didn't dawdle. In her condo, she looked around and it felt slightly darker than usual. A little less comfy and cozy. Too quiet. She turned on the lights and music before a quick shower. After applying fresh makeup, she checked her tablet one more time before meeting Samantha. Nothing that couldn't wait until the following day. She closed the door and locked it behind her and, of course, checked to make sure it was secure.

CHAPTER 66

Lindsay walked into the Coastal Grille at exactly 6:30. She was punctual, if not early most of the time, believing habitual tardiness was inconsiderate.

Sam was sitting at the bar talking to the bartender when she spotted Lindsay. Waving her over, she asked for two glasses of Lindsay's favorite Cabernet Franc as they made their way over to the usual table off in the corner.

It was getting crowded by the time the bartender showed up with tuna tartar, but their only focus was the nonstop chitter-chatter about lack of a love life, fear of a love life without a prenup, their mutual interest in business, organizational dynamics, and human behavior, and yes, even politics. All on the table, until they were talking about the latest happenings with Lindsay's firm and the workshop. She looked up and was stunned by the sight of Adam standing in the doorway. He was scanning the restaurant when a beautiful brunette motioned him over to her table. She stood and gave him a kiss on the cheek before they sat down together.

Lindsay's face went flush and she felt a disappointing twinge in her stomach. Sam immediately noticed the change in her, and asked, "Lindsay, what's wrong?"

"It's Adam. He just walked in and he isn't alone. He's with a woman," she hesitated before continuing, "a beautiful woman." She motioned to the table with a nod of her head.

"That's him. Wow." Sam uttered the words, not thinking before speaking.

"Oh well. That's that. All the good ones are taken, aren't they?" Lindsay shrugged, with a smile she didn't feel. Lindsay couldn't hide her disappointment from Sam. She might have been able to hide it from anyone else, but not Sam.

"If he is a good one. It is a little suspect based on the interest he has shown in you. But, yet he's out with her." Sam's glare was directed on their table.

"Stop looking. They might see you. Maybe I misread the entire thing and he wasn't interested at all, other than as a client. Maybe I wanted there to be a connection and I took it out of context."

"I don't know Linds. You're pretty perceptive."

Lindsay let out a deep breath and sat up a little straighter. She said, "This isn't such a bad thing. For the first time since all that happened so long ago, the thoughts of being interested in someone else finally surfaced. I was paralyzed by the fear of getting close and thought I'd never have those feelings again. I had even accepted that maybe I was destined to be alone and I should be grateful that I have a good life, a great life."

Sam touched Lindsay's hand and said in a low tone, "You're making progress, sweetie."

Lindsay hesitated and stared down at the wine glass before looking up. "I didn't think I could get better after losing him. I really didn't. When Patrick said it would happen, I can't say that I believed him. I felt hopeless. Then, I get this feeling that I could be ready to live again, move on."

"I'm so glad to hear you say that. I think…"

Lindsay put up her hand to stop Sam. "And then, there's this other part of me. I've always had a fear of commitments, even with him. I finally gave in, let myself go with it, and look what happened. I lost him. Maybe I actually am better off alone." Lindsay laughed and took another sip of wine. "God, I am such a contradiction."

"You don't mean that. You were the happiest I've ever seen you when he was alive." Sam hesitated and said with expression in her voice, "You were alive."

Lindsay didn't speak at first, staring at the legs in her wine glass as she swirled it around in her hand. "I guess you're right. I'm tired and being melodramatic." She continued with a shrug and almost a smile, "I WAS happy. Oh well, next time."

Sam was more than a little pleased to hear Lindsay speak about maybe thinking of love again, but it was too bad about this guy. She looked over at him and even she was almost mesmerized by his strikingly handsome features. He had beautiful crystal blue eyes that sparkled across the room, and a charming, but slightly devilish smile that took over as he was playfully chatting up his companion.

Sam asked, "So, how are things going with the workshop?"

Relieved to get the focus off her love life, or lack thereof, she said, "We've reacted even better than I thought we would. Our biggest change has been getting to know each other in an entirely different way. Going back to basics and building a foundation. It may just make us a more cohesive group."

"There certainly is something magic about a team that can pull it all together."

"Yeah, it's been fascinating. There are moments of real discomfort and vulnerability and you feel a little like you're naked, but it really works. The responses have been powerful so far. The connection or bond or whatever you want to call it is growing, evolving."

"That's awesome. Good on you guys for making the investment. I've been doing a little reading on human behavior and relationships, and this study made me think about you guys. It is about a company's demise…"

"Oh great. That's what I want to hear right about now."

"No, wait a minute. Let me finish. It's about failure attributed mostly to an inability of the team members to get along and talk through conflicts and challenges. It hindered solving even the most basic problems. No learning. No innovation. Attrition of the superstars. This directly affected operations, leading to high costs and decreased revenues when the environment required progressive thinking and greater interdependency. Instead, they became lifeless and irrelevant. You guys aren't doing that. You're acknowledging the need to address this head on. I admire it."

Lindsay nodded in agreement, listening so intensely to Sam describing the case study that she didn't notice Adam as he walked over to them. She had almost forgotten he was there. That all ended when he stood at her table with those gorgeous eyes and bright pearly whites staring down at her.

CHAPTER 67

It was ridiculous to feel like a teen with a crush, but she certainly was not going to act like one. Lindsay attempted to fend off a twinge of excitement as Adam stood over her. For once, she was at a loss for words, only interrupted by her social graces taking over long enough to introduce him to Sam. The three of them made small talk until the attractive brunette walked their way.

Lindsay felt a twinge of jealousy as she observed him watch the beauty walk to the table with a look that said adoration. *How could I have been so stupid?* He interrupted her admonishment by making introductions of his own. "I would like you to meet my sister, Angela."

Good thing Lindsay's wine glass was safely planted on the table and away from her mouth. The shock would have facilitated splattered red over the nearest victims, and that would have ruined the moment. She hoped her elation and relief weren't obvious to everyone at the table. She didn't realize until then how much she had started thinking about him. Sam didn't waste any time asking Adam and Angela to join them for a drink. Without hesitation, they agreed and the four of them talked and laughed for hours that led to dessert and coffee. They barely noticed how late it was until Angela looked down at her watch and excused herself, saying she needed to get home while she still had a husband and children.

Shortly after Angela walked out the door, one of the waiters approached Sam and asked if she could step into the kitchen for a moment. Quickly walking towards the back, she thanked the waiter, telling him his interruption was on queue.

"Your sister is quite lovely," Lindsay commented.

"Thank you. She's very special to me. We have been through some stuff together, for sure. She's my best friend. I don't know what I would do without her," he replied.

They started talking about their families and as the conversation became more personal, Lindsay witnessed a slight shift in his mood. She thought it happened when he mentioned his mother. He changed the subject with an abrupt turn that caused Lindsay to pause and wonder. *What was that all about?*

They were so engrossed in getting to know each other that neither of them noticed when Sam returned to the table. "Lindsay, I hate to do this, but I'm going to have to cut our evening short. We're having some problems in the kitchen that I need to tend to. Why don't you two have a night cap, my treat, and stay as long as you would like. I'm really sorry. I'll call you tomorrow." She hugged Lindsay and extended her hand and said, "Adam, it was so nice to meet you. I hope to see you again." She turned and walked back to the kitchen.

They talked for awhile longer, both hesitating to end the evening. Adam finally said, "I really enjoyed tonight. How about dinner sometime soon?"

"I would like that," she said, attempting to hide the excitement practically erupting from her physical being. She had to remind herself to play it cool, but act interested. This stuff was all so tedious.

"Great. I'll call you, if you don't mind giving me your number."

She delicately reached for her phone and dialed the number he recited. As any perfect gentleman would do, he escorted her to her vehicle. After saying good night, she watched him walk briskly across the street to get into his car. She liked watching his firm posterior in tight jeans, as he walked away from her. Yes, he was delicious, she smiled and giggled.

Who is this schoolgirl? What have you done with Lindsay? What happened to the fear of commitment, no-nonsense, I don't need anyone, powerful executive? Wimp.

She stepped into the car and touched the bluetooth icon on the dashboard. "Well played," she said to Sam. "I know what you were doing. Did I mention, thank you?"

"You're welcome. Thought you could use a little time together. What happened? Tell me everything."

"He wants to have dinner. Why is he still single? What's his story?" Lindsay said, with an excitement in her voice and her heart that she hadn't felt in a very long time.

"I don't know his story, but he is certainly a looker. And, really charming. I see why you're interested in him. Yum." Sam laughed jokingly.

Later that night, Lindsay lie in bed with yet another book about someone else's life. She thought about her own and hadn't realized how lonely she had become until she saw the possibilities of what could be. Maybe there were possibilities with Adam. If not him, then maybe someone else. It was time to concentrate on her own personal life as opposed to living vicariously through everyone else. Time to make changes. She had a smile on her face and drifted off to sleep.

CHAPTER 68

The sound of a horn to her left and a tailgater almost in the back of the trunk beside her startled Lindsay out of a daydreaming trance. About that time, she heard a crunching sound. She looked in her rear view mirror and grimaced as she navigated through heavy traffic and thought about the congestion that would cause.

The morning commute, lack of sufficient amounts of coffee, and a company to save. But still, what a great day. She almost bounced her way into the building.

"Good morning Lindsay. Were you in that mess on the highway this morning?" The receptionist asked.

"Hello Alice. I just missed it. A second longer and I would have been waiting for the next two hours." She smiled, and stopped at the front desk.

"This traffic around here is awful and people just don't know how to drive. It's crazy."

"I guess we're all in a hurry. How are you doing?"

"Really good. We're planning a vacation for next month and I cannot wait."

"Who's keeping Maddy?"

"My brother is staying at the house. That dog loves him."

"Golden retrievers are great dogs. I just love those big babies. Where are you going?"

"Hawaii, Honolulu and a couple of other islands. We've never been, it's on our bucket list, and we aren't getting any younger."

"Tell me about it. Sounds like a wonderful vacay. You'll have to take lots of pictures."

"Will do. Hubby bought a brand new camera for the trip and I told him he wasted money. We could use our phones."

Lindsay laughed. "You'll be happy with the camera. It'll take fantastic pictures." Lindsay looked at her watch. "I better get going. I have a meeting this morning. I'm grabbing a coffee, can I get you one?"

"Nah, I'm still sipping on this one." She pointed to her thermal cup and said, "Thank you anyway. You have a good day."

"You too. I'll see you later." It was people like Alice that made her want to fight so hard for this firm.

CHAPTER 69

Lindsay grabbed her coffee and stopped by David's office before venturing down the hall to her own. Once again, his assistant wasn't at her desk and his door was shut. She heard loud voices, one of which sounded like a woman.

Being a stalker wasn't part of her plan for the day so she kept on walking to her own office. She took a quick look at her emails and was a 'copy to' on one David sent to the new Operations Officer. *Ooh.* It was a little more direct and curt than she would expect from him, the guy that doesn't lose control, raise his voice, show signs of anger, or get emotional. He was usually the steady one, something she admired about him. With the fate of the firm, the collapsed building, and the embezzlement weighing heavily on his mind, who could blame him?

The possible demise of the firm didn't worry her so much for the other executives or herself. They were all talented and would get other jobs. It was David that had the most to lose. So much of his identity was tied to this company. Giving up his dream to be a doctor for a legacy his father demanded. All those heart to hearts late at night when they were working or traveling together, and he had never shared this with her. It wasn't until this exercise. Maybe the next few days could make a difference for all of them.

And then there was Adam. She was looking forward to diving into the mechanics of building better communication skills. He had said they were moving on to the single most important factor in the success of any relationship, and he made it all sound so simple. Something about communicating through it? She must have gone to the beach when he talked about that, or could she have been thinking about him? Was she losing her edge?

She chuckled at the simplicity of it all, thinking she was a fairly good communicator at work. She didn't shy away from directly addressing issues and attempting to resolve differences, and she wasn't afraid of constructive feedback or conflict. Her approach was non-threatening, caring and considerate.

Her personal life was a different story. Even with an understanding of the power of open and honest communication skills, she struggled when it came to men and intimate relationships. She had never been good at it. Then, she stopped trying. What was she really afraid of? Her assistant interrupted to remind her that it was fifteen minutes before her next meeting.

Usually she waited another ten minutes before heading out, but not this time. She walked with purpose into the conference room a little ahead of the others, only to be disappointed that Adam was not alone. She had hoped for an opportunity to have a conversation with him, leading to something, somewhere, but what?

Unfortunately, it didn't work out as planned. Adam and David were in deep conversation about a past client using communication tools to address their challenges and protect the value of their relationships. Authentic communications requiring honest and open dialogue, extinguishing the "taking it personal" by utilizing learning as the means of tackling tough issues, and providing constructive feedback, not bashing each other for their differences. Not to worry. They were going to learn a model to make them better communicators.

Lindsay couldn't help but smile as she thought about Adam's outlook on relationships and life. She recognized early on that he was a compassionate and caring man. He seemed to have it all together, and he was fascinating. Not to mention, very hot.

She was going to forget her fear, ask him out. This had gone on far too long. It was nonsense. After all, she was a progressive, take charge kind of woman. Not afraid to go after what she wanted. Yeah, she didn't get this far by being passive. She knew how to make things happen.

CHAPTER 70

He always hated this time. He had to make a withdrawal no later than close of business. Or, this whole thing would blow up in his face. His world was falling apart, and the danger, the guilt. There was rarely a moment that he didn't despise himself. He just wanted to go back to how things used to be.

Carefully and quietly walking through the office halls, avoiding the high traffic area, he started for another computer in a different part of the building. It was going to be tricky with people around. Maybe he should wait until evening.

No, now. Entering another cubicle, a strange cubicle, he logged on. Or hacked in. Depending on the viewpoint.

He was ready to make the transaction when he heard voices. His heart started beating out of his chest and he could feel the dampness on his forehead and under his arms. *Hold on one more second. You're almost there.*

He picked up a piece of paper and started writing a note. This would have to do for now. He exited out of the system.

CHAPTER 71

(Executive Training - Communications Session)

Adam waited patiently for a few of the last stragglers hurrying in and other people milling around the breakfast foods. These healthy looking execs could consume some calories. "Let's take our seats please. It's time to explore the powerful ingredient in maintaining relationships, the ability to communicate."

When the room was quiet, Adam said, "No secret - it's easy to communicate and relate when things are going well. Success or failure is gauged by how we react when the stakes are high, we have differing opinions about issues that matter to us, and things get uncomfortable or emotional. Poorly executed conversations and choice of words have the ability to cause irreparable damage, or stated more simply, we need to think about what we say and how we say it. Over the next few hours, we'll take care of facing conflicted conversation in a way that will not fail.

"And, the fear of confrontation. Many people would rather walk away, or run away, and sacrifice personal and professional relationships rather than confront issues or use communication as a means of problem resolution. They'll excuse it as toxic and rationalize an exit strategy. We'll talk about the discomfort of confrontation and how to make it less painful. Today's goal is to develop a new way of thinking about all of this.

"David and I have been doing some preliminary work over the last few weeks, and we've talked abut some of the past experiences of conversations and relationships gone wrong within your team. Before we get into the 'how to' discussion, David has agreed to share a conversation and relationship he felt he could have handled better."

Adam walked around the room describing the situation - an example of bad intentions? "How many of you have walked into a meeting and without any prior notification, you were blasted by a teammate about your Department's less than stellar metrics or performance, or some other thing that made you look bad? You were totally caught by surprise and you felt the purpose was indeed to make you look bad. Outrageous and unprofessional, right? True story."

A few hands reluctantly shot up. As if on cue, Patrick hurriedly entered the room, apologizing for being late due to the brutal traffic. David and Adam knew he was taking Stephanie out of town for medical treatment and might be slightly late, but he hadn't anticipated cutting it so close to his participation time.

Adam said, "Your timing is perfect." He paused and allowed him to settle in. Then, he nodded to David and Patrick to describe their experience.

Patrick sipped from the water glass in front of him. He said, "I'll start by saying this happened a long time ago and this person no longer works with us.

"It was a meeting pertaining to budget-type metrics. Our former VP of Operations didn't send out a read ahead prior to the meeting and hit us with a stoplight chart that displayed problems in performance. Of course, his metrics were accurate. But, we were not prepared nor given the chance to analyze the data, explain or defend ourselves, or talk about a corrective action plan."

Patrick sighed and continued, "He made us all look bad. We became defensive, seeing it as a dirty ploy. I thought better of saying anything in the moment, so I counted to ten. That didn't work, so I started measuring my breathing in and out. I remember thinking, I should have worked harder at meditation and yoga for times like this." Patrick let out a nervous laugh.

"But seriously, I vowed to myself, that's it. The last time I help him when he needs some information or something, and comes running to me at the last minute. No more favors, and there will come a time when he needs me. No more."

Adam asked, "So, there went the relationship. No more working together, helping him out. Is that what you're saying?"

"In a sense, yes. I still intended to do my job, but not go out of my way to support or assist him. This had happened too many times. We obviously didn't have a relationship because people in relationships don't act like that. He didn't care about me, and I certainly didn't trust him."

Adam nodded and scanned the room. He saw a number of faces with smiles and recognition as they remembered the event. "David, as the CEO, what did you think?"

"Of course, I wasn't happy. I thought it was intentional and inappropriate. In the moment, I made a decision not to call him out in front of everyone. But, we certainly had a discussion in my office after the meeting, and it wasn't my finest moment. Having an emotional conversation when you're as angry, well, we probably needed a timeout."

Patrick looked at David with a puzzled look on his face. He said, "That's interesting. I thought you were upset with the data, and us. Your expression and body language. You barely said anything. I thought we put you in a bad mood, and you aren't even moody."

David responded to Patrick, "No. I didn't want to make the problem worse by calling him out or calling you guys out on performance issues you weren't prepared to discuss. This was a better conversation for one-on-ones with the VP's."

Patrick nodded as he was contemplating how he had perceived the entire scenario in the Boardroom. The ambush and the misunderstanding. He remembered feeling bad about letting David down back then.

Adam walked to David and stood by him before saying, "David has agreed to share his conversation that took place behind closed doors."

"I asked him to come to my office after the meeting. I was angry. Didn't do a good job of controlling my temper. I jumped on him immediately. I asked why he didn't provide read aheads and what were his intentions? I didn't even give him a chance to answer before telling him it was a lousy thing to do to his colleagues. That it was unprofessional, and he better figure out a way to make amends."

"What did he say?"

"As you can imagine, I immediately put him on the defensive and he recoiled. Said he didn't do it on purpose and, even if he did, facts are facts and the data doesn't lie. He said none of this would have even happened if they had been focused on results and outcomes. Their own fault."

David paused and shook his head. "That fired me up even worse. We were intense and continued tossing allegations at each other. It didn't get us anywhere. I walked away from the conversation ashamed of my behavior. My failure to communicate through that heightened emotional drama. I shouldn't have handled it in anger, and I should have been a better leader. The relationship was never the same. The poor communication only exacerbated the lack of trust. As time progressed, we both agreed the company was not the right fit for him."

Adam chimed in, "I think most of us can identify with events like you're describing. Not at our best, we let the conversation get emotional, it spins out of control, and the damage is done. What would have been a better strategy for this encounter?"

David thought for a moment, "I should have cooled down first, prepared better for the conversation, and left out the "you" and "always" and "never" allegations."

He continued, "The cooling down period would have allowed me time to be more objective. I'm old enough to know that anger takes away any chance of that. I should have set the right tone - to talk about the facts and how we both felt about the facts. And, attempt to give him the benefit of the doubt before jumping to the conclusion that he was bad and his behavior was intentional."

Good so far, but Adam needed to revisit the initial meeting. That was the first missed opportunity. "Let's talk about how you could have handled it in the moment - in the meeting. Maybe address the Operations Officer with a question something like, 'I know we're trying to operate with a sense of urgency here, but we're not all prepared to talk about this. Didn't have a chance to review the data prior to the meeting. What happened?'

He continued, "This would give the guy on the chopping block a chance to clear up any misunderstanding, if it wasn't intentional. As you indicated, an opportunity to learn, gather all the facts and not immediately think the worst of the other person. As we know, things aren't always as they seem." Adam smiled, hesitated and continued, "And sometimes they are."

David said, "You're right. I should have done that."

"After letting Ops explain himself, David could have tabled the conversation on metrics for everyone to have a chance to prepare, review and analyze their performance before talking about it. That would put an end to it and would have sent a strong message about expectations for your culture."

Adam continued with his assessment. Second missed opportunity and the chance to curb emotion. "Now, let's shift back to the two of you in your office. You started the conversation in full combat mode, with no cooling off period or preparation. What could you have said and done differently?"

David answered, "Like we've been discussing, setting the tone is critical and guaranteed to take the conversation either north or south. I should have asked for his perspective about what happened. I could have let him know how important our working relationship is to me, and that I need to better understand where he is coming from."

Adam nodded, "Yes. Start with the learning dialogue. Invite him to share his views and you share yours. What next, if you didn't feel like you were getting anywhere after giving him a chance to explain himself?"

David thought for a moment. "I should have said" - 'Here is how it looked to me, and I could be totally wrong. I know you're under pressure, and I appreciate your hard work, but showing metrics charts without sending read aheads and letting people know in advance gave the impression you didn't care. Or, you were trying to intentionally catch them off guard. Whether that's true or not, that's how it looked. What actually happened?'

Adam nodded. "Sounds good. Basic process of back and forth to learn and resolve any misunderstanding.

"We've covered this extensively in our goal setting session. You're gonna get sick of me, but it's worth repeating. So simple. Prepare ahead of the conversation, think about the long-term relationship and what you need for yourself, what the other person needs, and set the right tone so you can navigate those requirements by way of a learning environment without misunderstandings from the start. Pay attention to your emotions throughout, attempt to see it from their point of view/burdens/what it would be like to be them, own the role you play in the problem, and look for common ground and solutions.

"That simple formula gives you the best chance of success. In this case, there was another issue. A really difficult one to overcome.

"There was clearly a lack of trust between the Ops VP and the other executives. Rather than immediately give him the benefit of the doubt, the others automatically believed he had ill intent. It was based on experience and the type of relationship he had established. At least, you realized he wasn't a good fit and took steps to correct it. You had to take action for the good of your team and the organization's health."

Several heads nodded. There was silence as Adam continued.

"There is another part of this I find fascinating. I watched an exchange between David and Patrick that clearly illustrates two people seeing the same situation entirely differently. Patrick thought David was upset about the metrics and performance. In reality, he was struggling to control his temper with the Ops VP, who wasn't playing well with others."

Adam asked Patrick, "How do you avoid this kind of misunderstanding?"

"I have a strong relationship with David. I should have flat out asked him about it." Patrick looked from David to Adam. He said, "We focused in on something important here today. I get the learning piece. Stop assuming and automatically accusing. Treat these complex conversations as a way to avoid misunderstanding, understand the other party's intentions and not expect the worst, and think about the importance of the relationship." What Patrick didn't say was that he should actually take his own advice. After all, these were important relationships.

Adam smiled to himself. They were making progress. They may have a shot at being a healthy environment after all. He gave them a fifteen minute break.

CHAPTER 72

David stopped Lindsay as they were both heading for the door. "Do you have an update on the collapsed building?"

"I'm talking to the construction firm's legal staff, but nothing new. The investigation is pressing along and there aren't any preliminary results, which makes me a little uneasy."

David shook is head side to side and sighed. "I'm getting more concerned as the time passes. I still can't help but worry about our design. We certainly can't withstand any culpability in this."

"Our designers swear we are on solid ground. They have examined it thoroughly. Concluded the collapse was not a result of our work. But, I'm with you. Still a little nervous. Is there anything we could have possibly missed?"

"We need to stay personally engaged. I certainly hope we don't have to launch into a legal battle against this construction company."

"You know, I had a strange feeling about getting involved with them in this partnership agreement. I couldn't figure it out, but I thought something wasn't right from the beginning. I should have insisted on taking the time to closely examine the terms and examine my concerns, but our guys were rushing us on the contract arrangement. I passed it off as me being paranoid."

"Well, it's worse than that. We should have been more controlled about where we save money. Getting involved with a company we don't normally work with, and making that decision to go low bid to save a few dollars isn't what made us successful." He sighed and continued, "It's like the relationship building we're doing here. Our reputation is based on solid partnerships and we detoured from our approach to save a few bucks. We won't do that again. It isn't the area to compromise. Building relationships with our construction partners is what made us successful and we're going back to it." He turned and walked towards his office.

Lindsay didn't move, but watched David walk away briskly. She didn't have the heart to make his already constant headache worse by telling him that embezzling funds wasn't their biggest problem. A law suit could push them over the edge and be devastating to the firm, if their design was defective. She hoped Peter was right.

CHAPTER 73

The intruder was observant, paying attention as he walked slowly, even methodically down the hallway. People were in and out of their offices and cubicles. Carrying coffee, tea or paperwork. Or both. They moved with purpose. Some faster than others. Some smiled and others had their heads down.

No one else was paying attention. That was the good part. It was the middle of the day, making it a little less tricky.

He stepped into a cubicle and bent over the desktop. He looked around. No one was there and the computer was on, making it that much easier. Only a few clicks of the keys and the transaction was complete. No trail. No problem.

It was getting easier, which probably wasn't a good thing. He stood and looked around. Checked both ways before leaving the cubicle.

He walked briskly down the hall, looking at his phone. He appeared to be on a mission like everyone else, until he pushed open the exit door and left the floor.

CHAPTER 74

The fifteen minute break stretched into twenty five by the time everyone returned to the conference room and settled in their chairs. Adam didn't waste any time. "Okay, the big day is coming up. Let's close with a summary of how we're going to prepare and conduct our challenging conversation, the budget crisis planning session.

"What do we have to do to achieve a successful outcome?"

There were basic responses like don't make it personal, be aware of your own emotions, and care about a solution as opposed to winning at all cost. These were all good answers, but not exactly what he was looking for.

Adam smiled. "Come on, we've talked about this - a big key is shifting our thinking to both an internal and external focus. This is not all about you." He pressed the buttons on the laptop and the wall illuminated with the plan of attack for the challenge ahead. The focus - the results all parties desired to accomplish, and the impact to their ongoing relationship.

They reviewed how to share facts and separate facts from fiction, ask for perspectives from all sides, listen to all views, approach areas of agreement and areas of differences, and continuously watch for emotion and tempers and bring the conversation back to calm and unemotional. They explored how they would look for alternate solutions that work for everyone.

And, they agreed upon the best way to conclude the conversation. To establish a specific action plan with a deadline, to include follow-up and appropriate accountability.

With their agreement in place, they adjourned. Their next session would be the Budget Crisis Planning Meeting. An opportunity to apply what they had learned in a real life scenario.

As they left the room, Adam smiled to himself. It all sounded so basic, but it would get real when the stakes were high. He was certain there would be fireworks and it would definitely get interesting.

CHAPTER 75

Back in her office, Lindsay couldn't concentrate in spite of several attempts at it. She couldn't get the embezzlement scheme out of her mind or the feeling that it could be someone in Patrick's Department. He was going to be crushed when he found out she knew all along and didn't say anything. Staring out her window and watching people hurriedly walking to their destinations, she wondered if their lives were as complicated as hers had become.

She turned away from the window and sat behind her desk. She ran her fingers through her long hair and leaned her head back against the chair. She sat in a meditative state for a couple of minutes, until she couldn't stand it any longer. Lindsay had to know. That's what friends did for each other.

She dialed the phone and it rang four times before Patrick picked up. "I was just thinking about you guys and thought I would check on Stephanie. How is she doing?"

He hesitated before responding, "Uh, thank you. She's fine. We should know the test results later this week."

"Okay, please let me know what you find out. If you need anything, you know where to find me. Anytime. Anything at all Patrick."

Uttering an affirmative and another thank you, he moved on to a couple of work questions, and it made her uncomfortable. *OMG, getting paranoid, and disloyal.* Deliberately changing the subject to their ongoing work with Adam, she detected what appeared to be genuine interest in hearing more about it. His mood improved and he sounded more like himself when they made a coffee date for Thursday.

Lindsay stared at the phone after placing it back on the cradle. How sick was Patrick's wife? Was he more worried than he was letting on? Sometimes life takes you right up to the tipping point on carrying more than you can handle. Was Patrick there? She certainly hoped not, but there was nothing she could do except offer her support to listen the next time they were together.

Until then, she needed to think about how this investigation and the aftermath would unfold. She had to have faith that David made the right call when he decided not to involve Patrick in the investigation. She and Mark had it covered. At least, she hoped they did. She couldn't shake the nagging feeling that human combustion was just around the corner.

CHAPTER 76

Lindsay was still in her office when the phone rang. She thought she recognized the number and grabbed it on the second ring. It was the attorney for the construction firm on the collapsed building project.

"Hello, this is Lindsay Thompson."

"Hi Lindsay, John Sutton again, the attorney representing RE Construction. I'm calling in regards to our collapsed building issue. I wanted to see if we can work out an agreement before we turn it over to the CEO's. I know neither of us wants our bosses to be forced to weigh in. I would rather provide them with a decision, a solution." He laughed slightly, pausing and waiting for her to comment.

"You have my attention. Please go on."

He continued with an uneasiness in his voice. "Ah, we've conducted another internal review, brought in some new experts since we last talked. We're certain this collapse was due to a design problem. We'll work with you on this. Hoping we can negotiate some type of an agreement. What do you say?"

Lindsay couldn't help but be annoyed at the drawl in his voice. She envisioned him sitting in a smokey cigar bar with a single malt scotch in one hand and the phone in the other. "John, I would love to resolve this between us, but I'm afraid we're in disagreement about what happened. We're standing by the fact that our design was not faulty and the problems were in construction. We aren't willing to accept liability."

"But, Lindsay, it had to be a faulty design. We've reviewed this thoroughly, and other than someone trying to blow up that building, we can't find any evidence of construction culpability. How sure are you about your investigation?"

Lindsay leaned forward in her chair and placed her elbows on the table. She was losing her patience and didn't appreciate his insinuation. Her voice was measured as she continued, "We've thoroughly reviewed our computations, considered and applied the proper loads for the structure, and we've examined the potential effects of stresses. Our internal investigations show we're on solid ground."

He let out a sarcastic laugh that made Lindsay even more annoyed and came across as insulting, but she didn't react. *Remember, he is a human being and there must be some degree of feelings in there.*

He said, "I hear you, but it doesn't look that way to us. What do you think happened?"

"Good question. This is not a complicated building. We've thought about it and have come to the conclusion the only plausible cause was defective construction materials. Maybe one of your suppliers?"

"Oh, I don't know about that Lindsay." There was a loud sounding sigh on the line and a break in conversation before he said, "We used the same suppliers for fifteen years. We have a relationship with them and we trust their work. We've never had a problem with them before." His voice became formal, with the drawl intact. He sighed, "I guess we'll have to agree to disagree. Let the third party investigation continue. I was hoping it wouldn't come to that. Letting the court system get involved is never good. The money. The time. Nobody wins under those circumstances."

"I completely agree. I wish we could come up with a mutually agreeable solution without the courts, too. I appreciate your call and the discussion, but I think that's what we'll have to do... John, if there is nothing else, I'm almost late for a meeting and I need to go. If you have any other ideas or you would like to talk some more, please give me a call back. I would love to explore some options with you." Without another word, Lindsay hung up the phone.

She was on the verge of being late. The conversation left them right where they started. Nowhere. *Couldn't at least one thing go right for the firm? They simply couldn't get a break.*

She murmured "*oh well*" and left her office. She hurried through the halls to get to the conference room.

CHAPTER 77

(Executive Training - Preparation for the Conversation - A Budget Showdown)

Adam observed the team filing in, talking and laughing. He smiled to himself. How long would it last?

"Let's take our seats, please. Prior to this meeting, you were given a homework assignment to prepare your proposed budget for the next year and a projection for three years. You were told to consider drastic measures such as potential organizational structure changes, opportunities for process improvements, identification of functions you will no longer do, and identify risk factors associated with process, functional, and structural changes."

Adam asked, "How did you get ready for the big day?"

One of the participants responded, "We met with our teams. Had a clear agenda and marching orders to examine the art of the possible for the future. Each executive had been given a copy of the overall budget for the past three years so there was full transparency." He glanced down at his notes and continued, "And, we all worked together on establishing a common goal."

Adam nodded and asked, "What did we agree on?"

Patrick answered like a true Comptroller, "Devising a budget that will result in this firm's survival."

"Okay. Let's make sure we keep that in mind as we move forward." Adam answered as he wrote the statement on the flip chart. He continued, "You examined your individual budgets to make sure you were ready for these discussions. You were instructed to think about the firm and conduct an objective look at the issue. Can we all agree on the main issue? What is it?"

"Simply put, deliberate budget cuts and changes to stay alive. Our operating expenses are too high. We need to determine where to best allocate our money for the out-years. A strategic look at the future since we can't operate like we did in the past," Patrick said emphatically.

Adam nodded in agreement and said, "Let me add the emotional stakes part we're not saying. There could be, no, there will likely be some view of winners and losers. Your job here is to allocate money to your individual business unit budgets, and the money may have to come at the expense of someone else." He paused before continuing, "So, what exactly did you do? David, what direction did you provide?"

"We put a substantial amount of time and effort into preparing for this meeting. Everyone looked at their budgets and proposed reductions of five, ten and twenty five percent. Based on that analysis, they performed a more measured, risk-based assessment of what their business unit could withstand, from functions they proposed no longer performing to more process improvement, and even possible functional and organizational structure changes.

"That is quite a tall order. Sounds like a major overhaul. Anything else?"

"Yeah. And, this one gets really emotional. Business units have resource allocation responsibilities to fund overhead percentages for those areas that are equally important, such as human resources, financial, legal, and purchasing. They were instructed to look at projected workload and address the percentages of overhead/infrastructure they thought we could afford in the future. Then, the negotiations would commence." David paused to think, knowing he was forgetting something.

"Oh, there's one more thing. I should have mentioned this. They were not only tasked with the budgeting process, but also instructed to consider who they are, who they want to be, and how to navigate to get there."

"Can you think of anything else?" Adam asked.

"Nope, I think that's about it." David laughed, "I think that's enough."

"I think you're right about that." Adam also laughed and went back to the flip chart and wrote four reflection points to keep in mind, to avoid a derailing:

FLIP CHART 3:

Emotional Checklist:

- *What is the common goal?*

- *What is the objective for the firm?*

- *What are the desired outcomes of the budget planning process?*

- *What about the relationships - what will success look like?*

Amidst all the budget churn and results-driven work, they were instructed to focus on the relationship. What they wanted out of the budget planning session for themselves, what they thought the other business units wanted and what they thought would work for them, and since they were engaged in a long-term relationship, what considerations and decisions would be best for the relationship, the culture and the overall firm.

Preparation was complete and they were ready to go into action. It was time to get down to the challenging part, actually conducting the conversation. It had the potential for explosion.

CHAPTER 78

Joe Jamison was the first up to brief his proposed budget. As the Vice President of the Government Infrastructure Group, his business unit captured thirty percent of the firm's revenue, one of the high revenue producing units. The longstanding joke was that he subsidized everybody else. That made him feel like big daddy during the good times. He actually liked it back then. But times change.

With money no longer flowing, he had not been looking forward to this, worrying about the tough decisions ahead. He wasn't sure how some of his favorite colleagues were going to feel about him after they heard what he had to say. He definitely would not win any future popularity contests. He just hoped they would still invite him to lunch.

Joe had poured over data, expended an exhausting amount of time and emotion thinking about it, and looked for creative alternatives. He second guessed himself, wondering whether or not he was reacting to the situation fairly. Attempting to put himself in their shoes, he continued to come up with the same conclusions. He had experienced enough leadership and communication training to know what to do. His strategy was planned and now it was time to be clear about his objectives, and setting the right atmosphere and tone for people to hear it. He even scripted his dialogue, figuring out what to say, what his colleagues might say, and making preparations for a productive back and forth exchange. It's not like he was void of any feelings.

He was going to have to accept responsibility. He had contributed to some of the pain he was about to inflict, but he had to do what was right for his business unit. And the firm.

Did he feel good about it? No. He had suffered more than a few sleepless nights. He didn't like what he was about to do, especially to Lindsay and Patrick. They would suffer the most. Or, so he thought.

CHAPTER 79

(Executive Training - Conduct the Conversation - The Explosion)

It was time for the show, the "put your money where your mouth is" opportunity to prove commitment…the budget conversation day. There was a tense aura consuming the room and sucking any idle chatter out of the atmosphere.

They had made necessary preparations for the dialogue that had started out with a focus on learning, researching, analyzing and reviewing data, and ending in a range of emotions from uneasiness, to fear of the inevitable conflict, to full blown panic. But, it was showtime and that meant putting fear in the rearview mirror.

They all believed they had a common understanding of the objective. Just in case anyone veered off course, the words were in bold red letters emblazoned on the flip chart.

They had their line-item budget spreadsheets scattered on the conference table in front of them. There were carafes of coffee, tea, water, cookies, chocolate, and fruit. Just the right foods to get a sugar buzz and sit through the next few grueling hours. No one was looking forward to the torture.

Joe took a deep breath before starting. His PowerPoint presentation appeared on the VTC screen as he looked at his notes. He peered over his reading glasses and started the conversation about the necessary reductions.

He began by stating that his business unit represented a substantial amount of the firm's revenue. If he had scanned the room, he probably would have made a mad dash to the bathroom to relieve the contents of his most recent meal.

He explained his analysis and extensive examination of alternatives he had considered, only to keep coming back to the same conclusions. If they were to continue providing the level of services they had in the past, his business unit could not afford more than a five percent reduction. Anything more would result in degradation of their engineering capability and expertise. After all, this was the government sector's bread and butter.

David was hesitant to bring up the question he knew would start a war, but it had to be discussed sometime. Reminding himself of the value of healthy conflict, he held his breath and thoughtfully asked, "What about the overhead functions you allocate funding to?"

He hesitated before answering tentatively, "Unfortunately, it means we need to take more reductions in the overhead functions. We can't afford it in the direct hours."

David's face drained of color, but there was no turning back. He asked, "So, what does that mean?"

Joe paused before answering. He was at the moment he had dreaded the most. His face felt hot and he sensed all eyes on him. He was certain his neck was crimson, sweat was beading on his forehead, and everyone would recognize his discomfort. *Do not look at Lindsay.*

As he started to answer, Bob Lowery, being from another direct billable unit, Vice President of Energy, came to his rescue. He sensed the need to be gallant and save him. Bob said, "Joe is right. We have an organization we can no longer afford. We have to start cutting these overhead functions. I know it sounds harsh, but it has to be done. They're not revenue producing and we can no longer subsidize at this level." He paused and looked around the room, glancing at Lindsay, Patrick and the others. He continued, "You guys will have to work on efficiency and effectiveness, of determining the level of risk we can accept. Get rid of some of our bureaucracy. It's killing us."

As if Bob hadn't already said enough to cause tension in the room, he continued with, "I wish it wasn't this way, but I think we've got to make the hard decisions. It's unfortunate. We have to accept that." He should have quit before the explosion.

One of the overhead participants spoke in a raised tone, without thinking about what they had learned in the communication session. They were operating purely on adrenaline. "Really? We need to change the way we're doing business? You direct guys are going to just keep on doing what you're doing and taking a meager five percent reduction and continue flying around the country on a whim, when it isn't even necessary. Your cut is about the size of my entire staff. Your departments are already too big." A couple of others chimed in loudly with similar assaults.

David was stunned by the quick turn to war and how these professionals were already acting like children. They had just spent days learning how to relate and communicate, but then it got real. He started to interject himself as their leader, but thought better of it. It was time to let it play out and let Adam do his job. The fireworks had begun.

* * * * * * * * *

Bob missed the previous meetings due to some personal conflict serious enough for David to give him a pass, but more on that later. Showing up for the budget planning session was his introduction, resulting in him missing the exposure to the relationship work and communication tools.

Bob's words and attitude didn't really surprise Adam all that much, but he couldn't shake the feeling there was more to it. Something else was definitely going on with this man. Adam's keen sense of intuition was working overtime. There were times when it was a gift, other times a curse.

Several sets of eyes glared at Bob as the atmosphere transitioned quickly to an emotional one. Adam had expected confrontation from one or more of the executives as this became more personal, but he hadn't expected the need for intervention this soon in the process.

Adam said, "Bob, let's take a pause here and think about the long haul for a minute - relationships intact and what's best for the firm. Before we dive into solutions, let's step back and talk about what we're trying to accomplish."

He called a thirty minute break and gave them two assignments. The first was to revisit their common goal for this budget planning session.

Secondly, a not-so-subtle reminder to consider other points of view, and to spend a few minutes thinking about what was good for them personally, for their colleagues, and the relationship.

They were supposed to have thought about these two important considerations before walking in the room to start the conversation. But, it's not all that unusual for people to underestimate the power of relationships and expend the bulk of their time on analyzing financial data, statistics, facts and figures, and not focusing on how to handle the human condition and their emotions. Then it's showtime and things get real.

When they reconvened, they spent the first few minutes of back and forth talking about their objective and common goal. They inserted ground rules that included caring about each other and each of their individual goals, needs and interests, and acknowledging respect for each executive and their department functions and contributions to the firm.

It took some time to revise the common goal and agree on one that was specific enough to translate into actionable items. It turned out to be more difficult than anyone had initially envisioned. It seemed so basic, so simple. After much up and down debate and a few scars, they landed on the goal of reducing costs by twenty-five percent and determining the most feasible method and places to take the reductions. Settling down and starting to build on momentum, they decided on a stretch goal to position the firm to not only survive, but to thrive. Be a leader in the architect and engineering industry.

Satisfied with the progress, Adam eyed his watch and called a lunch break asking them to return in an hour and a half. They had a long afternoon ahead and they were just getting started.

CHAPTER 80

Intentionally waiting for others to leave the room, Lindsay walked over to Joe and asked him to join her for lunch. Her face was emotionless, offering only an unsmiling invitation. She was disturbed and he knew exactly why. He would rather have a root canal at that very moment, maybe even without benefit of pain medication, but that wasn't an option. They had been colleagues for a long time and had the kind of relationship that was based on mutual respect, honesty, and trust. And, the morning took a turn that could undermine that relationship if it wasn't dealt with promptly.

They walked to an Irish Pub a couple of blocks from the office. It was one of their regular happy hour bars. Today, it was a familiar place, with a history of many good hours spent together.

"I wish we were heading for happy hour instead of lunch," he nervously laughed, as they arrived at the entrance.

"Yeah, I could use a drink," Lindsay responded, void of any emotion in her tone.

"Me too." He took in a deep breath and let it out as quietly as he could, while holding the door for her to enter the restaurant. They were seated almost immediately, successful at beating the rush of the lunch crowd.

The waiter was on his game, recognizing them and rushing over the minute they were seated. There was no need for menus, placing two orders for iced tea and salads.

Lindsay didn't waste any time with small talk. She leaned in and placed her interlocked hands in front of her, looking directly at his eyes. She said,

"Joe, I thought we should have lunch and talk about what took place back at the office this morning. Can we talk about what's bothering me?"

He shifted uncomfortably and said, "Sure Lindsay. But, before you start, let me say I'm sorry how things got crazy back there. I never intended for it to get like that."

She displayed a half smile before responding, "I know. I know you wouldn't do anything intentional and that's why I thought we could talk about it."

"Shoot. I deserve it," he said, with the look of a child waiting for his punishment.

CHAPTER 81

Peter and Tom were huddled in their Department's conference room talking about the next move. They were hovering over the laptop as Tom maneuvered through screens.

Peter stepped away and paced. He was sweating and his face was flushed. He frowned and thought he was getting a cold, or nerves, or something. "Hurry. We don't have a lot of time and I'm due back in the budget session within the hour."

"Okay, okay. Don't rush me. I can't mess this up and you're making me nervous. Please, go get some coffee, or something."

Peter looked at his watch and then glanced around the room. "I need to go to my office for a minute anyway. I'll be back," Peter said as he opened the door, to find David standing on the other side.

"Hi Peter. I thought we might talk for a minute," David smiled and said casually.

"Oh wow, you scared me. I didn't expect anyone to be standing there," Peter said, placing his hand over his chest and faking a laugh. "I was just heading to my office." Peter tried to remain calm, wondering if it was possible that David overheard them.

His boss studied him for a moment, placing his hands in his pockets. He smiled, before saying, "Sorry about that. I didn't mean to scare you. I'll walk with you. I need to get your thoughts on any liability for the collapsed building."

"Sure." Peter attempted to hide his relief, and get it together. He paused and said, "We're taking one last look, but David it has to be faulty construction. We've found nothing." Taking advantage of the opportunity for diversion from what was really going on between Peter and Tom, and hating himself, he continued, "In fact, Tom and I were just reviewing the design and doing some additional calculations. It just couldn't have been the problem."

David sighed, chewed the inside of his mouth and shook his head up and down before saying, "Yeah, that's what Lindsay said. We need this over with. The longer it stretches out, the more chance this is going to kill us."

"I know. The cynical side of me says someone is trying to cover it up. The longer this takes, the more I get worried about what's going on behind the scenes."

"Me, too. I'll exert some pressure. See what I can find out. It's like I told Lindsay, I could just kick myself for letting us partner with this company we haven't worked with before. I know better. All to save a few bucks." David looked at his watch and said, "I need to stop in my office before heading back to the conference room. Thanks for your time." David waved behind him and walked out, saying hello to some of the staff as he continued down the hall.

Peter sat for a moment. He stared down at his desk and put his face in his hands. He had to get a grip. His head ached. He liked David.

CHAPTER 82

The restaurant was starting to get crowded and the noise heightened to the point they could barely hear one another. Lindsay continued looking directly in Joe's eyes as she was about to speak. She began the uncomfortable conversation carefully, attempting to set the right tone and trying to keep it together. "Joe, I know we're both worried about the future and I believe we have the same goal here. To keep our firm's doors open. We just have different perspectives on how to make that happen and I think we need to explore both viewpoints. We need to talk about it. What do you think?"

Joe nodded and said, "We do have the same goal, and yes, we have differing opinions on how to achieve what we're after. I'm very concerned about the overhead, but I didn't do a good job of articulating it in there. I also feel strong about needing you and the other overhead functions."

"Well, I'm disappointed with how the budget planning session began today. Before your brief, I thought you valued the legal support you get from my department. Now, I'm not so sure. I felt you discounted the value of the overhead functions within our organization. And, personally, I thought we were friends."

He sighed, leaned in closer towards Lindsay. "We are friends. I never intended to hurt you or discount your value." He looked down at his hands, folded on the table. "This is difficult. I have spent sleepless nights over this, trying to figure out what we can do to salvage the firm and everyone in it. I just don't see any other way. With the budget situation as it is, I think we have to minimize the impact to the direct billing areas and revenue supply if we all want to keep our jobs. We're desperate here."

His tone became softer and he said, "I value what you do. I apologize if it came across that I don't. That's my mistake. My fault. I know I couldn't do my job without you. I'm sorry that I wasn't clear about that."

Deep down Lindsay believed he meant it. She said, "Thank you for clearing it up. I don't want any misunderstandings between us. But, we differ on the way ahead, and I would like for us to come to some agreement before we go back into that room. You and I have influence with this team and they will look to us to lead. We have the ability to succeed or fail."

"We certainly agree on that part."

"I don't think reducing all the overhead functions is the answer. We can do better than that. We're a creative group of people and it's time we act like it. Let's not settle. We can do what's right for the entire firm. I think we should try to come up with some type of resolution before returning to the conference room."

"I'm listening. What do you suggest?"

CHAPTER 83

Adam walked into the restaurant alone. He was standing in the entranceway scanning for a table, holding his tablet in one hand and waiting for the hostess when Lindsay spotted him.

"I have an idea. Maybe he can offer some thoughts." She pointed to Adam. With Joe's agreement, she walked a little too briskly to the front.

"Would you like to have lunch with us? We're just getting started."

He smiled, but said tentatively, "I would love to, as long as I'm not interrupting anything."

"Not at all. In fact, we have ulterior motives," she said, as she smiled up at him and teased, "While we would love to enjoy your company, we are actually hoping for your advice before going back into the room this afternoon. That is, if you don't mind." Lindsay said, looking at him and leading him to their table.

"Oh no," he replied and gave her his best disappointed look, "So this isn't about my charm?"

"Oh, my mistake. Of course, I meant to say, because you're charming." She winked and continued walking.

"Well, okay then. I'll do it. It sounds intriguing." He glowed, while following her and admiring her confident walk as she made her way through the restaurant. He couldn't help but notice a few of the patrons sneaking a peak at her. He shook his head. *Wow, she is a looker.*

* * * * * * * * * *

After Adam's lunch was ordered, Lindsay and Joe explained what they had been talking about. He listened attentively before asking questions, responding with suggestions, and acknowledging they were definitely stuck in respectful disagreement. He knew what to do.

Adam said, "Let's start the conversation over. Talk through your differences. Start the conversation with addressing areas of agreement, build on those points of agreement, and explore your differences rather than assert the other person is right or wrong. Get the entire story on the table, the facts, and then look for solutions that work for both of you. I like what you said about valuing each other, but afraid about everyone's future. Keep focus on your emotions and caring about each other's feelings throughout the give and take dialogue and problem solving process. You follow these suggestions, and you can't lose."

They spent the next hour working on Adam's advice. They talked and explored alternatives. The time passed quickly and they admitted it was much more productive, and they actually enjoyed it. They discovered it was less stressful and more fun when the issues were tailored to learning and taking into account the needs of others, as well as their own. Amazing and so basic - the results of mutual respect, kindness and caring.

They were almost late paying the check and had to hurry back to the office. They left the restaurant feeling better than when they walked in. They had come up with a few ideas and now they had to put them to action.

CHAPTER 84

When Adam, Lindsay and Joe returned from lunch, the other executives were already seated and quiet, reading and tapping away on their electronic devices. Adam walked in the door and didn't waste any time. "I don't think it's any secret we didn't do so well on our first attempt. Let's talk about it."

He grabbed a cup of coffee and scanned the room before continuing. "We've said the beginning of the conversation is critical. That's the time to do what?" There was silence. "Come on, we've driven it home several times."

"Set the right tone?"

He shook his head in confirmation. "And, be open to listening and learning, and making sure you've created an environment that invites participation and sharing of thoughts, feelings and perceptions. Based on this morning, what do you think we should do next?"

"Stop talking at each other and listen." Someone shouted out and received a few grunts and laughs.

Adam laughed. "That's certainly true and it would definitely help. The one thing that will make a difference going forward is getting back to the ground rules. So, let's spend the next few minutes talking about them now."

Instead of coming back from the break looking refreshed, the majority of the executives looked tired or distracted, or both. There was less talk than before, but it was after lunch. Adam said, "We've already experienced that this emotional stuff isn't always easy. However, I hope you can agree that we've also seen the power in it. So, please hang with me a little while longer." He continued, walking towards the flip chart and pointing. "Take a look at your ground rules and see if we need to modify them now that we've seen the crystal ball. Let's consider what took place earlier."

Joe stared at the rules on the flip chart. He said tentatively, "Based on my earlier debacle and scars to show it," he laughed and stood up, "I think we should refine our rules a little and then perhaps actually follow them," he joked on himself. He nodded towards the flip chart and asked, "May I make a couple of edits to the rules?"

"Sure." Adam handed him the marker.

"The one I could have benefitted from before is to emphasize the commitment to find a mutually beneficial solution, taking into consideration and attempting to meet everyone's needs. To welcome all ideas and get to shared understanding of the issues before making any decisions. Take time to learn. What do you think?"

"I think that's great. What do you guys think?"

Most of the participants in the room nodded in agreement.

The ground rules were revised and Adam continued to critique their earlier conversation before getting back to the actual budget planning. "Earlier today, we immediately went into action. We didn't start by discussing our common goal, we didn't use the opening conversation as an opportunity to learn from all the players, and we immediately went to a solution."

"It is obvious Bob and Joe have strong ideas about the solution, but maybe there are other alternatives worth exploring. I'm sorry guys." Adam shrugged and continued, "I'm sure it's no surprise to you that your teammates may not have received your dialogue in a constructive way. You guys want to give it another shot?"

Joe was eager to try again, to mitigate the damage. He began with an admission that he felt bad about his earlier approach. It had been insensitive, offered only one possible way forward, and he wanted to try again. He said, "I wasn't clear or appropriate before. I went about it all wrong. So I would like to try again, in a better way, with a different perspective in mind."

He drew in a deep breath and said, "I can't believe I'm actually nervous about this, but here goes." He cleared his throat and looked around the room to all eyes on him. "My initial thoughts are we can't assume more than a five percent reduction in our direct lines. I'm afraid about degrading our engineering and technical expertise. And, that's what led me to think we had to focus on the overhead areas for our reductions," he paused, almost pleading, "Look guys, that doesn't mean you aren't critical to the success of this business. We couldn't do what we do without all of us. I don't have the answers and I don't know what to do here. I'm open to learning and searching for other answers. So maybe we need to do a little more talking, and explore the options from other viewpoints. Maybe we need to brainstorm some alternate solutions that can meet all our needs."

Adam smiled, "That's much better. Explaining your thoughts, asking for the other participant's thoughts and being willing to brainstorm an alternative, creative solution."

For the remainder of the day, each executive was allotted thirty minutes to talk about their perspectives and recommendations. They used a facts-based approach to instill mutual understanding and learning. The central theme continued to be overhead as the target for reduction. All were key functions, but the revenue producing units had the largest potential impact on the firm's chance for survival.

So far, so good. They concluded their communication session without casualties. Communicating to learn actually worked. The next step would prove to be difficult; progressing to the decision making step with the team unscarred.

Adam told them to get a good night's sleep. They weren't done yet. The next day's work included examining alternatives, making the hard decisions, and creating an action plan.

CHAPTER 85

Everyone filed out of the conference except for Bob. He was sitting quietly in his chair, staring out the window.

Adam maneuvered around the conference table and took the seat next to him. "Bob, how do you feel about today's discussion?"

"It gave me some things to think about." He looked down at the table and didn't say anything else.

Adam said, "I was impressed how you changed your approach after the first round. In fact, I thought you embraced the idea of coming up with alternatives that worked for everyone. Caring about all the stakeholders. That was a powerful statement."

"I was an ass, at least initially. I wish I'd been able to attend the workshop over the last couple of days. I missed out on some good work on relationship building." He hesitated before saying, "But, I heard about the vulnerability exercises and I'm not sure I could have handled it," his voice cracked and he stopped himself.

"I'll be glad to go over the principles we worked on. And, I have a pretty good ear. We can talk about anything that's on your mind. Your call."

Bob stared off in the direction of the refreshment table and started to speak, but stopped. When he turned to face Adam, he wiped his eyes and his chin quivered. He finally spoke in a tone barely above a whisper, "I haven't been here because I'm struggling with some personal issues." He blew out a deep breath. "My wife and I are going through a tough time. Today has really driven it home for me…we're not doing a very good job of communicating."

Adam asked, "Would you like to talk about it? I'm happy to explore the communication challenges with you. You can trust me to keep our conversation confidential." He looked at his watch and said, "I don't have anywhere to be. How about going out for a drink or coffee, and talk?"

Bob thought for a moment before responding, "Yeah, I would like that. I'd like to learn and understand some of the principles we could use to be better communicators."

"Let's take a walk."

CHAPTER 86

The restaurant was overflowing with a happy hour crowd. Adam and Bob asked for a quiet table in the far corner. They made small talk and didn't resume the reason for their conversation until the waiter placed their drinks on the table.

Adam waited for Bob to begin. "It started awhile ago. Our two kids are finally out of the house. What an adjustment. I think we've both realized we focused so much on our children that we stopped focusing on each other. We don't talk much and it feels like we don't even know how to talk anymore. We've stopped paying attention to our marriage and even though we've recognized it, we don't seem to have the ability to get it back on track."

"Bob, I'm happy to share some communication tips and skills to help you get unstuck and start talking. It's a great place to start. I'm no marriage counselor but I've seen amazing results with this set of communication tools," Adam said.

"We're not ready to see a counselor anyway. Not just yet. I really believe our problems are in how we're communicating, or not. I just think we need tools. Learn to communicate better. At least, that's what I would like to try first."

Adam spent the next hour talking about the concepts from their executive sessions. He looked at his watch, thinking it was getting late and he was hungry. They ordered a couple of entrees and kept talking. Bob called his wife and told her he was having dinner with their firm's consultant.

After listening to Bob's story, Adam agreed with him. He thought maybe their problems might be solved by better communication skills. Even though he was not a psychologist or marriage counselor, he was a communications expert. He was fairly certain he could help.

"So, what do you think?" asked Bob.

"I believe it's the type of thing that can happen in marriage. More common than you would think. The children become the focus of the family, needing full attention on school work, sporting events, and other challenges of everyday life. Both parents work and become tapped out between the kids, the careers, and running the household. There is little time for the marriage space, unless you work really hard at the relationship. Easier said than done, the partnership has to be a priority. Sound familiar?"

Bob was shaking his head up and down in agreement. "That's exactly it," he paused, took a deep breath before saying, "I hope we haven't gone too far down that road and we can't turn back."

For a moment, Bob stared off into space and Adam watched him and thought carefully about his words before speaking. "But, you want to try?"

"I sure do."

"Then fight for your marriage, with her." Adam leaned in close, "Get vulnerable. Talk with her about making the marriage a priority and take the necessary steps to make it happen. An action plan. After all, what do you have to lose?"

"You're right. I'm not ready to throw in the towel. I'm interested in getting us back on track," he said emphatically, wiping his mouth with his napkin and tossing it on his dessert plate.

Adam smiled and leaned back in his chair before responding, "I think we can come up with a few ideas."

Bob grabbed a notepad and pen from his briefcase and they spent the next few minutes talking through a carefully crafted playbook. He had to get specific and decide exactly what he wanted out of a dialogue with his wife prior to starting any conversation. Preparation - thinking about the specific facts that led them to this place. Figure out how to make the marriage their priority in these busy lives and this new normal. When he knew what he wanted from the conversation and could articulate the facts from his perspective, he was ready to ask her to talk. Give her time to do the same thing.

Without paying attention to the flaming red head in the form fitting black dress walking a little too close and glancing a little too long in Adam's direction, he said, "Don't lose sight that it's critical to distinguish facts from perception. At times, we can be bad about that. Our interpretations often depend on the baggage we bring. Based on past experiences and the lessons we've learned about how things should and shouldn't be. They can be overly limiting and, to put it bluntly, false. Challenge the narrative in your head.

"Now, for the communication keys. Remember when we talked about a system approach to goal setting in the beginning of our time together. It's sort of like that.

"You have to start the conversation with the facts and say you want to use this as an opportunity to learn. Talk about how you both want the same thing, the common goal of getting your marriage back on track. The next steps involve inviting her to share her point of view, you sharing your point of view, and both of you clearing up any misconceptions. And, I don't think I have to tell you, there will be some. Ask what she needs, tell her what you need, separate the wants from the needs, and determine how to help each other through the challenges - a two way street.

"And, for some rules. You know I always have ground rules or principles, or guidelines. You've probably already figured that out." He laughed. "Some rules to consider - agree this is a no blame zone, accept that both parties are responsible for the challenges you are experiencing, and here is the kicker, accept an obligation to one other."

Adam didn't speak for a moment. Thinking about a different time, a different relationship. He stopped himself, shifting his focus back to Bob, and pausing long enough for Bob to finish writing. He continued, "Now for the real work throughout this process. Discuss areas of agreement and disagreement. As necessary, keep going back to your common goal. Refine it, add to it, if necessary. Work together and come up with solutions, devise a mutually agreeable action plan, and agree on follow-up to gauge progress along the way."

Adam concluded, "By the way, if you don't want the conversation to turn emotional, stay away from words like 'always' or 'never'. And, I'll say it again, state facts and the impact; how it made you feel. It is hard to argue with feelings. So, there you have it - conversation, action plan, and monitor progress. Based on what you've said about her, I really think you can do this."

"I think we can too. We still like each other," Bob chuckled and continued to scribble notes without lifting his head. "This is good stuff. I think it just might work."

Bob placed his pen on the table and looked up Adam. "You have no idea how much I appreciate this. Thank you for taking the time to talk to me," he continued with enthusiasm in his voice, "I am feeling good about the possibilities, and hopefully this new beginning with my wife. You've given me ideas that I can wrap my arms around. A strategy. An action plan. A new way of communicating."

Adam smiled and said he would be pulling for them. They finished their coffee, walked back to the cars, shook hands, and said goodbye.

Adam was thinking about Lindsay as he got in his car. He was good at giving advice, but not so good when it came to his own personal life. He was definitely going to be different this time around. The next time he saw her, he was going to go for it. Time was wasting and this was too good to be true. He was not going to have another missed opportunity.

CHAPTER 87

Adam arrived early the next morning. The traffic was better than usual, and he had intentionally left his house a few minutes ahead of time. He got out of his car in the firm's parking lot and glanced in the direction of Lindsay's reserved spot. She was already there. He had hoped to run into her. Maybe even have coffee together.

He stepped inside the busy Coffee Bar, looked around, and waited in line for his order. There was no sign of her there either. He picked up his 'to go' cup and took the stairs. He had a little extra energy that needed expending anyway.

Walking into the empty conference room and tossing his briefcase on the floor next to his chair, Adam glanced around the room and thought about the next few hours. He loved this work. This was an especially interesting group of people and he liked them.

The conference table was filled with papers and notebooks, even a few laptops. Everything was just as it was the day before. He looked at Lindsay's seat and observed that her papers were neat and orderly. He smiled.

People started filing in. Some in pairs and some alone. The room went from quiet to buzzing with chatter in a matter of a couple of minutes. Most stopped at the food table for breakfast and coffee and continued their conversations. Some laughing, some in serious discussion. Lindsay and David walked in together at the last minute.

The session barely commenced when the spirited conversation about reductions continued. The debate was centered around whether or not the firm could make sufficient reductions without resorting to organizational change. Did they even have a chance of survival? Were they wasting their time?

David shared a conversation that transpired between him and his wife the night before about the budget planning session. She was an auditor before they were married and her education and experience made her more than a little financially intuitive.

He had whined to her about the challenges they were facing and she was not one to mince words and flatly stated, "I don't think you have the culture or stomach to make the changes necessary for survival."

"What do you mean?" David had asked in a tone that said he didn't like her message.

"I'm just making an observation." She shrugged.

"Oh no, you're going to say more than that. What do you mean?"

"As an example, what about your executive suite? Do you really need an executive assistant and an administrative assistant when everything is automated? You know how to use a computer. You're savvy with all types of automation. Put your money where your mouth is."

David continued telling the group how the scene had played out, his face had turned red and the atmosphere had become a little tense. He was on the verge of getting defensive with her and made a few comments that are better left unsaid. She knew she had made him angry and decided they would both be better served by shifting the conversation to a different tone.

The softer, gentler, but candid continuation went like this. "I apologize for blurting out my thoughts. I didn't mean it the way it came out. I've listened to your concern and fear about the future of the firm for awhile now. You are fairly self-sufficient. You are a genius with a computer. Think about an ordinary day and visualize it without one of them. Do you think you could do with one less administrative person in your office? Maybe that could save a revenue producing job. And it's symbolic to your executive team that you walk the talk. What do you think?"

David hesitated before answering. "I hadn't really thought about it. You're right. I do most of my work on the computer myself. And, Joyce has been thinking about retiring. Spending more time with her new grandchild. Maybe I can talk to her and offer a retirement package."

"It could turn out to be a win-win. Something to think about. I know you'll do what's right for everyone. You always do," she said, with a smile and a peck on the cheek.

David finished his story with a chuckle. "She walked out of the room and left me sitting on the couch, thinking about what she said. Her initial comments had started to make me emotional and tense until she changed her communication style. She apologized, alleviating the tension and emotion. She changed her tone in the way she shared her thoughts and it made all the difference."

He continued, "Which brings me to our budget planning session. I'm going to do it. To reduce one overhead position in the executive suite. I've already talked to Joyce this morning and she wants to retire. She was waiting for the right time, but has wanted to leave for awhile. With everything going on, she didn't want to let us down. We'll work out the details and she should be retired and enjoying her grandchild by the middle of the year."

Without comment from around the room, their facial expressions illustrated they were impressed. Their boss was leading with action. Lindsay interrupted the silence with a question. "Your wife made a comment that I tend to agree with and I think we should explore. Do we have the culture or the stomach to make the decisions we will need to affect real change and fiscal responsibility?"

She continued, "We're all saying we need to reduce costs, determine what we're going to stop doing, and yet, none of us wants to take the real hits in our own areas. Until we do, we're not going to get anywhere."

The room was silent, until Jack responded. He said, "Lindsay is right. We have to change our thinking and our behavior."

* * * * * * * * *

Adam walked around the room, scanning faces and said, "Now, we're getting somewhere. Who is willing to share an actual example of a behavior that needs changing?"

The room was silent. Almost all faces were looking down at the table like it might come alive and move, tremble, or do something exciting at any moment.

The turn had all the markings of explosive territory with high stakes. At first, no one answered and the only noise was a ping from an incoming text on a cellphone that had not been silenced.

Then, Jack spoke. "Not to throw you under the bus, Bob, but I would like to talk about something that has been bothering me for some time."

"Uh oh. Go on," Bob said hesitantly.

"You come across as a fair guy and a team player, and that's why I've been surprised by your recent hiring practices. We all had an agreement to delay any new hires, except for the pre-approved few for succession planning six months ago. But you pressed on. Now, we're in a dilemma. You have a full staff and the rest of us don't."

Bob's face was turning red and he started becoming defensive. "Wait a minute, they weren't just any positions. We had designated them as critical positions to fill. I wasn't just thinking about my Department. I was also worried about the firm failing without them. And, why didn't you say something then?"

"Bob, they might have been critical but they weren't the pre-approved few." Jack looked down at the floor for a second before continuing. "You're question is valid. I should have said something. We all should have. When one of us doesn't live up to our agreements, we need to have a direct conversation to address the problem. As an executive team, we have the responsibility to hold each other accountable for the sake of this firm's success, and our relationships," Jack said.

Bob appeared ashamed. "You're right. I wish we had talked about it then. I wasn't thinking about the challenges you guys were facing, but I wasn't trying to hurt you either. I was thinking about survival of my business unit, and also the firm. I paused on hiring a couple of non-critical positions that were vacant. As for the critical ones, I was rationalizing that it was for the good of the firm. It wasn't intentional to hurt everyone else, but I see that it did. I'm sorry."

He thought for a moment before continuing, "I think I have a solution. I won't hire anyone else until I receive the green light. In fact, we'll look at the skill sets of the people I have and if there are other, more critical positions, we'll move them into those positions. How does that sound?"

They all agreed, and Bob was willing to do the right thing. They experienced the power of communication through open dialogue, getting to the facts, and seeing that Bob didn't have bad intentions. Unlike how it appeared, Bob said he wasn't trying to be inconsiderate or unfair to his other colleagues.

Adam pointed out to the group, "This conversation was extremely helpful on two fronts. Anybody care to take a chance at the answer?"

Jack started this exchange and he wanted to finish it. He said, "It allowed us to stop guessing about intentions and openly discuss our feelings about Bob's actions. It also gave Bob the opportunity to share his perspective, leading to a better understanding."

"And what is the other thing?" Adam asked the room.

David responded, "It led to an agreement among the executive team. We have given each other permission to hold each other accountable. I believe it's the makings of a stronger relationship."

"That's it." Adam smiled.

Adam called for a break. This next step in the process would be interesting. He couldn't wait to see the drama play out as they were putting words to actions.

CHAPTER 88

Hustling to her office during the break paid off. Lindsay picked up the phone and asked David if he would stop by and walk with her back to the conference room. She had some news that couldn't wait.

He stepped into her doorway and turned his head sideways like a confused puppy. "You look heavily engaged in something. I almost hate to interrupt you. Are you ready to go?"

She looked up and smiled. "I am. Let me hit send on this email." Her gaze shifted back to the computer screen, busily typing away before pressing the final button.

She stood up with a satisfied look on her face and joined him for the walk down the hall. Without hesitation, she said, "I have some good news. It's about the collapsed building."

He slowed and his face grew serious as he looked over at her. "I could use some good news. What's happening?"

"John Sutton, the construction firm's attorney called me a few minutes ago. They pursued a more comprehensive internal investigation and you'll never guess what they discovered." She nodded to a couple of employees passing by them before continuing.

"Go on."

"John apologized profusely, accepting liability. Said they will make it right immediately. He is working with their insurance company. If that isn't sufficient to completely solve the problem, they will throw whatever money is necessary to mitigate and take corrective action. In his words, 'to make good on this horrific catastrophe.'"

"Why the turnaround? What happened?"

"It was their Project Manager. He had worked with them for years. He was arrested today. He wouldn't give me all the details. Ongoing criminal investigation now, but he shared enough to let me know we have been exonerated from any wrongdoing."

Lindsay hesitated at the door of the conference room. She waited for a cue from David on whether or not to continue. "A criminal investigation?" He asked, leading her to the side of the door rather than entering the conference room.

She spoke in a low tone, "One of the home office auditors was reviewing invoices as part of their checks and balances system. They stumbled across some interesting entries in their purchasing system for material buys. The invoices, the accounting entries, and the materials didn't match up," she paused again and he nodded. "The auditor didn't think much of it at the time. Thought he stumbled across some data entry errors. He placed a call to the PM for clarification. When they didn't answer, he contacted the Superintendent. That's when it all unravelled. The PM and contractor were in cahoots, doctoring invoices and what was actually delivered. A scam."

"Wow. I hate to hear that's what happened. But, at least, it is a relief for us." He paused and continued in a low voice to avoid overly sharp ears, "Now we can focus on the other issue."

"I know. We'll get to the bottom of it."

David looked at his watch and said, "We'll talk later. We better get in there before we hold everyone up."

He motioned for her to enter the room ahead of him. She said she desperately needed coffee. They both went to the refreshments table and filled up their cups.

CHAPTER 89

Adam asked everyone to take their seats for another go at the budget planning business. He glanced at Lindsay to find her looking back at him. This time she didn't look away. *Excellent!*

"Okay - let's get to it. Process check."

The "oh no" groans and eye rolls made Adam laugh, feeling a familiarity, a comfort level that had been building over the last few days together.

"Well, if you hadn't, kind of, botched up the first round we wouldn't have to go over the process again. Am I right?" He smiled to a few "good point" and "you're right" comments that echoed around the room.

"Let's refresh on the key ingredients here. Create an environment of information sharing and learning before making any decisions. Understand the other person's perspective, share your own perspective, search for common ground, and explore differences. Thank you for indulging me. Let's go," Adam said with a sense of urgency.

Joe agreed to take the lead. After all, he said he had to fix some misunderstandings and he had some making up to do. He said, "As a direct line…"

Adam stopped him. "Joe, I know it's not intentional, but starting out that way can lead to a tone that separates/divides the direct from the overhead lines. This is a team effort. We're all in this together."

Joe shook is head and smiled before saying, "You're right. Let me start over." He sighed and continued, "I feel we're losing our competitive edge and we can't afford to reduce funding in our revenue producing areas if we want to stay alive. My goal isn't to reduce the overhead lines, but I'm having a hard time seeing any other options. We simply don't have the funding and we have to figure out how to save the firm. Any ideas on what we can do?"

Lindsay was next. She refused to let this get controversial. They were intelligent, creative people and they could figure it out. Would figure it out. She responded, "Joe, I agree our revenue producing areas need to be staffed appropriately, but I think everyone has to do some changing. We all have to figure out how to operate a little more lean." She continued, "I believe there is a direct correlation between your success and the support we provide. You can't get any work done without contracts awarded and that involves a legal review to protect you and this firm. If I continue to reduce, we will become a bottleneck for you. Then, we'll both be unhappy and unsuccessful."

Adam stepped in. "Good. This is the perfect time to reiterate you're all after a common goal."

They continued the dialogue about the firm's survival. Exploring contributions of all departments, eliminating non-value added tasks, and mapping out process and critical functions were all fair game and on the table.

Lindsay scanned the room as David was talking. Her eyes shifted over to Patrick, not saying much in a conversation that involved budgets. It wasn't like him. In fact, he would normally take over when it came to funding. They would even tease him and say something like, "Spoken like a real Comptroller." Why not now? What was he thinking?

David asked all of the other overhead department heads what they felt they could do before addressing the Legal Department. At last, he turned his attention to Lindsay. "I don't intend to take too much risk in this area, but is there anything you can do to reduce, alter the structure, or change processes without putting us in jeopardy?"

He wasn't worried about her response or whether or not she would be offended because he knew Lindsay was fair, prudent, and cared almost as much as he did about the firm. He should have said they were fortunate they weren't already in legal trouble over the collapsed building, some other careless move, or fallout associated with an embezzlement investigation. This last thought made him feel the heat rising up to the top of his head. He wiped the forming mist from his forehead, hoping no one would notice.

But Lindsay did. She picked up on the change in his facial expression. She said, "I have a couple of ideas. I think we can do some things. I know this is about survival and we'll do our part."

They soon discovered from Joe's second attempt at addressing budget reduction, the success was found in starting with agreement on the facts, diagnosing the problem, and introducing the challenge with an approach that said "we're all in this together, and let's find a solution together." And then, they were able to get somewhere. Be open to learn, to exchange, explore alternatives, and come up with solutions.

During this transition to a team approach of attacking the problem, there was a new energy emerging in the room. They shouted out ideas and Adam posted them to the flip chart. As pages were filled, they were ripped from the chart pad and posted around the room. Even the door opening and the smell of fresh cookies for the afternoon session didn't interrupt them.

Adam offered up a break, but they wanted to keep working. They were making progress. They stopped only long enough to grab a drink. The cookies were placed in the middle of the table to be devoured while the brains kept churning.

Once the sugar kicked in, there were a few moments that became a little shaky. After all, this was an emotional conversation that had high stakes for everyone. In those moments, Adam interrupted, reminding them to refer back to the common goal. Remind each other of their ground rules and taking the "personal" out of the conversation.

* * * * * * * * *

Then, the explosion occurred. The Operations Officer grew impatient with what she considered slow progress. But, this time a colleague called her out on it, not David. He smiled, as he observed them in action. The smile was short lived as his mind shifted to the days and weeks ahead. They were going to have to maintain this new culture they were building, and it wasn't going to be easy. It would take daily care and feeding and he hoped they had it in them.

Back to the eruption at the other end of the table. It was Eleanor and Paul, the VP of Operations and the Business Director at it again. Eleanor hadn't contributed much throughout the workshop. She believed in getting results at all costs irrelevant of the damage to relationships. Steamrolling was her style.

She was like a ticking time bomb that other executives just tolerated. She scowled, grunted, or sighed, unless she was raising her voice. At least she had the good sense not to spend the last few days glaring and sitting with her arms crossed. She sat quietly, making notes on her tablet the majority of the time. Up until that moment.

Eleanor finally reached her limit when Paul was going on and on about some new process. She raised her voice about two octaves and said to him, "We cannot afford to keep throwing good money after bad at process improvements that aren't even working. There is no time for that, and it's costing us a fortune."

The room grew quiet. Everyone stopped what they were doing to see what would happen next.

Paul's face flashed red, "What would you like to do Eleanor? Do away with rules, forget about consistency, and then have free reign to do whatever you want?"

"Oh, that's ridiculous. That's not what I said and you're being melodramatic," she continued loudly and passionately, "I would like to stop being a bureaucracy. It's killing us. I'm out there trying to get things done and everywhere I turn, there is a roadblock. I don't know what else to do."

"I'm sorry you feel that way, but we have processes for a reason, and by the way, they actually make us more efficient," Paul said as he glared at her.

"You and I have been down this road a hundred times. I don't know why I bother. I can't even talk to you," she said in a low tone and shook her head in disgust.

"Okay. Look, I'm sorry. I know you would like to have more flexibility, but we can't do it at the expense of our business practices. I know you think we're too conservative, but we have accounting compliance requirements. As a matter of fact, you may find this shocking," he smiled and lowered his voice, "But, I actually agree with you to a large degree. We can't do anything about a lot of it. I wish we could."

There was flicker of surprise in her eyes. She shook her head, as she spoke in a resigned tone, "I guess on some level I know that. I don't want to hear it, but I know it," she actually smiled, probably the first time in her entire life. "I'm sorry. I'm just getting a little frustrated here. You know, I'm sometimes impatient. I know it's a weakness of mine, but I feel like we're not getting anywhere."

Paul shook his head in agreement. He thought he saw a glimmer of hope and took advantage of the moment. He said, "Why don't we get together and talk about meshing our business and operational requirements. They're both valuable and critical. Let's explore how we can help each other. See what we can do for both of us to get what we need. I don't think you and I are that far off on our beliefs here. Look Eleanor, we need to be on the same page. Together, we can make a difference, or we can lead this company to failure. I'm willing to try and work through this. Our futures depend on it."

Eleanor actually shook her head in agreement. She wasn't making any promises, but she was willing to try. It was obvious this exchange made Eleanor uncomfortable. It wasn't normally her style for dealing with issues.

The room grew quiet. Not a word was uttered. Adam called for a break.

CHAPTER 90

Lindsay stopped Peter before entering the conference room after the break. "I haven't seen much of you lately. You usually come by and have coffee or talk. Are you doing okay?"

Peter faked a smile. "I'm fine. I've just been really busy lately."

Something is not right. That does not sound like him. She hesitated and asked, "How are the kids? Everything okay?"

"James is doing well for now. The other two are great. Petey is busy with golf and Janie is trying to figure out the basketball thing."

Lindsay attempted to hide her relief. Since Peter had confided about the struggles with James, she had spent more than a little time thinking about it. She worked on suppressing the fear that surfaced every time something wasn't quite right with Peter. That couldn't possibly be good for him, or her.

"I remember when they were just babies. And now, Janie is being recruited to play college basketball. Has she made any decisions?"

"Still doing the visits. I don't know what she's going to decide. She needs to figure it out and get it behind her." Peter looked into the distance, shaking his head, "It's taking too much time away from her studies."

"She'll figure it out. Not a bad position to be in."

"Oh yeah. No doubt. I just want it over for her, and for us." He was looking around as he talked to her.

"The last time we talked you were struggling with Tom. How is that going?"

"Tom is Tom. We're doing the best we can together. I'm not sure this is the right fit for him anymore," he said, but still didn't look at Lindsay.

"Peter, are you sure you're okay?" She studied him for a moment. Something was off. "You know you can talk to me. About anything. Stop by anytime."

"Thanks. I'm just tired and working through some things, but there's light at the end of the tunnel. I'm getting it together."

"I'm here if you need to talk."

As they walked into the room. She couldn't shake it. Peter was more than a little distracted, and there was definitely something wrong, and it wasn't James. He would have told her if it had anything to do with his son.

CHAPTER 91

(Executive Training - Conclude the Conversation - Extinguishing Fireworks and Cementing Success)

The executive team was seated around the conference table, working on the final rounds of their budget discussions and dealing with the emotional stuff that went along with it. They were nearing the end, coming up with an agreeable outcome, putting the final touches on their budget proposal, and creating an appropriate action plan assigning responsibilities, commitments and accountability.

There were parts of it that went smoothly, even easy, and others not so much. Some decisions required compromise and sometimes emotions ran high. At one point, Eleanor became so angry that she shouted at her colleagues and walked out. Adam called a break and the team members migrated to the food table.

Without saying a word to anyone, David left the room. When he spotted Eleanor, she was wiping her eyes and leaning over the water fountain. He stopped walking, giving her a moment, and the newly formed self-schooling habit within him said to take a deep breath, be gentle and speak softly. The voice echoed in his head to pay attention to the relationship.

He approached her, looking directly into glassy eyes. He said, "Eleanor, this is difficult for all of us, but we're in this together. You are incredibly gifted and I need you on this team. But, you've got to learn to control your emotions a little better."

"You're right. I'm sorry. I just get so passionate that I can't help myself. I have to do better and I'm really trying to work on it." She was looking down at the floor, shaking her head.

"I love your passion and I know you mean well, but you're an executive here and your job is more than thinking about your Department. You have to think about what's best for the team, and value the contributions of the others." David hesitated before continuing. His voice became firm. "You'll have to make changes if you want to have a relationship with them. And, I don't demand much, but I'm demanding a culture based on relationships, with mutual respect and the ability to work together."

She didn't say anything at first and they both stood facing one another in silence. She admitted, "I know. My impatience hasn't always served me well over the years. I can get things done, but at what cost. I want to do better. I really do. And, I know I have to change. You'll find this hard to believe, but I'm actually trying to use these tools Adam introduced. I can do it." She smiled up at him. "I just need a little patience. Isn't that funny coming from me?"

"Eleanor, we can work with that." He smiled back, and nodded towards the conference room as they headed back together.

When she entered the room, she apologized for her outburst. She vowed to do better and smiled as she looked around the room and asked for their patience, saying miracles don't happen over night. Almost all the heads in the room hit the conference table. What had they done with Eleanor?

CHAPTER 92

Adam broke the stunned silence by directing them back to work. He laughed to himself, thinking they were definitely an interesting cast of characters.

Joe was about to squabble with Lindsay and Patrick when Adam stopped it. He asked them, "What do you do when you're not getting anywhere finding a suitable solution?"

Lindsay said, "Continue asking questions - what do we each want? What do we absolutely need? What can we all live with? Do everything possible so we don't have to accept a winners and losers solution." She smiled at Adam and ran both hands through her long, silky blonde hair before sliding her reading glasses onto her head.

"That's right. I couldn't have said it better. Let's keep looking for the win-win solutions." Adam smiled back and continued walking around the room. *God, she was intoxicating.*

They spent the next couple of hours coming up with the last of the possible alternatives and looking for solutions. Faces looked tired, hair was mussed, and eyes were red. Determining budget reductions while keeping relationships in tact wasn't all that easy. After all, they were trying to save the firm.

Adam continued making notes on the flip chart as the team crafted their conclusions. He acted as a facilitator, but didn't have to interfere in many emotional tirades. They were learning the skill of holding each other accountability, and referring to the grounds rules and the common goal as often as necessary.

They still weren't quite finished. Once the decisions were made, it was the collective responsibility to own up to the solution. The Action Plan was established and documented, clearly delineating responsibilities and designating who was to do what by when, solidifying deliverables, and discussing the mechanics of follow-up.

They were starting to celebrate when Adam put up his hands in a motion that said, hold up. He said, "We're not finished yet. Coming up with the Action Plan is great but we have one final step. Anybody want to wager on what it is?"

David said, "Follow-up and accountability."

"That's right. Follow-up is critical to ensure accountability, and assessment of any need for redirection, if necessary." Adam smiled and nodded. "Your initial work on communications is almost done."

There were a few playful groans heard around the room.

* * * * * * * * *

An hour later, they reached a mutual agreement on the things they had to do. They accepted responsibility to be committed to the plan, agreed that performance objectives would be changed to reflect this agreement, and performance evaluations would be based on their contributions and compliance.

Adam put down his marker and turned to face them. He said, "You did it. You did some outstanding work here. Now for the easy part. Let's summarize your conclusions."

The overhead units agreed to take a larger percentage of reduction over the next two years, some more than others, depending on the function. However, if they were going to exceed their budget due to projected increase in business volume, they would charge back to the business unit asking for the overhead support.

As for the direct billing business units, they took a smaller reduction in their overhead, but they had to change their methods of operation. No free rides here. One of the changes involved direct vs. overhead billable. Employees had to be able to bill seventy five percent direct. If they couldn't bill at that rate because they were out of projects to work on, they had to go to the overhead billing pool. They had a period of time to market themselves and get picked up for projects. If they were good, they would quickly be solicited to resume the direct billing percentage. If not, the employee went to part-time and able to keep their benefits for a short duration. If they still didn't get picked up for projects, they transitioned to on call, as needed, and no benefits.

Administrative staff was greatly reduced at the Director level. They agreed to look for opportunity for job sharing.

Travel was to be curtailed and scrutinized much more closely for the upcoming year. Virtual connection was inserted as the first consideration.

Funding levels were greatly reduced and budget controls were much more restrictive than in the past. If they had a unique circumstance or anomaly that required increased controls, it had to go before the senior executive team for approval.

This was a good start. If these changes didn't realize the kinds of funding reductions they needed, they would re-enter budget planning negotiations.

Adam stepped back to look at their finished product, their plan to reduce funding and save the firm. It was impressive work.

How did they do it? Let's summarize…one more recap: They worked on being open and honest, and they shared a willingness to dissuade actions violating that environment. When under attack, they were reminded to tap into their own self-awareness and recognize their emotional state and fight the desire to lash out. They kept reminding each other about the common goal and what they wanted for themselves, their colleagues, and their ongoing relationships. They vowed to keep learning and stretching, they explored alternatives, they brainstormed solutions together, and sometimes it got heated. When they sensed the conversation slipping away, they returned to the areas they agreed on, identified areas where they disagreed, and continued to look for alternative, creative solutions. When they struggled, they went to inquiry and discovery until they came up with solutions. Throughout, they openly discussed what was best for the relationship and their firm. They became all about building the foundation for win/win solutions.

Adam scanned the room with satisfaction. There was an undeniable energy, maybe even an excitement. He saw it in their faces. They were wide eyed, engaged and focused. Shirt sleeves were rolled up and suit jackets draped over chairs. There were papers scattered everywhere. Notes scribbled on tablets. Crumpled pieces of paper that were ideas discarded. And, the sun was shining brightly through the windows, overlooking a fast paced, electric city.

People were continuing to talk about the approach for the different facets of their plan. They addressed ways to assist each other in meeting their individual goals as well as their collective goals. Colleagues were making concessions and talking about ways to support one another. He almost hated to call for a break, afraid it would impact their momentum. But, he didn't intend to let them lose this kind of chemistry, at least not on his watch.

* * * * * * * * * *

Some went to the back of the room for refreshments, others talked, and some left the conference room. Adam's eyes drifted to Lindsay. She wasn't talking to anyone. She was reading her tablet. He wondered if she worked all the time. He was certain she was driven. That much was obvious. And, gorgeous. He was running out of time. He stopped, internally admonishing his lack of professionalism at a moment like this. The team just finished making some amazing progress and he was thinking about the girl. *Get your mind back in the game. Focus.*

These executives had the capability, the skill set, and now the tools. They thought they had a winning formula for survival, and to perhaps drive them to success. They even established a stretch goal - to restore their place as an industry leader. Time would tell.

CHAPTER 93

"Let's summarize. So, your relationship is on the path to getting stronger. Why do you think that is?" Adam asked.

Bob was quick to jump in since he was becoming a believer and had been on the dark side. He said, "The emotional and human element to addressing the issues. It's about respect and considering everyone's viewpoints and value prior to making any decisions. We're starting to look for options together, being heard and feeling like what we say matters to each other. Like we are all in this together."

Before anyone could chime in, Bob continued, "This is stuff you can relate to, anyone can. I don't think the principles or tools we've learned are all that complicated. They're packaged in a way that makes it easier to put into action. It's not rocket science, but it requires awareness and focus, and sort of a new way of thinking about the purpose of a conversation. When we're more conscious about what we're trying to accomplish with each other, it's easier to address our positions, intentions, and feelings." He took a breath and continued, "We sometimes get so caught up in what we want that we forget about the other person. Look what we accomplished here." Bob looked around the room, at the faces staring at him. He said quietly, "Yeah, I'm sold. There is something to this human connection and relationship building business."

Many people in the room were nodding in agreement. David stood up to refill his coffee cup at the table in the back of the room. While walking, he said, "Well said, Bob. I like it. And, it's getting easier the more we do it. It's like we're building a habit."

Adam nodded his head in agreement. "I like that - building a habit."

Joe responded quickly, "I like it, too. We all should know how to behave, but...it's paying attention to basic behavior that we don't always practice. Respect, kindness and caring."

Jack piled on, "Definitely agree with that. And, I know we've been harping on it, but I think the opportunity to learn and the way we went after it was powerful. Breaking the communication process down into three distinct steps of preparing, conducting and concluding the conversation and requiring certain actions at each step. It was approached in an organized fashion with a set of tools."

Lindsay added, "I really liked the Communication Model. It's a great way to ensure everyone is heard."

"How so? Do you mind expanding on that?" Adam asked.

"Starting with the facts alleviates the emotions of the situation. I'm with Jack, I love this idea of building a learning environment as the method of asking the other party to share and explain their views, feelings and assumptions, and then you doing the same. Once all that is on the table, you start dissecting agreements and disagreements and work through a sort of gap analysis. And, I particularly like that you engage in problem solving and looking for alternative solutions together," she continued, "I know I have oversimplified it, but I can see how it works and it's an approach you can use in every facet of life."

Adam was almost giddy inside, but calmly said, "I agree. I'm a big proponent of this basic model focused on the need to be human. I've observed the range of success with athletic teams, disagreements between parents and their children, sibling rivalries in the care-taking of an elderly parent, couples work, and a host of other business/workplace setting challenges and conflicts."

He paused and looked around the room for a moment. They were getting it, and liking it. He smiled and said, "You guys were great today. I am impressed with your potential for handling difficult conversations. When communication skills are strong and you can address issues or conflict openly and authentically, then you are well on your way to building a relationship, with trust as the foundation."

"Our final session will be about relationships in the long haul. It's the final principle you won't want to miss. That's it for today. I will see you tomorrow."

CHAPTER 94

Lindsay had been planning for that moment. She had gathered up the nerve to ask Adam to join her for a drink. *This stuff is so tedious.*

She glanced his way while waiting for the others to file out of the conference room. Before walking towards him, she looked down at her tablet as if she was working. Then, she admonished herself. What had she just learned about communication and being genuine, vulnerable and open? She frowned and thought, it is one thing to learn the principles, quite another to make them a habit. There was still work to be done.

Adam was at the front organizing the flip chart pages for the next day. While he had his back to her, Lindsay's eyes shifted to his firm backside. She couldn't help but admire his tall, lean physique. When he turned around, she looked away quickly, hoping he didn't see her gawking at him.

He caught the glance out of the corner of his eye and smiled. He must have read her correctly. She was definitely looking at him. Good sign. Today was the day to ask her out for a drink.

He put the rest of his papers in his briefcase and felt his heart quicken. He took a deep breath and looked at her. *Here goes.* He asked, "Lindsay, I had a great time the other night. If you're finished working for the day and free, do you want to join me for a drink at The Grille?"

Before she could answer, her phone interrupted with an annoying buzzing sound. It was a text from David, asking to see her so they could finish their earlier conversation on the collapsed building. It couldn't wait. He wanted to close the loop and get the word out to the workforce.

With a look of disappointment she didn't hide, she let out a sigh, lifted her phone into the air and replied to Adam, "I would really like to join you, but it looks like I may be working late tonight. Raincheck?"

"Absolutely," he said, noticing that her smile lingered for a couple of moments before saying goodbye. Adam smiled as he turned the lights out and left the room. At least she was willing to say yes. That was a promising sign.

CHAPTER 95

Lindsay left the room thinking about missed opportunities. Was this how it was always going to work for her and relationships? Timing rarely seemed to be on her side. Who was she fooling? She was slightly relieved.

She stopped by her office to pick up her notes. Her assistant had left for the day, but taped a reminder to her computer. It read, "Go home on time." Smiley face.

She grinned, turned off her light and walked to David's deserted outer office. Everyone had left for the day, no doubt on their way home to be with their families. Lindsay walked to his door and tapped on it before entering. He motioned her in, as he was finishing a phone call.

She overheard his conversation with his wife. She tried to ignore it, but she was drawn to the words. "Yes, dear. I won't be late. I have a meeting with Lindsay and I'll be on my way in thirty minutes. A dinner date sounds great. I'll pick you up in an hour. I love you, too." He smiled and winked at Lindsay.

"That was sweet. It kind of makes my heart melt. I sort of envy what you two have - in a good way, that is." She smiled at him, opening her notebook and turning the pages to find her notes. She glanced up to see him looking at her. She knew what he was thinking. "I said sort of."

He studied her for a moment before answering. This conversation could get deep and he wanted a little bit of wine for it. He asked if she would join him. She politely accepted, making a signal with her finger and thumb for a small one.

He walked to the bar and poured them both a half glass of red and carried them to the sitting area. He handed one to her while saying, in a measured, careful tone, "You can have that, too. That is, if you want it. I worry that you don't want it. That you're okay with letting work be your life." He hesitated and said, "I'm concerned about you."

She swirled, observed the legs, and sipped her wine before answering. "I'm happy with my life the way it is. I'm busy. I have great friends. No complications. David, I'm a really good friend, but not so great at romantic relationships."

He studied her. He started to say, *That's not true. I saw how you were with him,* but stopped himself. Instead he said, "You know, it will be different the next time." He held her gaze until she looked down.

She carefully placed her wine on the coffee table and reached back for her notebook. "So, you wanted to talk about the details of what happened to the collapsed building. I'll tell you what I know."

He sat back in his chair and looked at her before speaking. He started to say something, but accepted her cue and remained silent.

She cleared her throat and said, "As I started to mention earlier, the problem was twofold. One, they used salty sand to make the concrete, and two, they substituted the steel from their normal supplier with inferior steel."

"Why? Kickbacks? Revenge?" he continued, "You know, it's usually one of the two."

"Bingo. The PM was taking kickbacks from a college roommate's company. The supplier had worked with them for years, but things changed recently. He was a gambler that stepped up his game and needed to get his hands on quick money. At the same time, the PM was going through a terrible divorce and needed money. His wife cheated on him, and left with his two kids. Of course, he was devastated and bitter. He started drinking too much and it led to developing a heroine habit. They were drinking one night and came up with this grand scheme. They never planned on the building collapsing."

David said, "That's crazy. Even an excellent design and constructed structure can't withstand a bad foundation."

"You're right. They probably would have gotten away with it, if they didn't muck up the foundation. Alter the stress distribution."

He shook his head and said, "Desperate people. Just incredible. Tell me again, how did they discover what happened?"

"The auditor talked to the Superintendent and he started looking into the prices and thought something wasn't right. He inspected the materials and compared them to the billing invoices. A manufactured purchase order." she smiled, closed her notebook, and said, "That's all the attorney would tell me. He said he couldn't go into all the details since it had been turned over to the police. Bottom line, we're off the hook."

"That is the best news I've had in a long time. Thank you for the legal research and the work you and your team did on this Lindsay."

"Thank you. They did a great job. Both legal and our designers. They believed in our design," she paused before saying, "David, we're a great company with a lot of fantastic talent. I would hate to see anything happen to what we've built."

"Me, too." David looked out in the distance momentarily and turned back to her and said, "That's why we can't let that happen."

They spent the next few minutes coming up with their communication plan to let the company know the collapsed building was not a faulty design. Once satisfied, David sent the email.

He gathered his things and locked the door on their way out. He turned to Lindsay and said, "Why don't you get out of here? You are putting in way too many hours. Do something for yourself."

"I have one more call to make and then I'm out of here. Enjoy your date." She winked and he smiled, watching her leave. The one small, playful moment between friends.

CHAPTER 96

The place was too quiet and most of the lights were off. Lindsay experienced a sudden feeling of loneliness as she walked to her office.

She sat down at her desk and picked up the telephone, dialing a number she had been dreading. An unpleasant conversation with a subcontractor's attorney. Lesson learned already - just say no to contractors you don't have a long standing relationship with. How many times did they have to get burned to learn?

After a few minutes of getting nowhere, the call ended. Her stomach growled loudly as she slammed the receiver back down on the cradle and then schooled herself on temperament control.

Hunger and not feeling like going home made her pick up her cellphone. She scrolled through her favorites and hit the second one down.

Sam answered before the first full ring. There was restaurant noise in the background and Lindsay got right to the point. "Are you free for dinner? I could really use your company and a bite to eat."

"You sound wiped out. Are you okay?"

"It has been a long day. A long week. I could really use some time with my best friend."

"Just so happens I'm available to you. I'm at the restaurant. Do you want to eat here or would you like to go somewhere else?"

"I would love Thai. How about the little Thai restaurant on K Street?"

"Ooh, that sounds good. I can be ready in 15 minutes. When can you be there?" Sam responded with excitement in her voice.

"I'll see you in 15. Thanks for catching up on such short notice." Lindsay loved that Sam was flexible and willing to drop everything when her friend wanted to talk.

This evening was less about talking and more about just being together and one topic was definitely off the table. She wanted to tell Sam everything, but couldn't. Sam was normally her sounding board, her confidante. But, she couldn't share this.

It was still hard to believe this was even happening. She picked up her purse and walked to the doorway. Hesitating, she glanced at a book on her coffee table about leadership, relationships, and trust. She stared at the cover for a moment.

An employee amongst them embezzling money. How could someone in their firm do this? How could one of their own justify such an egregious crime? It didn't make any sense. She felt a shiver run throughout her body. She turned off the light and walked to her car.

CHAPTER 97

This has to be the last time. This has got to end. Most of the office lights had been turned off. The workday was over and most people were leaving work to join their families for dinner. Probably peaceful and quiet evenings involving food, a little television, or a good book. People feeling safe at home.

Not for him. Just an ordinary day and hacking into the financial system of a company comprised of good people, sound leadership and funding short-falls. *It will all be over soon.*

Walking to a different cubicle on the same floor, he spotted a computer screen illuminated. Sighing and almost frustrated, w*hat is it with all these computers being left on at the end of the day?*

He moved closer and sat down. He took off his jacket and placed it on the empty chair next to him. It was way too hot. He felt the heat as he pressed the keys to get to the screen he was looking for. *Come on. What is taking so long? The computer shouldn't be slow at this hour. Probably another software update, or … has someone realized what's going on so they're monitoring trans-actions? Oh stop, people don't do that in real life. Way too much television.*

Perspiration dripped down the side of his face and onto the desktop. *Not a good thing.* He wiped his shirt sleeve over the puddle until it was dry. Not a trace of ever being there. *Definitely stop watching so much television.*

The screen he had been waiting for finally appeared on the monitor. He was both relieved and scared. Looking up at the ceiling, he let out a deep breath before the next move. Running hands over his face before touching the keyboard. *Breathe in, Breathe out. Please forgive me.* Click, click and the task was done.

CHAPTER 98

Lindsay was only driving a few blocks and probably could have used the walk, but she opted for efficiency, enabling her to leave the restaurant and head directly home. Although she wasn't sure why that was the deciding factor since she really didn't want to hurry home. She usually loved going home.

When she stepped into the packed entrance, she saw Sam seated at a table in the corner. Lindsay waved, smiled and walked swiftly to her. They hugged and started their incessant conversation about this and that.

Lindsay's mood immediately lightened being with her dear friend. She felt safe and relaxed, exactly what she needed.

They ordered a bottle of buttery Chardonnay and were looking at the menu when the waiter brought the wine and told them about the specials. As foodies, this was one of their favorite things to do together. It involved sharing an appetizer, a couple of entrees, wine, and friendship that felt more like sisters. On this night, they selected fresh Thai Spring Rolls, a Thai Seafood Salad, and a grilled Seafood Curry dinner. The waiter nodded in agreement and said, "Splendid choices."

When he left the table, Sam's face changed and became serious. She focused her gaze directly on Lindsay's eyes. "So, what is going on? Tell me about your week. What happened that has you so concerned?"

Lindsay shook her head and said, "It's something I can't talk about. You know I want to tell you and would if I could, but I can't. It's a legal matter at work. Confidential nonsense with all kinds of potential fallout. I just need your presence and easy conversation tonight."

Sam looked concerned. "As long as you are okay. That's all I need to know."

Lindsay reassured her with a smile, "It's nothing like that. I just can't get into it. Suffice it to say, it means many hours of hard work and late nights in my future."

Sam stared for a second and started to ask more, but stopped. She knew to leave it alone. She twirled her wine glass in her hand and eyed the legs before speaking. She asked in a teasing way that only she could get away with when it came to Lindsay. "So, what's going on with that hot consultant you're working with?"

She frowned. "Absolutely nothing. Every time we have attempted to make a date, we get interrupted by someone or something," she sighed and continued, "With this latest problem, I doubt I'll have any free time. He'll probably finish up his work with us and that will be it. It's probably better off that way anyway."

"Oh no, you don't. There was a spark between you. I saw it. You need to act on it. Lindsay, what are you so afraid of? You look for ways to sabotage the possibilities. Don't do it this time. I've met this guy, and I think he may be worth it. He is handsome, sexy, successful, and seems compassionate and empathetic. You deserve someone like him, you deserve him," she said sternly, as she leaned back in her chair and sighed, staring at Lindsay. She let a couple of seconds pass before leaning back in and speaking softly, "Do you really want to go through your life without finding love again? It's one thing when there isn't anyone good enough that is available, but this guy? Really? I'll say it again, what are you afraid of? Lindsay, I know you. Don't do this again." she warned, shaking her head no.

"Sam, the timing is all wrong."

"When will the timing be right? Next year or the year after. When?"

CHAPTER 99

Adam was in his study, leaning over his desk and staring at his laptop. He read the same thing over and over without any chance of comprehension. He scanned the room and thought about the masculine decor and all the books lining his bookshelves. He must have read two hundred books over the last couple of years. He really had become married to his work. Was that so bad?

The ringing of his cellphone was a pleasant distraction. His sister was on the other end, chatting about the plan for his nephew's upcoming birthday party. Adam assured her he wouldn't miss it. He had a rule not to schedule business trips when it involved family events. He loved his niece and nephew as if they were his own. They were good kids. They were his family.

Before hanging up, his sister asked, "Has there been any progress with Lindsay?" Without letting him answer she said, "I think she is a good fit for you."

"Thank you, sister."

Before she said goodbye, she instructed him not to let this opportunity get away. She teased him by closing with, "seize the moment."

He smiled and thought about Lindsay. He couldn't stop thinking about her. Sexy and gorgeous, but had an aura of power about her unlike anyone he had ever been with. A woman on top of her game. She was passionate about things that meant something and didn't mind acknowledging it.

He was drawn to tough minded women. Spent his childhood years and most of his life surrounded by them. He loved strong women. Maybe she could fill that void he didn't want to admit was there. What if she could be the one? What if he was blowing the chance to find out?

He was getting ahead of himself. The first step was to get it started.

CHAPTER 100

Taking a sip of wine and a deep breath, Lindsay tried to remain untouched by Sam's remarks, but she knew she was right. Changing the subject was the only palatable option in the moment. "Let's talk about something else. I can't handle this tonight."

Sam wanted to say more but knew better. Subject closed. She stared across the table before answering, "I won't bring it up anymore. At least, not tonight. Can we at least talk about the workshop?"

A rush of relief flooded Lindsay's face. "Yes. It is really good. We spent the day actually living the direct connection between strong communication skills and success in relationships.

"I realized something today. I didn't even think about the extent, but it's amazing to observe the degree of fear associated with addressing issues with other people. Sometimes we would rather pay the price of walking away or remaining in discomfort in a relationship rather than confronting an issue. The fear can make you shy away from any type of conflict resolution, and severely restrict the possibility of a deep bond with another human being."

"I am fascinated by people and how they think, communicate, and act. Tell me more about what you've discovered," Sam said.

As the waiter brought the first course of their meal, they barely stopped talking long enough to acknowledge him or the food. He poured more wine and they kept speed chatting.

"You would love being in the room while we're going through our budget planning meetings. It's grueling, but the dynamics of the human behavior is intriguing. I find I'm paying attention to the relationship piece more than the details of the budget session sometimes. I admonish myself for it, but then I realize I need to be mindful of that, too."

"What do you mean?" Sam asked with an inquisitive excitement displayed on her face.

"I was ready to blast Joe when he briefed his proposal for budget reductions. And then, Bob piled on. Let me say, they did not get an 'A' for effective communication skills." Lindsay smiled and continued explaining what transpired in the conference room.

"What happened? I love a good story." Sam moved in a little closer as she listened to Lindsay.

"Joe and Bob talked about reductions in the overhead business lines. They said we should take the biggest reductions because we aren't revenue producing. Never mind that we keep their butts out of trouble. Needless to say, the environment grew a little shaky. Looking around the room you could see some tense, angry faces on the verge of eruption. Several of us in the overhead category were holding our breath and trying to keep it together."

"Oh, I can see Joe now." Sam laughed.

"But, it didn't become nearly as explosive as it could have. We recessed for lunch and Joe and I had a little talk off line. It was interesting. It had come across as Joe thinking overhead departments didn't perform important functions; therefore, had to be slashed. He said he didn't mean it that way at all. He felt bad. In fact, he had some sleepless nights over it. In the end, we all learned from it. There was a breakdown in the learning part of our conversation, misperceptions, and he and Bob could have delivered their message in a much more non-threatening way."

"Poor Joe. I like him. I'm kind of surprised."

"I like him, too. But, both he and Bob were over the top. I'm actually not surprised by some of the behavior we're witnessing. This is bringing out the worst in people. High stakes issues leading to emotional conversations. We haven't been used to conflict and we're not all that good at handling it. But, we're learning."

"So, how did you resolve it?"

"We're focusing on caring about each other." Lindsay continued talking about her exchange with Joe. "Joe and I were seated and getting ready to order lunch when Adam walked into the restaurant. We invited him over to join us."

"What? Wait a minute, you left that part out all this time," Sam said, with a teasing smile.

Lindsay held up her hand to stop the silliness. She said in her business-like tone, "Simmer down. Nothing happened." Lindsay frowned at her. Her face saying, *do not go there.* "We talked about the mistakes in Joe's delivery and Adam said he would give him another opportunity after lunch. Fast forward, the conversation was much improved the second time and we actually had some good exchange."

"That can be emotional stuff. An opportunity to go to misinterpretation quickly. Explosive."

"Yeah. Adam prepared us for this kind of reaction. Up front, he warned us about the importance of preparation, thinking in and outside of ourselves, and preparing a strategy for an emotional, high stakes encounter. Think about what we want out of the relationship. He said it's a common mistake to not think it through ahead of time, completely sabotaging the open and safe environment and instinctively spouting off rather than learning. Lots of chances for misunderstanding. Sounds common sense, doesn't it?"

Sam contemplated and answered, "Oh yeah, but easier said than done. Been there. When it comes to relationships, you can't just think about yourself when you're entering into a conversation. And, so many people get caught up in the emotions and trying to win that they lose sight of the big picture, and what they really want."

The waiter took away their dinner plates and brought two decaf coffees. Temptation did not win out, no dessert.

Sam poured cream in her coffee and took a sip before continuing. "I had similar takeaways from a couple of classes in college. God, that feels so long ago. Let's check my recall." She looked up towards the ceiling and then back at Lindsay before continuing, "We talked about the importance of creating an environment inviting diverse viewpoints, and making sure the people involved in the conversation were open to listening to these different viewpoints and perspectives. Not, you're wrong and I'm right."

Lindsay nodded and smiled. She loved these conversations with Sam.

Sam continued, "Determining what you want, what you think they want, and exploring ways to get what you both want. A critical part of preparation is to do your homework and anticipate the likely questions and responses from the other party, but not in a manipulative way. Pretty basic stuff, and very effective."

Lindsay thought about what Sam said. These really were the keys to good communication skills. And, the beauty of it, anyone could learn. It's the same thing Adam said. *Adam,* she smiled.

Her thoughts of Adam were interrupted by Sam continuing on with her philosophy on communicating. "Can you imagine what the world would look like if we were all able to openly discuss opposing views, and really listen and understand each other's perspective? Not necessarily agree, but at least understand each other. Respect diverse views. To not show anger or hostility because of disagreements on politics, religion, discrimination, or any other difference that brings out the worst in people. Not pass judgement. It's just sad we can't communicate with a more open mind and appreciation for others' beliefs. We're all human beings with feelings and trying to do the best we can. We would be a much better nation if we could all do that. We would be much better people. Imagine the impact. We might actually get things done.

"And it all begins with communication. What a powerful tool that is so under-appreciated and under-valued."

Lindsay listened as Sam talked, appreciating her knowledge about organizational development, human behavior, leadership, and communication. She had certainly missed her calling. She could have been an outstanding consultant or even a therapist. Lindsay felt like she could use a therapist right about now, she smiled to herself.

Her mind shifted back to Adam, wondering what he was doing. He would enjoy this conversation. She would have loved listening to the both of them trade thoughts. She knew Sam was right. She should stop running.

What was she really running from? What was she afraid of? Was she fearful something would happen and she would lose him, too? Or, was she so used to being alone that she had become afraid of losing the autonomy? Or a piece of herself?

Oh no, not tonight. The internal conversation was a bit much for this evening. She was too drained for this heavy topic and way too busy these days to even think about it.

"Lindsay, are you listening?" Sam asked, "Where did you go?"

"Oh, I'm sorry. My mind wandered to, ugh, work, for a second."

Lindsay shifted her attention back to Sam as she continued talking about the impact of bad communications. She tested Lindsay's intelligence on human behavior in an engaging way. She made her think differently.

On a roll, Sam said, "Look at the restaurant business. Totally communicating and building relationships. I want repeat business and I want people to feel like the restaurant is comfortable, like home. I love when someone comes into my place and does something like hug me. It makes me feel like we know each other, care about one another. I've never understood restaurants failing to build relationships for repeat business and part of that is addressing or communicating through mistakes that have a direct impact on customers. In my business, it's customer satisfaction and a great experience, while still making a decent living. If we screw up, it seems like a no brainer to own it. Comp a meal, drink, or dessert depending on the error and be clear that we are really sorry and want them happy. That they matter. Even in the restaurant setting, effective communication is a great customer service skill that costs nothing. I'm adamant about it. Oh well, I've digressed and it's getting late," She said as she drained the last of her coffee.

They continued talking until the check arrived. After paying the bill, they stepped outside and said their goodbyes. Lindsay watched her friend going in the opposite direction.

She continued thinking about her as she walked to her car. Sam was interesting, bright and funny. Her tall, but slender frame was intimidating to some. Or maybe it was her beauty. She was stunningly gorgeous with red shoulder length hair and sparkling green eyes that were lively and intense. Her face full of expression.

To be so engaging and sociable, she was an introvert and a bit of a loner. Lindsay couldn't remember the last time Sam had a romantic relationship in her own life. She was always worried about everyone else and the restaurant had become her love, her life. She worked too hard. Lindsay had an idea. Yes, a very good idea.

CHAPTER 101

Lindsay had a day off from the workshop and couldn't stop herself from wondering how Adam was spending his time. Was he moving on to another client or still devoting his energy to them? What did his other clients look like…Why did she care? She scolded herself back to work.

It wasn't until late afternoon before she could break away from endless meetings and talk to Mark about the embezzling investigation. She walked to the conference room where he was leaning close to the computer screen, reading glasses perched on his nose, pouring through electronic financial files. He didn't see her standing there.

"Is there anything I can do to help? Do you need coffee?" She leaned against the doorway watching him work.

He looked up, appearing distracted. "No thank you. I'm fine," he answered, pointing to his Cafe Bar coffee cup. "This has to be the last one of the day, or I'll be up all night."

Lindsay stepped inside the door and closed it. She spoke softly, asking about the status of the investigation. He ran his hand through his jet black curls and let out a sigh, "Lindsay, it's strange. I am finding absolutely no audit trail at all. Names are missing from the system at various transaction points. Definitely some shoddy data entry work. I am having a hard time getting even a small tidbit of information to pinpoint to anyone."

She moved closer to his computer screen. "What have you found so far?"

"Most transactions are initialed by authorized personnel in the system. However, there are a number of large unexplained accounting adjustments with no sign of who made them. And guess what? The one common denominator is they are all tied to the same corporation. The one that David discovered, ZZ Corporation. I'll do a little more cross checking. I'm coming up with nothing but dead ends, except for what we already know."

She drew in a deep breath and let the air out as she lifted her head towards the ceiling. She looked back at Mark and noticed that he looked about as tired as she felt. She asked, "What next?"

He hesitated, rubbed his eyes, and said, "Lindsay, I need a list of all employees that have had access to the financial system."

"I can get that for you." She paused and thought for a moment before continuing, "Mark, I overheard an odd conversation we may want to check out. It's probably nothing and I may have taken it completely out of context, but I can't shake it. It involves an exchange I overheard between Peter and Tom. I feel horrible about even bringing it up. Peter is my friend. God, please, I hope I'm being silly and paranoid."

"What happened?"

Lindsay told him what she heard and how Peter was visibly nervous. And, there was another troubling conversation that took place in Tom's cubicle. She couldn't hear that much of it, but heard enough to know that it was suspect. Something was very strange about it.

She continued, "Peter has been acting a little different lately, but I've passed it off as stress. He has been in and out of the workshop, with the collapsed building fiasco eating his lunch, and I know he has some personal things going on. Look, I'm being crazy. I know Peter is the last person that would ever hurt this firm. He is frustrated by the way we're headed, but who isn't. He is certainly the 'company man' kind of guy. He would never." Lindsay didn't finish the sentence.

"Yeah, I know Peter. It would be hard to believe he could be involved in anything like this." Mark thought for a moment before continuing, "It's going to be a little more challenging to look at Peter and Tom without raising suspicions since they aren't part of the financial group. But, I'll figure it out. I'll look into it."

"Mark, it may not be our financial department."

Shaking his head in agreement, "Oh, I know. I'm uncovering every rock in that group first. If we get to the point where we're looking at others, we won't have much luck keeping it quiet. People will find out, and then it'll get harder and very messy."

Lindsay thought for a moment before speaking. *What happened to this firm? To her? Suspicious of Peter. Really! Paranoid much!* She said, "The more I think about it, I must have misinterpreted what I heard. Not Peter. It doesn't make sense. It's probably nothing," she continued, "As far as the financial staff, I'll get you the list. It would be so much easier if I could get it from Patrick, but I'll get it. I hate this. I feel like I'm being disloyal to Patrick. To Peter. And, Patrick has a right to know what's going on in his Department."

Mark started to speak, but stopped himself as she lifted her hand in a halting motion. She continued firmly, "I know. I know. I think it's time we talk to David. Figure out the remainder of our investigation strategy. It's not likely this will get resolved quickly."

CHAPTER 102

Lindsay and Mark walked into David's office as he was finishing his last meeting. His executive assistant closed her notebook and stood to leave. She spoke to them and gave Lindsay a look that said, *he is in a mood.* David motioned them in and stepped from behind his desk to greet them, undoing his tie, and moving to the chair facing the couch where they were instructed to sit.

Lindsay didn't waste any time. "We haven't found a trail linking to any of our people. Now, it gets a little more complicated. I'll give Mark a list of employees that have access to our systems and it looks like we will have to undergo the interviewing process. We need a communication plan for what we tell people."

"Let's do what we have to do." David said quietly as he crossed his arms.

They strategized the details to keep the investigation under wraps, and David signaled the meeting was over when he stood and started towards the door. Lindsay asked if she could have one more minute of his time on an unrelated matter. She waited until Mark was out of range before starting the conversation.

* * * * * * * * *

Lindsay turned and faced David without speaking at first. Then she stepped closer and looked him directly in the eyes. She said in a low tone, "David, I'm worried about you. With the investigation and all the other things going on. I've come to your office a few times lately and the door has been closed and voices were loud. I know you are under a great deal of stress, but this is not like you. Is there something I can do to help? Do you want to talk about it?"

His eyes had dark circles and he looked like he might have lost a couple of pounds. His face looked a little more drawn, a little thinner than usual. She knew him well enough to see that he was weighing whether or not to get into it. He sighed and said, "The investigation will be what it is. I've come to terms with that as much as I can. But, two key executive leaders, Paul and Eleanor, have been at odds with each other and it's been getting worse."

Lindsay asked, "What do you mean at odds?"

David smiled and grunted, "Up until today, it means they can't be in the same room with one another and they can't get it together. But, I thought they made good progress today. All I can say is that they better keep it up. If they can't fix it, one of them has to go."

Lindsay was surprised he would even consider getting rid of Paul. He had been the Business Director for as long as she had been with the firm. Paul was very effective, easy to get along with, and had a soul. Then, there was Eleanor, the fairly new addition that had been hired to get things done. She had already succeeded in using her position as Vice President of Operations to be results-driven, take no prisoners, at all costs. She was brilliant and forward thinking. Unfortunately, she was also impatient and easily frustrated, leading to direct, and sometimes caustic remarks, regardless of the recipient. But, she was definitely talented.

"What are you thinking?"

"I'm thinking I don't want to lose her. She is really good, exactly what we need during these tumultuous times. So, I've started working with her, helping her develop better interpersonal and communication skills. I don't want it to come down to her or Paul. We need them both. Adam and I are collaborating on a coaching/mentoring plan."

"How are you approaching her development?"

"Placing the emphasis on people. Working with her on being more aware of her words, her actions, and her ability to think about the value in relationships, without sacrificing progress. She tends to go into a conversation believing she is right and the other person is wrong. A bulldozer approach has no place here."

"What exactly are you doing about it?"

"It's what she is doing. Concentrating on thinking outside of herself. She has strong opinions, and that's okay, but she has to be willing to listen, learn and understand the other person's point of view, and how they got there. And, accept that she might be wrong and there might be other alternatives. Listening carefully to understand. Asking questions. That's where she needs work. That's what I'm drilling into her head, and urging her to practice and make it habitual."

"Sounds good in theory, but how is it working? What are the mechanics?" she challenged.

"Changing her communication approach to operate in her relationships. Nothing earth shattering, but we've given her a script to start using. It goes something like this." David paused before answering, "We have different views. I would like to understand your view, help you understand my view, and see if we can build on mutual ground and come up with an alternative that works for both of us."

She smiled. "Sounds familiar."

"It should." He continued, "She needs to think about the common goal and feasible alternatives that may or may not have started from either viewpoint. And, she is not to deviate from the script." he smiled and said, "Sounds easy, doesn't it?"

Lindsay chuckled and responded with sarcasm, "Yeah, real easy until you add people to it." She looked puzzled, hesitating before asking the next question. "I'm confused. If you used this approach, why all the yelling in your office?"

He laughed, "Seems changes don't happen over night."

"No, they do not," Lindsay agreed.

The focus on Eleanor almost made them forget the real reason they were in David's office. To talk about a very personal crime committed against the firm. One that could destroy them. But, it would not be solved on this night. She said good evening and left.

* * * * * * * * * *

Walking down the hallway, she saw Peter and Tom working in the conference room. She started to stop in, but noticed them in deep conversation leaning over a laptop computer screen. She was too tired to interrupt. Of course, she had been wrong.

She stopped in her office long enough to grab her purse and her briefcase. She turned out the lights and headed home.

CHAPTER 103

Peter and Tom hadn't noticed Lindsay. It was a good thing Peter didn't see her. That would have been enough to push him over the edge. The only way he was able to go through with this was knowing his colleagues were likely on their way home for the evening. His heart was pounding. He wasn't cut out for this. He said, "Tom, this is making me nervous. It is *not* a good idea. It's making me crazy. I'm not sleeping at night. Someone is going to find out and then we're both in big trouble."

"Boss, calm down. It's going to be okay. Don't get cold feet now. We're too far in. No turning back. Just relax," Tom said, without looking up from the computer screen.

"I can't believe I let you talk me into this. These are good people. David has been good to me, and you. I have a family to think about." Peter was shaking his head back and forth. He walked to the conference room door and turned back around. He stared at Tom working. This wasn't bothering him at all. *What kind of person was he?*

Tom sensed Peter's eyes on him and looked up. He said almost too sternly to be talking to his boss, "Look, we are in too far now. You have got to get a grip. Do you want me to stop? You say the word, but say it now. Before it's too late."

Peter said in a low, hopeless sounding tone, "It's already too late. We really don't have a choice at this point, now do we? We're in too far. Go ahead."

CHAPTER 104

It was Thursday morning and Lindsay hadn't slept well, tossing and turning before finally giving up around 3:30. She got out of bed, made coffee, and grabbed a few papers from her briefcase. Reading the same sentence over and over led her to the conclusion that lack of focus was becoming a habit and the concentration part of her brain slept better than she did. How was she going to do this?

She was more than conflicted about David's decision to hide the truth from Patrick. She was having coffee with him later in the morning and was actually nervous about talking to him. She wasn't used to keeping things from him. And this was big.

It felt a little like the walls were narrowing in around her. At least the investigation of the collapsed building was behind them. Although painful, it was finally over. But embezzling funds and tackling the budget of a firm that was barely hanging on was not part of her plan. And, she still had a nagging feeling about Peter and Tom but kept telling herself she was just being paranoid. *What else can possibly go wrong?* Oh, there is definitely more.

She gave up and showered. It was darker than the color of midnight when she left her house. It wasn't often that she went to work looking up at a black sky. At least the traffic would be light.

She pulled into her parking space at 5:30. The lot was completely empty except for a couple of cars. To her surprise, Patrick's car was parked a couple of slots away. He wasn't normally a morning person. The inability to sleep must be going around.

After a few minutes of sitting in her office and reading, she glanced up at the clock. It was a little before 6:30. She picked up the phone and placed it back on the cradle. She could use the walk. And the energy to fire up her courage for this big fat lie of omission.

She stopped short of entering his domain long enough to look upward and breathe in and out. When she got it together, she peeked her head into his office door and saw him studying spreadsheets that covered two thirds of his desk. He jumped when he saw her.

"Hi, I'm sorry. I didn't mean to startle you," she said, timidly.

Patrick smiled and recovered, "No problem. I wasn't expecting anyone. It's so quiet this time of morning."

"You're in early. I was surprised to see your car."

"Yeah, I couldn't sleep."

"I guess that's going around. Since we're both here, I thought you might want to get coffee early. Are you able to go now?"

He looked at his computer screen and said, "Sure. Can you give me a couple of minutes. How about I meet you down there?"

"That's fine. I'll go down and order for us. Do you want your usual?"

"Yes, please. Give me another ten minutes."

She walked briskly down the stairs and was almost out of breath when she reached the Cafe Bar. *How could anyone that works out this much, get winded going DOWN the stairs?* She made a promise to shake up the workout. It was time to mix it up.

CHAPTER 105

Lindsay ordered drinks for the two of them and scored a table at the far end of the room, the best place for privacy and less noise. Probably not the most strategic location for the dreaded conversation. She might need more of a distraction than baristas calling out various combinations of caffeine-laced drinks to energize the veins.

She was gazing at the news on her tablet when Patrick walked through the door, already looking fatigued and void of color so early in the morning. *What could that be about? How serious was Stephanie's illness?* Lindsay intended to find out.

Patrick and his wife were the perfect couple, with a wonderful young man for a son that was an exceptionally talented basketball player. Their family seemed to have it all. When she and Patrick travelled together, she found it endearing the way he called home before and after dinner. He stayed engaged with his family's events and they did the same with him. Stephanie cared about what he ate, how he felt, and what he needed. That was a loving partnership.

There had been moments when Lindsay longed for a relationship like that. But, other times…Commitment was terrifying. Could she ever let it happen? Her interest in Adam had brought all those old feelings back to haunt her. She needed to face the fact that Sam was right. She looked for excuses to sabotage relationships at every opportunity.

"You looked deep in thought. Is everything alright?" he asked, as he sat across from her.

"Truthfully, I was just reflecting on my life. But, that's a little deep for this hour. Let's talk about you. How is Stephanie?"

"Good. We are guardedly optimistic about her prognosis. She has been undergoing some treatments that are working well," he said, as he scanned the incoming people, standing in line with eyes glued to their phones.

"Excellent. I've been worried about you both. Is she almost finished with the treatments?"

"We're not exactly sure yet. We'll see how she responds. Thank you for asking, for caring," he looked down and said quietly.

"Of course I care. We're friends. You know, you can tell me anything. If you want to talk about Stephanie, I'm here, but I'm not going to pry. I get the sense you don't want to talk about it. I just need to know that she'll be okay and you have all the support you need," she said, looking deep into his eyes.

"Thanks. She'll be okay. And, I feel the same about you." He looked around the room and down at his hands wrapped around the warm cup. "I haven't really wanted to discuss it. I'm superstitious about it all and it's one of those female things that I don't like to talk about. I'm a little stressed these days. But it will work out," he said, his voice cracking.

Lindsay didn't press. "I understand. The invitation is always open. I'll always worry about you, you know."

He smiled, "I know and it's one of the many things…about you."

She changed the subject. "How is Andrew? Isn't the big opener coming up soon?"

"Yeah. He is shooting the ball really well. I'm excited for him. I hope you're up for dinner and drinks before the game."

The feel of old times. She said with a grin on her face, "Absolutely. I wouldn't miss it. I can hardly even wait. I need to give him a call and wish him luck."

They discussed a couple of work issues, but not the one she really had to talk about. She couldn't shake the feeling of being deceptive or the guilt that he had a right to know, but David had been clear. It had to be this way. Protect him and his interests during this investigation, and make him understand when it was all over.

For now, more deception. She had to tell him something. She had dreaded this moment.

Lindsay's heart stopped momentarily. She felt the perspiration escape every pore on her body. She wasn't cut out for this. *Here goes. God forgive me.* "One other thing. Mark contacted David and asked if the CPA firm could do some preliminary work on our mid-year inspection. They are trying out some new processes, a new model, and they want to try it out on a couple of their clients. David agreed to it. Said it's a free service that will yield lessons learned. Enable us to improve our overall business processes," she said, awkwardly, in a monotone voice. She couldn't believe she was actually saying this to him. It sounded like she had rehearsed and was performing an infomercial.

Patrick put down his coffee cup without taking a drink. "Really? Why didn't David talk to me about it? Those kinds of things are usually my decisions."

Lindsay's face felt hot and she could definitely feel a bead of sweat on her brow. She hated herself, but had to stay the course. "You were out of town. He didn't want to bother you with this, considering what has been going on with you. He knew you would agree to it, so he simply said yes. I told him I would talk to you about it. It's really no big deal. And, it's actually much broader than just financial. There are some other processes that will also be looked at." *Really? Your ability to lie is scary.*

"What does it entail?" he asked quizzically.

"I don't know all the details, but I think Mark is doing some review of our financial systems and he mentioned interviewing you." She shrugged, no big deal and waved her hand in the air. She continued, "Oh, and he'll interview a few others to process map what they're doing. Look for improvement opportunities. You know, that sort of thing."

Patrick was visibly annoyed. He frowned and asked, "When was David going to tell me about the interviews? He could have called me so I could prepare my people. Frankly, I'm a little irritated. This is so unlike David and it's a little weird."

"David asked me to tell you, and I'm telling you now. Look Patrick, it's no big deal. He was going to tell you today, if I didn't. As I said before, he didn't want to disturb you with this. You have so much going on and he was certain you would want to do it."

"Well, of course I would support it, but still he should have been the one to tell me." He looked down at this coffee before continuing, "I'm sorry. I'm just really tired. I haven't had much rest lately. In fact, I didn't sleep at all last night. That's why I was in the office so early."

Lindsay looked at her watch and realized it was time to get to the conference room, to discuss the final topic on trust. *So much for trust.* This wouldn't be the easiest session to sit through these days. Hiding the truth, embezzlement, what next?

She and Patrick dropped their coffee cups in the trash and walked to the elevator. When the elevator stopped on their floor, she left Patrick to stop by her office. Or, so she said.

CHAPTER 106

David and Mark were waiting for her. They made it through the first big hurdle, telling Patrick enough to keep him from becoming suspicious. Lindsay let out a deep breath and said, "It's done and he is NOT happy. Do we really need to keep this from Patrick? It's his Department. He has a right to know. And, I feel like we're really violating his trust."

Mark answered, "Lindsay, I agree with David. If anything, you have got to protect him from any fallout or he won't be able to lead his team. He will be the one they trust and he will have to provide strong leadership after the investigation. Assuming it is someone in his Department, he will have to pick up the fragile pieces."

All that emphasis on the word 'he' and what 'he' will have to do just made Lindsay more annoyed. Getting sufficiently irritated and ready to respond, she checked herself.

David piled on, "Lindsay, I hate it too, but it's the only way."

"Okay. Okay. I get it. I don't have to like it. We're deceiving him and it makes me feel terrible. We have always had trust, been completely candid with one another."

David stood squarely in front of her and lowered his voice. He said, "I'm sorry. I know how difficult this is. It will be over soon. We'll talk to him when we get some answers. He will understand."

"It's time to get to the workshop. I have to go." She walked to the door.

* * * * * * * * * *

David started to follow, but stopped as if he had forgotten something. He motioned for them to go without him. He waited until they were far enough out of his sight before leaving. He cautiously peered out of the entranceway to his office suite, looking right and then left. Both of his assistants were away from their desks.

He closed the door and walked swiftly towards the Comptroller's shop on his way to his final destination. He looked at his watch. He would just have to be late.

This was not something he ever imagined having to deal with. It was not easy to reconcile, but he had planned every detail. What he would do, what he would say if the cubicle was occupied, and why he would do it. He had considered every alternative. This was best. He looked around and didn't even see anyone in the near vicinity. *Where was everyone? No wonder we're in trouble.*

He walked to a cubicle he knew so well. He hated this. Naturally, the computer was on. It was the workday. It should be on. Good. It shouldn't take but five minutes. He could get out of there before being seen. No sign of anyone, or so he thought.

CHAPTER 107

Lindsay was almost late. Adam was talking to Jack when she walked through the doorway. He looked at her and smiled. She nodded and smiled. There was that tingly feeling again. He had an overwhelming affect on her and it was ticking her off. It was unlike anything she had ever experienced. What was she going to do about it?

She stopped and diverted her attention to the environment in the conference room. It was a little noisy with people standing around and talking with one another. The room had a positive energy. She felt it. She wasn't sure when it happened, but something was changing. Not nirvana or anything, but improvement. It had the feeling of a group of friends gathering together. It was certainly a different feeling than usual. The atmosphere was a little more relaxed, laughing and joking. Maybe there was something to this.

CHAPTER 108

This act of crime. Before the last session - trust. It would be laughable, if it wasn't so real. Doing this, taking this action. He had looked for every alternative until he was sick. But, there weren't any. Desperation made people act in ways they didn't recognize within themselves. There wasn't anyone that could help.

Same narrative, the only way, lives at stake. It couldn't end without a fight. He couldn't let it end this way. There was no turning back.

It was getting easier. Once the decision was made and after the first time, it was almost mechanical. It was another time, another transaction. A simple press of a few keys. Maybe five minutes.

The system said, input initials. There was a frown, smile and shaking of the head before overriding. *Why can you override initials? That really needs to be fixed.*

The guilt returned, but he had learned to handle it. Halted it more quickly this time. *Remember, no turning back.*

Transaction complete.

CHAPTER 109

(Executive Training - Trust - Really?)

The final day of the workshop. It comes down to trust.

"Without trust, what do you have? How can you share any kind of relationship? Let's find out." Adam grabbed the remote and pointed towards the large screen attached to the wall. "This video is based on a real life story of people being thrown together in a work environment, trying to make the best of the situation, making mistakes, having no trust, building trust, and finding workable solutions. We have all kinds of dynamics at play. Let's listen in."

The setting involved an introduction to three different offices at various levels in an engineering firm. The headquarters in Washington DC, a regional office in Richmond, Virginia, and a subordinate office in Dallas, Texas.

The DC headquarters focused on strategic and lobbyist issues. The Richmond office focused on compliance, field oversight, leveraging the human capital of this interdependent organization, and providing approvals and support to their offices spread throughout the country.

The Dallas office was one of eight field offices located near critically important clients. Prior to a recent reorganization, they reported directly to the headquarters with a substantial amount of autonomy, empowered and in charge of their own destiny. The transition proved challenging with the injection of a middle layer resulting in two bosses and two tiers of management. They fought the Richmond regional office most of the way. Initially, they didn't know each other very well and that was okay with them.

The video began with a phone call to Dallas. There was an irate voice on the other end, the Richmond boss. Word had leaked about the field office bypassing them and going directly to the DC headquarters to get permission to enter into negotiations for a teaming arrangement. And, it gets worse. The Richmond office had already disapproved the request.

It was the third infraction, and the immediate perception was they intentionally elevated to DC to get a different answer. Sound like a child going to a chosen parent with the greatest likelihood of a desired outcome?

The conversation from Richmond to the Dallas Operations Director went something like this, "You guys ignored our direction for the last time. I've already told you no to the teaming arrangement. You continue to go behind our backs. You tell your people the next time they do anything like this, there will be serious consequences. I'm done with playing nice. I've really tried here."

The Dallas Director attempted to defend his team, without knowing all the facts. But, it didn't sound good. He told Richmond he would check into it and heard the clicking of the phone on the other end.

He blew out a deep breath and slammed his phone on the cradle. He shouted for his assistant to get the Deputy in his office.

The Deputy walked in a minute later. "You wanted to see me."

"Yeah, it's about the teaming arrangement. Richmond is really mad. Said you went to DC around them after being told no. What happened?"

He laughed and his right eye twitched. "That's not exactly what happened. One of the DC analysts reached out to me on a totally unrelated issue. While we were on the phone, I asked what he thought of the teaming arrangement and the possibility of making it happen."

"Well, that's not good. You shouldn't have done that. What were you thinking?" He put up his hand and said, "We'll talk later. I need to call them and see if I can straighten this out."

He called back to Richmond attempting to defend his team, calling it a big misunderstanding, trying to explain the DC office had initiated the call on an unrelated issue, and it wasn't what it looked like. The Richmond Vice President of Operations didn't want to hear it. He knew exactly what they were trying to do. It had happened too many times. Once again, the call ended abruptly.

* * * * * * * * * *

Adam flipped the light switch and pressed the button on the remote. He said, "I'll start with the obvious. What is the problem?"

"They don't endorse the change in organization structure and they certainly don't care for each other." Joe shook his head. "But, that wouldn't be an easy transition to accept and expect to just happen."

"Good point Joe. What else?"

Jack answered, "There is definitely a trust problem. This kind of thing happened before, leading to the perception that Dallas wasn't trustworthy. They weren't team players and they lost their credibility."

"Joe and Jack are both right. Actually, there were several problems that tie into what we've been talking about over the last few days. First, Dallas didn't really want to accept the transformation, but they had to get over that. The Richmond and Dallas people didn't start with a relationship and neither of them seemed to care about building one, making everything they were trying to accomplish more difficult. Plus, they didn't use good communications skills, and, as you said, there was no trust between them."

Adam continued, "Tough environment to survive. It takes excruciating effort just to get anything done. By the way, this company recognized they couldn't go on like this and did something. It took some time, but they did it. We'll see in a few minutes how they made it happen. Before we do that, let's talk about the mistakes they made."

Lindsay subtly glanced around the room and looked at Patrick. She thought about their relationship and how important he was in her life. She felt terrible about not telling him the truth about the investigation. *Trust, ugh, betrayal. He had a right to know.*

She returned to the moment as Adam asked, "Did they try to cover up what they had done?"

Lindsay's voice conveyed no emotion and she shifted her eyes to look directly at David. Holding his gaze, she answered, "No, they didn't."

"You're right. They didn't lie, but they did something else a little more subtle. It was basic, everyday actions and behaviors that kept them from building trust."

David looked away from Lindsay's gaze. He knew what she was thinking. *This had to end soon. There was too much damage. But, there was no going back. Not now.*

Neither realized that Adam caught this peculiar interaction between them. *What was that all about? What is going on with these two?* He reprimanded himself for even caring, continuing towards the flip chart and getting his head back in the game. He said, "Let's get specific about the mistakes that were made."

Discussing the topic of trust with this group was unsettling. The embezzler scanned the room. There were too many players, too much going on, too close, and too painful. His face felt hot. He thought it had to be visibly red - people would figure it out. He looked down at the table. He couldn't face them. Some of these people were even friends. Trustworthy people. *How did it get this far? Should have turned to them. Trusted them enough. Too late now. No going back. Not now.*

∗ ∗ ∗ ∗ ∗ ∗ ∗ ∗ ∗

Adam asked, "So, what were the mistakes?" This was an easy one. The executives around the room were not shy. *It's certainly a lot easier to Monday morning quarterback others than perform self-reflection, isn't it?* The critiquing went like this:

"They didn't respect their other colleagues. Trust and respect did not align."

"They aren't operating from a common goal or the good of the company."

"They get a failing grade for self-awareness they could have managed. Stopping, pausing the mind, and considering how their actions and words affect each other. Starting with the benefit of the doubt, and choosing to believe the best in one another instead of immediately jumping to negative conclusions that may be wrong or unintentional."

"They aren't taking advantage of the value of this new interdependence. The ability to pool diverse skilled resources and accomplish amazing things."

Adam asked, "How could Richmond address this trust issue more appropriately?" More critiquing:

"Not immediately accuse the field office of bad intentions. Start with finding out what happened. Leave judgment out, and open up discussions rather than being accusatory from the start."

Adam nodded his head, "Yes, we love judgement, don't we? They immediately jumped to conclusions about bad intentions. Granted, they did it based on history, but it can be misleading, most often incorrect, and paranoia wreaking havoc. Downward spiral in action. As we mentioned a few minutes ago, you can't build trust without first giving the benefit of the doubt. What else?"

"Trust begins with trust. The higher levels of the company had a responsibility to build a culture that valued trust. Leaders demonstrating the importance and demand for trust, communicating the expected behaviors, and integrating that into the culture. More valuable than any single wins or losses along the way."

"Good. What you don't know from the video is whether or not the Richmond office was hypersensitive or suffered from some degree of paranoia. Regardless, they owned part of the responsibility for the damaged relationship. Respect evolves. It begins with making a choice to respect others and communicate by open and honest sharing of information. Talking through conflict and problem solving scenarios. None of this is rocket science. It is so simple, but we sure know how to botch it up, don't we?"

Adam pressed the start button to resume the video show in action. "Let's see how they started building trust."

The setting resumed with the executive players of the three offices coming together. They admitted this couldn't go on and something had to be done, and fast.

What did they do? It started with an off-site similar to what Adam was doing with this group of people. Training, tools, and exercises to get to know one another on a more human level, working on mastering communication skills, and building an infrastructure for trust. All of it was geared towards recognizing the value and importance of building and maintaining relationships.

How did they fare? Well, success didn't happen over night.

They started getting to know one another and discovering they weren't all that different. Talking and opening up about their hobbies, families, personal interests, and yes, the office too. Traveling and dining together changed the way they began to view one another. The two Operations Officers from the phone altercation became whiskey drinking companions when they traveled together. Called it "whiskey night". Didn't see that one coming.

They spent face-to-face time and were required to operate in groups, working on the relationships. The more time they were together and forced to depend on one another, the more they started experiencing the benefit of interdependence. The possibilities of success in relationships when a collective number of colleagues worked for the common goal. Terms were thrown around like "we" and no longer "us and them." Human beings with good intentions. They were evolving, communicating, and starting to address conflict. This was progress, but it was just the beginning. They would face tests, conflicts and challenges. It would take time. After all, trust doesn't happen overnight.

* * * * * * * * *

Adam glanced around the room. There was definitely something going on between Lindsay and David. If they weren't staring at each other, they were exchanging glances and quickly turning away from one another. *What was happening?*

Reverting back to focus on the video, he asked, "This is all critically important stuff, but what do you think they actually did that put them on the road to building trust?"

Lindsay said, looking out of the corner of her eyes at David, "They made an attempt to be open and honest, regardless of the topic. They started down the road of believing, trusting they could believe in one another, and they wouldn't let each other down. They could handle anything."

Adam was struck by the passion in Lindsay's response, over enunciating and varied inflection that said more than the words. He followed her look to David, who had his head tilted downward, looking at his hands. *Uh oh. Yes, something had definitely happened.*

With a nod of his head, Adam said, "They had to take some steps and missteps before getting there. They needed a strategy and an action plan. And, because trust had been a major challenge for these colleagues, they established a set of business rules. It became the contract they all agreed to live by."

Adam walked back to the flip chart and began writing, "The Rules of Trust. They aren't difficult or complex. It's more or less a focus on how to treat people. We can all use it like a checklist, but be gentle with yourself. There will be times, well…you know. We're all human."

FLIP CHART 4:

The Rules of Trust:

(1) Be open, honest, transparent, and direct in conversation. Practice authenticity. No hidden agendas.

(2) Share information in real time. The good, bad, what, and why. Timing is everything and holding back can diminish trust quickly.

(3) Honor Commitments. Be dependable. Do what you say you'll do.

(4) Practice striving for the common good. Looking for opportunities where everyone can win. Serving everyone's best interests.

(5) Admit mistakes. Own it. Apologize. No blame. Be vulnerable - share shortcomings and weaknesses. Be accountable.

(6) Don't take the credit for the team's accomplishments. Acknowledge and give credit where credit is due.

(7) When you speak of people, talk as if they are in the room. Be courageous, upfront, and speak directly to them.

(8) Confront conflict directly and honestly. Opportunity to learn and look for mutually beneficial solutions. Acknowledge opposing views and perspectives by thanking them for trusting you enough to be honest.

(9) Trust begins with trust. Be open to trusting and believing in others first. Choose to give the benefit of the doubt before jumping to conclusions.

(10) When trust is broken, confront it. Admit your part, demonstrate a willingness to work on it, and offer possible solutions to re-establish it. Trust is a continuous process that will be challenged and tested.

Adam smiled, placed the marker back on the ledge, and turned back to them. "How do you ensure everyone accepts responsibility for these rules? Each of you has to perform a little self-reflection along the way. Ask yourself, am I following the rules? Am I being the best version of myself? Don't let yourself off the hook. Be accountable. But, be gentle. You will make mistakes."

He picked up his glass of water and took a sip, giving the audience time to finish jotting down notes. "If you follow these rules, you will have trust," he said quietly.

Adam hesitated a moment to let it all sink in. He looked around the room and said, "What if someone breaks one of the rules? What's the plan for accountability for broken trust and how do you restore it?"

No response. He looked at his watch and knew why.

"Uh oh. I'm losing you. I know, I'm the only obstacle between you and lunch. Stay with me. We're almost finished," he said before continuing. "The good thing is that trust can be restored. A facts-based discussion about what transpired and it shouldn't be personal since you can point to actual violations. Then, it's up to the parties to care enough about each other to be all in on modifying behavior and re-establishing trust."

Peter asked, "Okay, so what do you say? How do you handle something as highly charged as they had in the video?"

Adam smiled and said, "You have to explore it through communicating. Think back to the Communications Model. Have a conversation, confront conflict, and determine a solution and way ahead together. If you find any of the steps are not applicable to the circumstance, then skip to the next step. It's a good template to follow."

He continued talking, while writing on the flip chart, "Let's recap the model:

FLIP CHART 5:

The Model:

- *Start with the facts to set the right tone,*

- *Ask to establish a common goal,*

- *Ask the other party to explain their point of view, feelings, assumptions, and intentions,*

- *Explain your point of view, assumptions you made about their intentions, how it made you feel, and clarify your intentions and accept your part of the responsibility*

- *Discuss areas of agreement and disagreement, and*

- *Engage in problem solving; brainstorming and looking for creative and alternative solutions.*

Adam placed the marker in the tray and turned to face his audience. "Now, we'll talk about the difficult part. What do you do if you can't restore trust? Anyone want to take a shot at it?"

"You cut your losses," Eleanor responded a little too loudly.

Adam nodded. "Actually, it is something like that. There will be instances that no matter how hard you try, you will be dealing with someone who is unwilling to build a meaningful and trusting relationship. In that case, you have to be willing to minimize the contact, know what you're dealing with, and if you can, walk away or cut the ties. The last resort.

"Let's take a break and come back after lunch. We'll spend the remainder of time talking about trust and your relationship. I think you'll find it eye opening and fun. I know I'm looking forward to it. See you in an hour."

CHAPTER 110

Peter didn't move while his colleagues filed out of the room. He remained still, looking down at the conference table in front of him. His stomach did flip flops and he thought he was going to be sick. He couldn't help but feel guilty. He had spent most of his working hours with these people. They were almost like family. They had become friends.

The last thing he had been ready for was a lesson on trust. He was feeling many emotions, but mostly he felt like a hypocrite. How did he get here, to this place? He knew right from wrong, and he and Tom shouldn't be doing this. Desperation was his most powerful enemy. There was nothing he could do about it now. They were too far in. He picked up electronic devices and left the room.

CHAPTER 111

The embezzler crept around the corner even though he didn't need to. No one would get suspicious at that hour. He went to the computer and sat down, as if he were writing the cubicle occupant a note.

He quickly entered a passcode and the financial system appeared. The transactions were fast at lunch time. This was almost routine. A few clicks on the keyboard and it was done.

He just couldn't think about it. It was too late to worry. He knew what to do when it was all over. And, it would be over.

He exited the program and walked slowly down the hall. He wondered, where to go for lunch. He didn't have long.

CHAPTER 112

They were all arriving at different times, but everyone was early. Some were gathering at the refreshment table. Others were looking at their tablets or phones while continuing to talk and laugh together.

Adam asked everyone to take their seats. "I think you're making progress in a short amount of time. I like the changing dynamics. But that's my observation, what do you think?"

Jack was quick to jump in. "For me, it has certainly been eye opening. I'll be the first to admit I wasn't interested in connecting with colleagues. Now I know what I've missed. It feels good to get involved. Be part of something. A community."

David asked before Adam could speak, "What made you feel," he paused before continuing, "uh my word, disconnected?"

"Fear and the painful experience of my buddy and his baby haunting me. But something happened here when we shifted the focus to us as individuals with life experiences, challenges, and imperfections. We started opening up, sharing, and even being vulnerable. I have a new appreciation. I want this more fulfilling work life."

Several others piled on and agreed. Jack found his voice and wasn't planning on being silenced without a final surprising comment. "The best part, I think we've demonstrated we're willing to invest in us, even if it's hard work."

"I couldn't have said it better." Adam paused and looked around at the attentive faces gazing at him and again thought about how they were an extraordinary group of individuals. The energy in the room was undeniable. They might just have a chance at success. He smiled and said, "But, there is still work ahead for you. Make it part of your daily life to consider and think about each other. Don't leave anyone out. Take some responsibility for your team members."

He continued, "And, dedicate to the good of the team. You have to believe you are part of something more than yourself. Collective accountability and responsibility for your everyday successes and failures. The 'we're in this together' mentality. You're never alone."

He let his words sink in before continuing. "It will be challenging at times. Like any other relationship, it will be tested, when you let each other down. We're human beings with flaws. Don't let it take over and cause permanent damage. Communicate and course correct."

Adam asked, "Do you trust each other?"

A number of heads nodded up and down. "Any reservations?"

At first, no one answered. Then, one of the executives spoke apprehensively, "I think I trust this group, but I'll have to wait until real challenges and conflicts occur, requiring us to put the interests of the company above our own. I need to see it tested."

"Yes, there will be opportunity for tests. Your success will be based on your response."

Adam looked at his watch, knowing the end was near. "When team members trust one another, they will take measured risks and not condemn a risk gone bad, tackle real issues, and look at healthy conflict as an opportunity for growth. Not let each other down. At least, not intentionally. It is based on the relationship you have built and continue to build everyday. I can't emphasize enough that daily maintenance and nurturing is essential to your long term success. Needless to say, that is trust."

He paused and walked around the room scanning the faces looking back at him, contemplating his next move. He said quietly, "Care to guess what happened that made me know you have a real chance?"

Lindsay responded, "I think Jack hit on it. When we opened up to one another. We shared some intensely intimate details of struggles in our lives.

I personally experienced real empathy and connection. The relationship started to feel different after that. At least, I feel different."

Adam asked, "Anyone else?" Most of the participants were nodding in agreement and a few commented affirmatively with their own similar accounts of what transpired for them.

"That's it. Those exercises we did were actually good trust exercises. You could have gone through the motions and talked about fairly benign stuff, but you didn't. You showed up. You opened up, shared a part of you. Be proud of where you are headed and stay on that path together. I think you have what it takes and you can do it."

Adam started to say goodbye, but stopped himself. It was nagging at him. He had never felt this before. The need to be more naked, raw and vulnerable with this group than he had ever been in any of these sessions. He wasn't sure why, only that he had to do it, in this moment, or it would haunt him forever.

He continued, "In closing, I want to go back and revisit the video on trust, the question, 'how did they fare?' There is more to the story, a more intimate testimony of relationships. Do you want to know how they fared?"

A few heads nodded, others looked confused, and Adam was stalling for time. This team merited the right to know. What a way to end their time together, a glimpse at possibilities. Caring about other people, really caring. After the stories they shared over the past few days, it was only fair. But, could he be this exposed, tell this story?

He knew the story. Lived the story. Knew her. For the first time as a consultant, it was his turn to share a tragedy that hit way too close to home.

Adam looked down at his hands. Not sure he could get it out or that it should be told, but he couldn't stop himself. They deserved to visit that experience, a momentary glimpse into the value, the real power of relationships, human connections, and the results of trusting one another. And, she deserved for her story to be told. He sat down and leaned forward, telling her story.

On her dying bed, and not afraid. She was one of the leaders from the Dallas office described in the video. Over time, she built relationships with employees from all levels of the organization by spending time and getting to know them as real people with names, families, and hobbies. Her name was Dee.

On the last night of her life, there were local colleagues in her hospital room, even a few from out of town that wouldn't allow her to depart without knowing what she had become to them. Others in the higher level offices across the globe were invited in through virtual means. Some of these were people that started out almost as adversaries, or at least as unknowns. Dee never did fear the unknown.

She was in a daily battle with her own mortality when she performed the selfless act of reaching out to a man whose father was dying. Being there for him. She had no interest in living with a victim mentality. Where did she find the emotional capacity, mental space? She just did.

In that room, her last night, colleagues that had become friends were gathering around to be with her. She did what she always did, thought about them, and pleaded for them to go on, to flourish and luxuriate in life. She was unafraid, promising she would see them again. She embodied breathtaking beauty, an amazing positive outlook, insurmountable courage that most people can only strive for, sheer will, and yes, friendship. That will forever be ingrained in the minds of people left behind.

She spoke these last words across the globe on a tiny little screen that housed immense responsibility in the last hours of her life. Propped by pillows, her weakness looked more like strength, if only for a few moments. Knowing her, she was attempting to spare pain. Her message was not about her. It went like this:

"I don't want any of you to feel sadness about what is happening here. I've accepted this, I'm ready, and I'm going to be okay. I need you to be okay.

"I hope you'll choose to focus on the good, the laughter, love and friendship, and the lessons we shared along the way. And, I hope you'll be kind to yourself and to those around you. Our relationship has turned out to be one of the most precious gifts this life has given me. I hope you'll use this as an opportunity to take advantage of the power you can find in connection, relationships, and friendships. Share it with everyone you meet.

"Please don't worry about me. I'll be fine. Our separation is temporary. The next time we see each other, we'll have an epic celebration. Our love and friendship will never be forgotten. Until we're together again. I love you all."

The screen vanished and all that was left for the rest of us were the tears and goodbyes. Thoughts about a cherished colleague and friend that understood.

He still carried the written tribute in his briefcase, a reminder of the good in people. It was etched in his memory and it read like this: Dee, We are trying to follow your lead, your outlook, your practice of gratitude, your passion for life, and your urge to care and be kind to others. We're still waiting, hoping for a time when our pain is replaced with endearing memories we can carry on and make a part of our daily lives. Your deep friendship and love is an amazing contribution, a teaching, and it will never be forgotten.

What he could only say to his inner self, "I still think about her."

Adam wiped his eyes and he wasn't alone.

* * * * * * * * *

"I would like to thank you for our time together. This was a special experience for me and I had the pleasure of learning from you. I am excited about your potential, your future. Keep doing what you're doing." Adam looked across the room, not wanting to linger too long in Lindsay's direction. "Thank you. Until we meet again. Have a good evening and good luck."

David stepped up to the front of the conference room and publicly thanked him for working with them. Others followed David's lead. All, except Lindsay.

She didn't move from her chair. She tried not to be obvious. She waited around looking at her tablet, but not paying attention to it. She was thinking what to say to him. No. She should get up and walk out. This wasn't a good idea. But she couldn't help it. Tug of war with her mind and heart in conflict, once again. But, something made her stay. Lindsay didn't want this to be their last goodbye.

CHAPTER 113

Adam and Lindsay were the only two remaining in the room. Her heart pounded so hard she thought it would leap out of her chest. She could feel the heat rush to her face and knew she had to calm down before making a total fool of herself.

The seconds seemed like minutes. Neither made a step at first, probably not knowing how to make the next move that could change everything, or nothing. It shouldn't be this hard for two people with behavior that screamed they were both interested. And let's not forget, they are supposed to be adults.

Adam was slowly shuffling papers and placing them in his briefcase, feeling his heart beat way too fast. He thought to himself, just dive in and stop messing around. And, that's what he did. He cleared his throat, walked over to where she was sitting, and said, "Lindsay, I've really enjoyed these last few days together. About that raincheck, would you be interested in having dinner with me?"

She hesitated only slightly, smiled and said, "I would really like that."

"Would I come across too anxious if I asked about tomorrow night?"

Okay, I'm really doing this. "Would I be too anxious if I said tomorrow would be great?"

They held each other's gaze for a moment and made a date for Friday, a great lead into the weekend with no deadlines. Adam suggested he pick her up at 6:30 for dinner at The Grille at 7:00.

He finished gathering up his things and stuffing them in his briefcase as he watched her leave the room. He smiled to himself. *That wasn't so hard. So far, so good.*

CHAPTER 114

Lindsay stepped out of the conference room and moved far enough away before stopping and leaning her back against the wall. She let out a deep breath and looked at the ceiling. She was, once again, overcome by fear, dread, and yes, excitement. She was going to take that first step and get to know this man. What if there was something between them? What would it be like to date and maybe even have someone care about her day, her ups and downs, her life? Someone to lean on, to simply be there. But, what if…?

Ugh. Stop it. She felt like a ping pong ball in the middle of a match. Why couldn't she get her mind around it, get it right?

She knew why. She had been down that road before and it was way too painful. It left her with a heavy fear of commitment, of getting involved and loving someone only to have it end or be taken away. Maybe it wouldn't happen right away, but someday. She would come to love and depend on him, and then life would happen and he would be gone. And, of course it would happen when she was at her most vulnerable place.

She knew she had a habit of pushing men away, especially when they started to get close. Good men. Made excuses in her head about why it wouldn't work. It wasn't her, it was them. He was too tall, too short, too lean, too heavy, too...

Who was she fooling? Yes, she needed to get her head around it. It had been long enough. She had to stop being afraid of love, of commitment. There were no guarantees. *Stop. Live life. Take a lesson from Jack.*

Yes, that's exactly what she would do. Embrace life, at least until the next wave of fear overwhelmed her. She frowned and walked down the hall towards her office.

CHAPTER 115

The conference room door was closed. Prior to the investigation and being set up as Mark's office, it had been the main conference room for the attorney staff. The place where lawyers could gather to connect, meet, each lunch, and strategize. Lindsay had hoped the current occupancy would be a little more temporary than it had become. Assuming the closed door meant Mark was conducting interviews, she didn't want to interrupt progress. Controlling her impatience, she returned to her own office.

She placed her suit jacket on the hook behind the door and walked over to her coffee pot, but decided against it. She chose work instead. She sat behind the desk staring at her laptop. When that didn't work, she leaned her chair back, ran her hands through her hair, and stared at the ceiling. Her mind wandered to her upcoming date. She still felt uneasy. Adam was great. Handsome, charming, intelligent, and definitely successful. And, he possessed traits most women adore in a man, empathetic and compassionate. Why did she keep doing this? *Make up your mind.*

She stopped herself. She was thinking way too much. They might not even hit it off. She scanned her spacious office, taking in the scenery that had become her life. As the day was turning to evening, the room was dimly lit with two floor lamps symmetrically spaced in corners and a desk light emitting a golden glow.

She glanced at the two leather chairs facing a couch against the wall in front of her. She had spent many hours in those chairs, late hours talking with colleagues or her leadership staff. Over to the right side of the room, was her long rectangular shaped cherry conference table where she met with other lawyers and clients.

On the walls, there were ocean pictures, landscapes, and inspirational pieces, but no family pictures. She had spent enough of her life alone. It was time to change. She was going to push the demons away and do something about it, starting the next day.

She forced herself to get up and leave for the evening. She grabbed her briefcase, a mound of work papers, and headed home.

CHAPTER 116

By the time Lindsay reached her condo, the colorless sky added to the feeling of loneliness. She opened her door, turned on the dimmer switches for as many lights as she could reach, and pressed the remote for the fireplace. She wanted, no needed, a little more of something this evening. It felt cold and damp inside.

The day left her exhausted, but she still had the urge to cook before reading some legal documents and getting to bed early. After changing clothes, she poured a glass of bordeaux and turned on the music. Vivaldi quieted her brain and made her breathing a little slower.

She lathered a mustard-based rub on one piece of salmon and placed it in the oven. Making a spinach salad and adding blueberries, crumpled cheese, and a drizzling of homemade balsamic vinaigrette put a smile on her face and calmed her mind. *Cooking was definitely good for her soul.*

With the finished product on a television tray and remote in hand, she flipped a few channels and gave up on some rerun of a comedy that she had seen too many times to count. It didn't matter. It was noise.

She took her first bite of salmon and slowly chewed, closing her eyes and making a sound that celebrated perfection. She thought of Adam and how nice it would have been to share this meal with him, until reality set in. *He might not even like salmon. Simmer down girl!*

Dinner, paperwork and bed. She turned out the light. She really did have to get a life.

CHAPTER 117

Adam woke the next morning not thinking about action items and "to do" lists. For the first time in a long time his initial thought of the day was not work and what he had to accomplish. He was going on an official date with the hot blonde that he could not get off his mind.

Then, panic. *Flowers? Do men even do that anymore? How pathetic.* He hadn't been on a date in so long, he almost forgot how to behave. All of his energy had been expended establishing himself as a successful entrepreneur with a thriving consulting business. Too bad he didn't have the same success in his relationships with women. He was normally unflappable, yet found himself nervous about a date, even if she was a beautiful, successful, intelligent and well-educated woman. He would have to be on his game and they definitely didn't teach that protocol at Harvard Business School.

Deciding yes to the flowers, he placed the order before leaving for the office. Having too much work to do between now and the date with Lindsay, it was time to get moving and get focused.

He was starting another project the following week and had to make contact with the client concerning last minute details. The demand for better communication and a more people-focused culture was increasing as a result of companies, athletic programs, government agencies, and even public officials suffering, and accepting the direct correlation between human relationship skills and potential success. Finally, and harder to digest, the surrender that many people aren't really all that good at it as part of our human condition.

His consulting firm was growing exponentially. It had become increasingly profitable over the past five years and his staff had grown along with the company. He had a steady client base, along with an insurgence of new ones with different needs outside of traditional areas of leadership, organizational dynamics and human behavior. While he had a passion for the work and stayed engaged by personally working with some of their clients, he exclusively handled the projects of high powered players that hired him, not the firm, for his unique capabilities and skill set. It sometimes took him to remote and threatening parts of the world with captivating assignments, and he loved it.

Working with Thurmond & Hollingsworth had been special for a different reason. He knew David, admired him, and liked his senior executives. Impressed by their emotional capacity, he had experienced their progress. They had the potential to build a great system.

Of course, meeting Lindsay was a bonus. She was really something and the way she… *Stop. Too much to do before thinking about a date. That would have to wait.*

CHAPTER 118

Lindsay's goal for Friday was efficiency and lots of it. Get tasks accomplished, leave the office on time, and start the weekend without worry about work left unfinished. For the first time in awhile, renewed energy and passion was everywhere and everything, any subject.

She intended to spend the day in her office reading emails and reviewing contract documents. She had coffee in hand and was pacing around the room, analyzing the legalities of a business arrangement. They weren't making the same mistakes of the recent past. This was a partnership with a firm they had worked with for years. Minimal risk.

Looking up to find Mark standing in her doorway, she hoped he was not going to ruin her day. She did not intend to let anything spoil any part of it.

Mark's brow furrowed, lines formed on his forehead, and he frowned before he spoke. He let out a deep breath and said, "Lindsay, I have to tell you something is really strange here. I've interviewed a number of the staff and I'm coming up with nothing. I'm convinced this is someone who has been with the company long enough to know something about the accounting system and it's practices. I doubt it's one of the new staff members. They wouldn't have as much latitude and authority in the systems."

Lindsay didn't speak right away, letting Mark's comments sink in before saying anything. She leaned in closer to him. "Have you interviewed the senior managers? I have a nagging feeling, some random thoughts swirling through my head that I can't make any sense of," she said and waved her hand in the air. "I feel like we're missing something."

"I know. It's frustrating. I'm interviewing the senior managers today."

"When are you questioning Patrick?"

"I don't think I'll get to him until Monday. His interview will be a little more delicate and I haven't determined exactly how I want to approach it yet."

"It won't be easy. He is a bright and perceptive guy. He may see through it immediately."

"Let's hope not." He said as he headed back to the conference room to resume interviews.

There was not a trail and the longer it went on, the harder it would be to keep it confidential. No matter the ending, there would be collateral damage and they were running out of time.

CHAPTER 119

Lindsay's hibernating day in her office resulted in very little contact with the outside world. She was immersed in a stack of papers and didn't even look up from her work except to have a thirty minute mentoring meeting with Tyler.

When they finished talking business, he asked, "Do you have plans this weekend, Boss? And, please tell me you aren't working the whole time."

She smiled. "No, I'm not working all weekend, thank you very much. I am actually looking forward to the next two days and no work."

"Really? I'm shocked. Every time I walk by here at night, and I'm leaving pretty late, your light is still on. You work a lot."

"You're right. I need to do something about that. It doesn't mean I expect you to keep my hours. I want you to have a life and balance. Speaking of…"

"Ugh, nothing is going on. My life couldn't be any more boring. I'm going out with the guys tomorrow night, some new bar in town. I'll probably just have a pizza and a couple of beers with my roommate at home tonight. I'm a little tired."

"Well, that sounds like fun to me. Enjoy it while you can, my friend. Someone fabulous is going to snatch you up before too long and it will change everything."

"Yeah, yeah, I hear you."

When he walked to the door to leave, he turned around and wiggled his finger at her before saying, "Don't stay too late."

She nodded and he swiftly moved through the door with hands in his pockets, heading back to his office. She had grown quite fond of Tyler over the years. There was a comfort level between them from the very beginning. He was charming, intelligent, and adorable, but he had her work habits. He just needed balance.

CHAPTER 120

Lindsay looked at her watch. The day had flown and she was getting closer to the time for her date and the anxiety was kicking in.

A knock on the door interrupted all of that. She glanced up and waved for Mark to enter. Two times in one day. That can't be good.

She smiled, "What did you find?"

He plopped down in a chair next to her. His tied was loosened and his sleeves were rolled up. He ran his hands through his black hair, leaving a few strands standing up. He sighed and said, "Nothing, absolutely nothing. The people I interviewed weren't aware of any abnormalities tied to their accounting practices. We talked through their processes and I didn't find anything unusual. Other than, an accounting trail is required and we didn't find one in our embezzling transactions. No surprise there."

He continued, reciting what he heard from one interview after another. "They all agreed that each step involves an approval process, with initials of the authority approving it. They all said the exact same thing on the review and approval. So, that leads me to the next big step. Someone is a very good liar and should win an Academy Award for their acting ability. No one so much as flinched through the discussion. In fact, many of them came across as proud of their work."

"That's not good news. I mean, except for the pride part. What now?"

"We step up our game. We let David know we need a second round of questions. A little more invasive. We don't need to go into embezzlement, but we need to point out some bad accounting practices and have a couple of 'what if scenarios'. I'll interview Patrick before we step it up."

A sudden pause led Lindsay to sense there was more. "Is there anything else?"

He answered somewhat tentatively, "I think I need to interview David, given his expertise and knowledge of the systems."

"You can't be serious. Why, you can't possibly think he did it?"

Mark laughed uneasily, "No. I meant he might be able to shed light on the inner workings of the financial systems. Things others may have missed," he continued, "No, I'm not suggesting he did it, but, he could have. If I let my imagination run, I could think he was trying to throw us off his trail by calling it an embezzling scheme. We both know he is a computer genius and could successfully pull it off. And, it would be a great way to solve a money problem. Pay yourself. Who would think of him?"

Lindsay laughed. "You need to write mystery novels."

"I'm just saying it's possible, but I certainly don't think he did it."

She thought about it before moving on. She said, "Of course he didn't do it. David will agree to stepping up the interview questions. Let's decide on the questions and then we'll have a meeting with him to discuss our plan. You might as well interview Patrick today."

"He left for the day. I called him and he asked to delay the interview until Monday."

Lindsay shrugged and said he often plays golf on Friday afternoon. She frowned, thinking that he usually stopped by to wish her well for the weekend. Especially odd since he knew she had a first date that night. No big deal.

As the conversation shifted to idle chatter, her mind wandered to a very charming and handsome man. Smiling at the thought of having somewhere to be, she wished Mark well for the weekend, turned off her office lights and left. She desperately wanted to look forward to the evening and be open to possibilities of new beginnings. *Don't run from this.*

CHAPTER 121

Adam was sitting at his desk staring at the laptop as he hit the send button. Satisfied, he pushed back his chair and placed his feet on the desk and his hands behind his head. He took in a deep breath and let it out slowly.

His work was finished for the day, but it had been a struggle to stay focused. With several stops and starts he finally managed to meet the weekly deadline to his editor. He didn't like to miss deadlines, and agents and editors were bossy. He smiled.

On to the subject that had begun to consume his thoughts lately. He went to his closet to select the right pair of pants, shirt and jacket. He was almost ashamed he was taking so much time to decide what to wear. After all, he was a guy and they weren't supposed to do that, were they? He was clearly out of practice.

He stared at the clothes on the racks. He thought about blue, then black, no khaki pants. *Is the white shirt or color better? What about a sweater instead of a shirt?* His sister would know what to wear. Still standing in the closet, he grabbed his cellphone out of his pants pocket and called her.

She told him to wear the black pants he wore to his niece's dance recital along with that light weight creme sweater. She teased, saying the pants fitted his bottom nicely. He muttered, "Stop it. Not words you want to hear from your sister. But, thank you for the fashion advice."

On the way to Lindsay's house, he stopped by the local florist to pick up the flower bouquet that was arranged in a variety of bright orange, yellow and red colors. He thought about roses, but it was too soon.

His heartbeat accelerated as he pulled into her driveway. Could this possibly be the start of a new chapter in his life? Representing everything he wanted in a woman, she was fascinating, brilliant, and yes, gorgeous. Learning from his past, he wasn't going to make the same mistake this time. He would be open to the possibilities.

CHAPTER 122

Lindsay's doorbell rang precisely at 6:30. She glanced in the hallway mirror and fluffed her hair on the way to the front door. She looked through the peep hole at the man standing between her and the hardwood barrier. He was shifting his weight from side to side. He looked jumpy.

What am I doing? This can't possibly be smart. What was I thinking? Her tummy did a flipflop as she drew in air, smiled and opened the door.

Adam was standing on the threshold displaying shiny white teeth and cute little dimples. He said hello, and "these are for you," as he handed her the bouquet.

"Well thank you. They're lovely," she said, blushing as she took in the springlike fragrance. Stepping out of the entryway, she motioned and said, "Please, come in."

Adam complimented her stunning appearance. What he intentionally didn't say was that she was breathtaking and very sexy in the form fitting, yet classy dress. *Wow! Simmer down boy!*

* * * * * * * * *

On the way to dinner, they talked easily and spoke mostly about work and the impact of the workshop. She agreed with Adam about the possibilities. She was starting to feel closer to her colleagues. They were definitely transitioning into relationships and he was largely to thank for that.

When they arrived at the restaurant a few minutes before 7:00, Sam greeted them at the front entrance. She escorted them towards the back, away from the main area that tended to be more open, lively, and sometimes noisy. When Adam had called Sam for the reservation, he asked for the table in the back right corner. It was clearly the most romantic location. Sam had smiled to herself.

As Lindsay and Adam maneuvered their way through the restaurant, Lindsay observed a table of women shifting their eyes in Adam's direction. He didn't notice them as he walked with an aura of confidence and focus dedicated to his date, touching her arm to lead her to their table.

He held the chair for her. His style was gentlemanly, but not too much or insulting. She thought he was progressive, but had observed an old fashioned sense of manners that she admired.

They were talking about the wine selection when Sam came to the table and suggested a bordeaux on the house. Adam attempted to decline, but Sam insisted. After some back and forth dialogue about the free wine, he reluctantly accepted that he wasn't going to win this battle. *Note to self - don't do battle with two strong willed women.*

The conversation between Adam and Lindsay continued at a comfortable pace. She felt an easiness being with him unlike past experiences with any man this early on.

Lindsay loved hearing him talk about his consulting business. She didn't see him as consumed with his work, but he had a respect and passion for it. He appeared to have a genuine interest in assisting corporations and observing them evolve through their challenges.

Adam shifted the conversation to focus on her, looking directly into her eyes when she spoke. Lindsay had been right all along - his sense of compassion and empathy were refreshing, and frightening. She didn't know him well, but was a little unnerved by the thought that she could possibly fall for him. *Could she really do this?*

They were interrupted by the waiter arriving to take their orders. Adam looked up and said, "I apologize. We've been talking and haven't had a chance to look at the menu. Please give us a couple of minutes."

"No problem, sir. Take your time. I'll be back in a few," he smiled and left their table.

They continued talking, still without looking at the menu. By the time the waiter came back a third time, they still had not opened it. They all laughed and Adam sent him away again and promised they would be ready in five minutes.

Adam ordered the filet and Lindsay ordered the fish of the day. They agreed to share the entrees so they could sample a little of both specials. While it might seem a bit unusual for two people on their first date to share meals, it didn't feel that way.

For the remainder of the evening, they talked without any moments of awkwardness. The space was filled with interesting chatter about all sorts of topics. The conversation was not deep and personal, but it was engaging and interesting.

The food was delicious and time passed too quickly. They were having coffee and splitting a piece of sinfully rich chocolate cake when Lindsay noticed how late it was. Her keen sense of always knowing the exact time was out the window. *Oh Boy!*

When they returned to her house and he walked her to the door, not many words were needed. They had a wonderful evening and said goodbye. There would definitely be another date.

CHAPTER 123

Lindsay couldn't sleep, lying in bed, tossing and turning and reflecting on her evening with Adam. The feeling of excitement she hadn't experienced in a very long time. She had been interested in getting to know him, thought he seemed like a great guy, but this? How could such a kind, gentle man be so sexy and masculine at the same time? At that moment, she knew she had to find out.

She thought back to earlier in the evening when he picked her up. It was raining and he came around to her side of the car with an umbrella to shield her from the weather. At the restaurant, she stepped out of the car and her sandals splashed in standing water at the curb. When they were seated at the table, Adam signaled the waiter for a towel and asked Lindsay's permission before proceeding to dry the tops of her shoes. She smiled to herself and immediately thought, *he must be a serial killer*. He was simply too good to be true. She thought, *now, I know I'm in trouble*.

CHAPTER 124

It was Monday morning and Lindsay jumped from her bed before the alarm sounded. She had abruptly awakened from a nightmare of an embezzler standing over her, but didn't recognize them. She didn't believe in that sort of thing anyway. But she knew one thing, snapping back to reality, they had to figure out who was behind embezzling from the firm before the staff became suspicious.

Groaning her way to the shower, she still wasn't sure what to do. This was new territory and in the next couple of hours, she and Mark were going to figure out their next move.

She arrived at the office a little earlier than usual thinking Mark would be there. She saw the light on in the conference room and walked in to find him working on his laptop. "When are you interviewing Patrick?" she asked, with two coffee mugs in her hands.

He looked up and reached for the coffee. "Ah, thank you. You are saving my life," he said as he sipped the steaming hot coffee. He continued, "I'm interviewing him at 9:00 this morning."

"Good luck. Be…" Her voice cracked and she couldn't finish.

"I'll be careful." He smiled and thought he noticed her chin quiver. His look changed to serious as he crossed his arms and stared at her for a moment. He finally said, "Lindsay, I know this is difficult. I am really sorry about the position this puts you in with Patrick. I've developed a relationship with him too, and I hate it. But, it's best this way."

"I just wish there was another alternative. We've always completely trusted each other. I hope he'll understand. Mark, he is a special friend to me," her voice cracked again and she walked out.

Lindsay returned to her office and didn't want to think about Patrick's reaction to finding out they kept this from him. She had to push it out of her mind and get back to work. She kept telling herself, it will all work out.

When she finished for the day and walked out of the building, her cell phone rang and the display read Adam. She grabbed it on the second ring, and they talked for most of her drive home. Before getting off the phone, they agreed to a second date on Saturday night.

She hung up and smiled, relieved he had called. It was the first good thing that happened all day. She hadn't heard from him since their Friday night together and she was beginning to think she might not hear from him at all. *Really? Worried that he might not call. Acting like a school girl. Come on, Lindsay. Ugh!*

CHAPTER 125

The first stop on Tuesday morning was to see Mark and inquire about his interview with Patrick. Lindsay wasn't interested in any conversation except getting right to the point. "How did it go?"

"Dead end. He didn't tell me anything I didn't already know." Mark told her that Patrick said department policy was to provide electronic initials on completion of each transaction step, but the system didn't force it. This was a vulnerability and he had intended on allocating funding to initiate a system fix, but it wasn't a high enough priority. They weren't having problems in that area. It was a risk-based decision that had worked out well so far. Blah, blah, blah.

Lindsay told him to hang in there and keep trying, as she looked at her watch and left for a meeting.

Mark threw his hands in the air and put them behind his head and stared at the ceiling. All of the interviews were turning out to be dead ends. They weren't leading to anything or anybody. They were definitely dealing with an expert who didn't leave trails.

CHAPTER 126

Lindsay was busy tapping on her keyboard when Patrick poked his head in her office and asked her to join him for coffee. She towered over the laptop, continuing to hit the keys rapidly. Without looking up, she smiled and said, "I would love to. Give me a sec."

It was mid-afternoon and the Cafe Bar was packed with the after lunch crowd. Lindsay spotted a favorite table in the corner and hurried to it, recognizing and nodding to a few people along the way. Patrick delivered their coffees, his with all kinds of additives, disguising it so much that it was barely even coffee anymore. Lindsay snickered.

He placed the drinks on the table and gave her a look that said, don't say a word. He smirked and took the seat across from her.

"So, how is Andrew doing? What is he saying about the basketball team?" Lindsay asked.

Patrick shrugged and said, "I haven't seen much of him lately. When I talk to him, he doesn't say a lot other than they're working hard, conditioning harder and he is busy with school." He looked down at his coffee cup, shook his head and looked back at Lindsay. "I don't know how he does it all. Playing basketball is like a job for college kids these days. But, it's an exciting time of year for us. I'm looking forward to the season."

"Yeah, me too. I can't believe he's almost done. I remember when he was a little boy. What happened?"

"Tell me about it."

Their next topic of conversation was about Stephanie and the health condition Lindsay wasn't supposed to inquire about. Patrick unexpectedly brought it up and said she was doing much better, expected a full recovery.

"I'm so happy to hear that. You must be incredibly relieved," Lindsay said, with a wide smile that took over her face. She left out the part that she had been really worried about him. That he hadn't been himself lately. But, on this day he seemed better, more like the Patrick she knew and loved. It was like old times. At least, for a moment.

"We are. It's a load off my mind. I've been worried, but it looks good." He glanced around the room. "Can I change the subject and ask you something about Mark?"

"Sure. What do you want to ask?" she replied, trying not to hesitate too much or show the panic she was feeling. Her heart was beating faster and faster. Thank God it was on the inside of her body.

"What's the deal with him? He interviewed me today and it was strange. I thought he was doing a process improvement initiative, but some of the questions were odd. Do you know anything about this?"

Lindsay, be calm or you will blow it. Breathe in, breathe out. She shrugged, "Not much. Just that he is looking at our financial processes."

"I have a feeling he has discovered some problem areas."

"What did he say?"

"It's more of what he didn't say. Maybe I'm just paranoid. After all, this is my Department we're talking about. I'm a bit possessive, feel some ownership over it. If there is a problem, I want, no need, to know about it."

"I'm sure if he discovers anything, he'll let you know." She said to herself in disgust, *at some point.* She gulped down her last drop of coffee and stood. "I need to get back to work so I can get out of here at a decent hour today. I'm glad we had time to chat. We don't seem to find time to get together as much as we used to."

"I know. We'll have to change that. I'll be around more now. I think I only have a couple more trips over the next few weeks," Patrick said, as they walked to the elevator.

Lindsay and Patrick walked in opposite directions when the elevator doors opened. She reflected back on the second half of their conversation. He hadn't seemed suspicious and appeared satisfied with her response concerning Mark. They wouldn't be able to keep this from him much longer. He was too smart for that. She really did hate this.

CHAPTER 127

For the remainder of the week, Mark continued to interview and re-interview personnel in the Financial Department. He couldn't find any details or potential wrongdoings to implicate anyone. He wasn't sure what to do next. He sat for a couple of minutes before pushing back his chair and walking to Lindsay's office.

He tapped lightly on the door and asked, "Do you have a minute?"

She looked up from her computer screen and nodded. He dropped into the chair in front of her desk and placed his elbows on his knees. He leaned forward and said, "I'll have to interview the senior leaders and Patrick again next week. I've come up with nothing. How can this be so hard? There are only a few senior executives that approve payments.

"I was wondering about the Deputy Comptroller, but he was out of the office during two of the payments. It doesn't necessarily mean anything and I won't rule him out. But, I have this feeling. There has to be someone else who has access or has figured out how to tap into the system. I'm even contemplating some IT guru at work here."

She crossed her arms and shrugged. "The transactions could have occurred remotely. We don't want to rule it out."

"Yeah, I was thinking that too," he said as he stared beyond her and out through her office window. He hesitated before continuing, "After we talked, I decided to look into the Peter and Tom thing. The more I thought about it, the more concerned I became."

The mention of Peter peeked her interest and she leaned in closer, placing her hands on her desk, giving him her full attention. She asked, "What did you find?"

"Well, it was interesting. For once, my timing was good. I spotted Peter returning to his office from the conference room where he left Tom. I walked to his door and found the guy sitting behind his desk, sweating, with his head in his hands. He appeared to be overly anxious, having a heart attack, or something. He looked like he was about to blow. I asked him if he was okay and he passed it off as a bad day. As it turns out, he had just finished a heated argument with Tom."

Mark looked back at Lindsay and smiled before continuing. "I pressed him to tell me what was wrong. I talked about how long we had known each other and I was a good listener, and wanted to help. And, I guess it got to him because he spilled it. He said he and Tom were going against direct orders from David on the level of effort, even to the point of extravagance, on a particular design Tom was working on. He initially thought he could help save the firm, but as it turned out, it's probably going to cost the firm more money."

Lindsay stopped him, "How?" She continued without waiting for an answer, "Well, that's bad, going against David, but it's not the absolute end of the world. He thought he was doing something good."

"There is a little more to it. He said his original motivation was he thought they could save the firm and assist with the funding profile. Make money for the firm and get them back into the creative/innovative position they were used to. Then he realized Tom's motivation was not about the firm and Peter was too far in to stop it."

"What did he do?"

"He told Tom he was having second thoughts and wanted to scale back the design. Talk to the client and negotiate a different deal. Tom threatened to expose him for disobeying the order of the CEO."

"Are you kidding me? This would sound like high school stuff, except that it is blackmail."

"I wish I was kidding. But, that's not the best part."

"It gets better? Go on."

"As you can imagine, Peter wants to take steps to fire Tom. He's coming to see you about it. To come clean," Mark said, shaking his head back and forth before continuing. "I didn't realize what a nervous guy that Peter is. He needs medication before he has a nervous breakdown, or the job is getting to him."

"He isn't normally all that nervous. He is a good guy with a lot going on. I can't believe I actually thought he could be capable of embezzling money. I should have trusted him more than that. Going against David's direction in the spirit of helping the firm is one thing. Embezzling money is in an entirely different league."

She was quiet for a second, trying to think about the next move. Tired after a long week, clear thoughts weren't easy. She could say the same for Mark. He looked drained and had dark circles under his eyes. Lindsay continued, "We knew this was going to get complicated. Let's take the weekend to think about what we know and where to go from here. You and I can get back together Monday morning. We'll figure it out. Hang in there." She tried to be positive.

"Yeah, let's talk Monday. We need to rethink our strategy. We can't keep operating under the guise of a process improvement initiative. Someone is going to figure this out and jeopardize any chance we have of finding out what's going on. I'm tired and going home."

"I think that's a good idea. You look like you've had a rough week. Get some rest."

He left Lindsay's office and stopped by the conference room, packed his briefcase, locked the conference room door, and left for the weekend.

CHAPTER 128

It was late Friday afternoon and Lindsay didn't want to go home alone. At least, not yet. She wanted some company, maybe a drink with a friend. Her first thought was Sam. She could always count on her.

Sam answered when Lindsay's number popped up on her cellphone. Coastal Grille, glass of wine, fifteen minutes. Sam's mother was in town so she couldn't stay out long, but she had time for a quick happy hour. She was cooking dinner for her mom and promised she wouldn't be late.

Lindsay politely declined an invitation to join them. One drink and a little social interaction with her best friend would fill the void. The week had been long and she wanted to get to bed early. The next morning, she was going to the gym and then shopping for something to wear for her date with Adam.

They were barely seated when Lindsay broached the possibility of what she thought was an exceptional idea. "I've been working with our CPA lately and I've been thinking of you. He is really cute. Intelligent. Works hard. I think you might like him. What do you think about me bringing him in for a drink one night next week so you can meet?"

"No Lindsay. That's the last thing I need right now. I am way too busy at this restaurant to start dating."

"Oh, but you can provide advice to me about dating. When will you have the time? Since you're planning on keeping this restaurant, when will be the right time?"

"Oh great. Now that you're dating, you've all of sudden become cupid. An expert." Sam replied with a sigh and roll of her eyes.

"No, I just think he is a great guy. And he's single and charming, with a good job. Might be quite the catch. Isn't it worth at least meeting him? I won't say anything. I'll just ask him to join me for a drink to talk about the work he is doing with us. Oh come on. No pressure. You have nothing to lose. Please," she begged.

Another roll of the eyes, "I know that look. You're not going to let this go, are you?"

Lindsay smiled and shrugged. "Probably not. What do you say?"

"Oh all right. I know when I'm beaten down by you. But swear you won't tell him anything about this. It's just a drink between the two of you," she pleaded.

"Agreed. I won't say a word." She showed her mischievous grin.

They continued talking for the next hour before Sam looked at her watch. She was going to be late. She offered Lindsay one last chance to join them. She thanked her for the invitation, they hugged in front of the restaurant, and walked in opposite directions to their cars.

It didn't take long for Lindsay to get home, drop her keys on the foyer table and head straight to her bedroom for a pair of yoga pants and a faded college sweatshirt.

Dinner consisted of a salad and lean piece of chicken. She smiled. *Eating salads, going shopping, diet and appearance, hmmm.*

She went to bed early and attempted to read, but was distracted by thoughts drifting to Adam. She was excited about the next night. She gave up on the book. Adam was her last thought before turning out the lights.

CHAPTER 129

It was finally happening. Maybe even a new beginning. The sun shone brightly through Lindsay's bedroom window and she woke to the sound of her coffee maker and aroma of fresh java. It was barely daylight and she was excited about getting up. Having an early start on what she hoped would be a fantastic day.

After a trip to the gym, she drove to the mall. It was probably one of the last standing malls since city centers had taken over. It was not very crowded for a Saturday. Lindsay spent most of her time in a couple of boutique like stores trying on almost everything in her size, looking for the perfect dress.

She considered black, but thought it might be a little boring and too traditional for this date. She considered blue to enhance the color of her eyes, but didn't like the shape of the dress. Red was a power color, but she didn't feel that either. She finally picked out an elegant, but subtly sexy dress the color of merlot. It was perfect. She laughed and shook her head, thinking she could not possibly be so concerned about what she was wearing on a date. *Really?*

She looked at her watch while waiting patiently at the cash register, shocked at how the time had flown. She must have tried on every dress in the store that came in her size. She couldn't even remember a time she had shopped for hours. She hated shopping. *What was happening to her?* Oh, she knew.

It was lunchtime and searching for the right dress left her famished. She walked out of the store and started towards a nearby restaurant that served fresh organic seafood salads. She loved the food and had been thinking about it since leaving the house.

On her stroll towards lunch, she spotted Patrick's wife Stephanie looking at a clothes rack outside of a major department store. From a distance, she noticed how good she looked, radiant actually. About that time, Stephanie looked up and saw her walking in her direction and a big smile spread across her face. They moved towards one another and hugged and held on with an intensity of missing an old friend.

Stephanie spoke first, in an excited tone, "How are you? We haven't seen you in such a long time. I have thought about you so much lately."

"I'm good. I've been thinking a lot about you too."

"It's funny we ran into each other, I just told Patrick to talk to you about coming over for dinner when his schedule improves."

"I would love that," Lindsay paused and cocked her head sideways. "How are you feeling? You look really good."

"I'm doing well. I've been a little slow getting back into the swing of things since my procedure, but I feel great now. And, I've been working out more and eating better. I hope it's paying off. "

"Well it certainly shows. You look fantastic. Patrick has been really worried about you. He's had a tough time thinking about much else lately."

Stephanie laughed and waved off the comment. "Oh, he is such a worrier. I'm doing fine. He has enough on his plate at the office without worrying about me, too," she said, and changed the subject, "Back to dinner. We need to have you over soon. We would have already done it, but Patrick has been traveling so much lately."

They talked about scheduling a get together and promised to be in touch before saying goodbye. Lindsay couldn't get over how good she looked. Knowing Patrick and their son, Andrew, she probably had received all the love and caring she needed to nurse her through the past few weeks.

CHAPTER 130

As Lindsay was making her way to the restaurant, thinking about the seafood salad, her phone rang. Sam wanted her to meet her and her mother for lunch. Since she hadn't seen her mother in awhile, she felt like she should accept the invite. So much for the seafood salad.

She left the mall and drove to a nearby cafe. She walked in and they waved her over to the table. Hugs all around. Sam's mother looked great. She had hardly aged since the last time she saw her. They laughed and talked nonstop about fashion, shopping, dieting and men. The subject of organizational development, human behavior, or business in general didn't come up. They spared Sam's mother.

The lunch and laughter was a nice distraction from thinking about work and the anxious feeling she was getting about her upcoming date. Nerves about a second date. *Really? Who is this person?*

When Sam's mom asked about dating, Lindsay responded carefully, "I've been on a date with this guy I met through work."

"Oh, that's exciting. Tell me about him."

"He's a consultant. Owns this firm we hired to help us out. Let's see, he is handsome, intelligent, charming so there must be something wrong with him. We'll see," she shrugged, crossing her fingers under the table.

Not wanting to talk love life with her mother, Sam said, "You mentioned seeing Patrick's wife. How is Stephanie?"

"She looks fabulous. You wouldn't know she had been ill. She's really something."

"Did she ever say what was wrong?"

"No. And, Patrick has been so secretive about it, I was afraid to ask. I didn't want to come across as prying."

"That whole thing is odd. Patrick usually tells you everything."

"I know. But, he says it's a female thing and I could tell it made him uncomfortable to talk about. Even a little bit."

"Well, tell him I asked about them. And, get him into the restaurant for dinner or a happy hour. I would love to see him," Sam said, thrilled there would be no discussion about her own love life.

CHAPTER 131

When Lindsay got into her car, her mind wandered back to Stephanie and her illness. Guilt struck. She should have insisted. Visited her while she was sick. Mentioning it to Patrick, he had said Stephanie wasn't feeling up to seeing anyone, but he would pass along her well wishes. Keep her in the loop. They would get together as soon as she was better. Lindsay didn't want to push or be intrusive so she had dropped it. Still guilt struck.

Stephanie made a comment about Patrick's travel that just popped into her head. Had she heard her correctly? She must have misunderstood. She really needed to pay closer attention.

You would think she could have mastered the art of listening after finishing Adam's workshop. She smiled, thinking maybe she could get a one-on-one refresher.

CHAPTER 132

He looked even more flawless than the last time she saw him, if that was even possible. Adam stepped in her front door with a bouquet of dark chocolates, filled with assorted cremes and nuts. An Italian delight. How did he know?

He handed her the bouquet. "These are for you. I know you have a special connection with dark chocolate, so I thought you might like these. They are exquisite with a full bodied red. I just happened to have one of those, too," he said with a grin, as he pulled the bottle of wine from behind his back.

"How did you know one of my worst, and best, vices is dark chocolate?" Lindsay pursed her lips as she was thinking back to a time she may have told him.

"You talked about it the first time I saw you at Sam's restaurant. The night I was there with my sister. The topic of dessert came up and you said something about dark chocolate being your divine obsession."

Lindsay laughed and her face turned flush. She couldn't help but show how much this meant to her. *Oh boy, a man that listens.* She said, "Thank you. It was very thoughtful. I love it."

He smiled and nodded, "I hope you enjoy them." He stepped back and took a long look before saying, "My, you are absolutely stunning."

"And, you are handsome," she blurted out before thinking. *Ugh! Did I really just say that? It must sound so cheesy.*

"Thank you," he nodded and bowed slightly.

Recovering from what she hoped would be her only rookie move of the night, she asked, "Since our reservations are not for an hour, why don't we open the bottle of wine and have a glass before dinner?" She read the label on the back and continued, "It sounds fantastic. I would love to share it with you."

Adam looked at his watch. "If you think we have time to make it to the restaurant by our reservation."

"It's only fifteen minutes from here. I think we're good. I'll get the glasses?" She paused for agreement, and handed him the wine opener on her way to the cabinet, leaving behind a hint of a familiar perfume he inhaled deeply while trying not to be obvious.

They sat at opposite ends of the couch and exchanged easy conversation. Lindsay talked about their progress at work and Adam talked about spending the past week with a new client in San Diego. She didn't realize he flew a private plane almost everywhere he went. He had failed to mention that part before. *Easy on the eyes, charming, and a lucrative businessman, with an eight passenger Leer jet at his disposal. And, not a big ego. Oh yeah, he is definitely a serial killer.*

Adam attempted to give her words his full attention, but his mind kept wandering to thoughts of how all this made him feel. They had only been on one official date, but when they worked together he had observed her powerful presence and strength balanced with the ability to be empathetic and vulnerable. He found her demeanor intoxicating.

He didn't know exactly when it started, but he was already beginning to develop feelings. He was trying to remain cautious, guardedly optimistic. He kept telling himself they needed to get to know each other fully before any possibility of advancing the relationship. The last thing he wanted was to conjure up false perceptions and have a bad reality set in, leading to disappointment for either of them.

Adam worked hard and was dedicated to his profession. He believed in what he was doing and the possibilities of changing people's lives. It excited him and he thought he saw glimmers of the same in Lindsay. Only time, and time together, would tell. He was looking forward to it. He wondered, *is this too good to be true?*

* * * * * * * * * *

Adam and Lindsay continued talking for the next hour while drinking the bottle of wine. They weren't paying attention to time. It was cozy and comfortable, yet exciting and neither of them wanted to change a thing. The time escaped them.

He finally looked at his watch and said, "Oh wow, we missed our dinner reservation." He stood up quickly and said while pulling his phone out of his jacket pocket, "Why don't I see if we can get a later one?"

"Why don't we eat here? If you aren't afraid of my cooking, that is. I'll bet you didn't know cooking is one of my favorite things to do. You can be the judge, but if I can say so myself, I have skills," she said with a smile before continuing, "I can throw a couple of salads together and tuna steaks on the grill. I bought fresh tuna earlier today. I was planning on preparing it tomorrow, but I would love to cook for you. I'm really enjoying the wine and company. Are you brave enough for my cooking?"

Adam replied with a hint of pink in his cheeks, "Well, I'm a bit embarrassed since I asked you to dinner and now you're cooking for me. I will accept under one condition."

"What is the condition?"

"You go out with me again. I'll take you to a special dinner at one of my very favorite spots. Is it a deal?"

"Deal. Now, if you'll excuse me, I need to light the grill and get the salads started."

"What can I do? Let me help. I'll pour the wine and light the grill." He stood and walked through the french doors leading to the patio.

She was in the kitchen preparing two caesar salads when he returned. He was watching her move around the kitchen in an orderly fashion, swift and graceful. She glanced over and smiled at him watching her work.

He smiled back and said, "You do know what you're doing in the kitchen. I'm quite impressed. Is there anything I can help you with?"

"Have a seat and enjoy your wine. I don't have much more to do. I'm hoping you like your tuna steak rare?"

"Rare is perfect."

"Good. I had them marinating in a new ginger and soy marinade I discovered. I think you'll like it, if you like asian food."

"Asian is great."

They set the table together and stepped out on the patio to finish grilling. They talked and laughed. Adam had a calming nature and did not appear to take things too seriously during the workshop, but she hadn't realized the extent of his wonderful sense of humor until now. Warm hearted and comical. *Could it get any better than this?* She stopped herself, inward admonishment to remain cautious.

They ate dinner by candlelight with jazz playing softly in the background. The atmosphere of a romantic evening with a wonderful man was an unfamiliar feeling for Lindsay.

After dinner, she served coffee in the living room. They shared dark chocolate from the bouquet and continued talking. It was after 11:00 when Adam reluctantly said he had to get home. He was flying back to San Diego the next morning and had to get some sleep.

He stood and said, "I had a great time tonight. And yes, you are quite the cook."

"It's hard to mess up a tuna steak on the grill," she laughed.

"I'll be back in town next Friday. Are you available for dinner at that favorite restaurant next Saturday night?"

"I am. That would be wonderful."

"Then, it's a date. Are you up for a surprise?"

"I am. Sounds intriguing."

Lindsay walked Adam to the door. They experienced the first sign of awkwardness between them. He hesitated and looked back at her before saying, "Can I call you while I'm away next week?"

She answered quietly, "I would like that."

He kissed her on the cheek. "I'll call you. Thank you for tonight." With that, he walked to his car. He looked back and waved before getting in.

She closed the door and said quietly as she leaned against it, "On boy, I am in trouble. This was so not supposed to happen."

CHAPTER 133

Lindsay and Mark met early Monday to discuss the questioning process that would take place later that morning. After a couple of legal questions, he ended the conversation with a "wish me luck" and went to the conference room.

The last senior manager was interviewed late in the afternoon. Mark wiped his eyes and leaned back in his chair to think about what he heard. The answer had to be there, somewhere. Where was the connection, he kept asking himself.

He had a meeting with Patrick in the conference room after all the interviews were conducted. Mark cut to the chase, "Just so I'm clear, the only people with the authority to authorize payments for the firm are David, the Deputy Comptroller, and you. Is that correct?"

"Yes. We keep a tight control. In fact, most of the payments are authorized by me. We only turn them over to David when I'm out of the office and my Deputy is out of the office. Why do you ask?" Patrick asked.

"Just trying to make sure I understand the process and any vulnerabilities. It sounds like you have a strict control on the authorization," Mark tried to sound casual.

"Yes, we do. We've talked about the only weakness in the system. The signature approval process to move to the next transactional step is too flexible. But that takes money and reprogramming to make a system fix. My long term plan is to budget for it and fund when we can."

There was silence for a moment as Patrick stared at Mark, trying to think of the right words. Finally, he just asked, "Mark, what's the problem? I sense there is more than you are saying? Are you telling me everything?"

Mark shrugged, "I'm trying to tie together some final loose ends. That's all. I have found a couple of vulnerabilities within your accounting processes. I agree with you. I recommend tightening up some of the controls. Continue to restrict the number of people having transactional approval in your financial systems. I also agree the system needs to be reprogrammed so each transactional step cannot process without the required initials. I saw a number of postings without them," he said attempting to sound a little nonchalant.

"Really? Well, that concerns me. I've been clear about the requirement for initials. You didn't find any signs of intentional wrongdoing, did you?" Patrick asked.

He hesitated, "No, just looking for steps to prevent any future opportunities for misuse or hackers. There are a few other measures you may want to put in place, institute some minor process changes. I'll help you with that."

Patrick's face softened. He smiled, "Thank you. I'm sorry if I appear defensive. I don't mean to be," he continued, "I should appreciate the feedback. We're always interested in improving processes that are vulnerable. Have you discussed this with David?"

"Not yet. I have to report out to him when I'm finished," Mark answered slightly uneasy by the increasing number of lies.

"I would like to be present for the meeting with David. Since it's my Department, I think I should be there. Be part of the solution and make the necessary changes. I'm assuming my presence at the meeting is okay?"

"I don't think there is a problem. I'll let you know," Mark answered.

Mark thanked him for taking the time to meet and Patrick offered his support if he had any additional questions. Mark made a few notes before continuing.

CHAPTER 134

Lindsay stuck her head in the door and interrupted Mark's note taking. "Hi. How is it going? Are you feeling better?"

He smiled up at her. "I'm not sure. I had the strangest conversation with Patrick. We were like strangers. Is he okay?"

Lindsay thought before answering. She didn't want to say too much at the risk of being disloyal to her close friend and colleague. "He is frustrated that he didn't know about this audit up front. And, his wife has been ill, but she is doing much better now."

"I'm sorry to hear that. Is she okay?"

"She seems to be. I ran into her when I was out shopping last weekend. Appeared to be doing really well. Based on Patrick's concern, I was a little surprised. As her husband, I guess he has the right to be overly cautious and worried. I probably would be too."

"Yeah, I've never been married, but I can see how it would be difficult. Trying to deal with a partner's sickness and everyday life. I've watched it impact a close buddy of mine. It can really be draining."

"Patrick is very devoted to his wife and son. Stephanie has been undergoing some treatment out of town and he has been with her every step of the way while trying to keep things going here at work." She continued, "Stephanie mentioned something about him worrying about her and traveling with work lately. I guess I didn't realize he had been traveling that much. I have been caught up in my own stuff and didn't pay enough attention," she said with a frown.

"Where has she been receiving treatment?" Mark inquired.

"I'm not sure actually. I think it's in Philly or outside of Philly. It's really been tough on them going back and forth, in and out of town. As I mentioned, Patrick hasn't been at work as much lately, but it's been fairly seamless since his Deputy, Frank has been covering. I guess I just didn't realize some of this was work travel. Shame on me for not being a better friend."

"What do you know about Frank Anderson?"

"Dedicated and hard working. I've known him for awhile. He is a good guy." A light went on in Lindsay's head and she abruptly asked, "You don't think Frank could have anything to do with this, do you?"

"Do you?" Mark inquired.

"He can be introverted and keeps to himself, but I can't see it."

"I haven't discovered anything implicating him. I don't have any reason to believe he is behind this. I'm just covering all the bases," Mark reassured her.

"No, I've worked with him for years. I can't believe he could be involved in this."

"There are only three people that have the kind of access necessary to approve payments. We've ruled out each one of them. That leads us back to the possibility of someone else having one of their passwords or the expertise to tap into the financial systems. I've interviewed everyone. Nothing. I need to go over my notes again and figure out what I've missed, if anything," he said with frustration in his voice.

Lindsay sighed and urged, "Keep looking. I don't want to put the pressure on you, but we need to solve it. Time is becoming a strong enemy here."

"Lindsay, I hate to say this, but the possibility exists that we may not solve it."

"Keep looking. We have to," she said emotionless as she walked back to her office.

Mark spent the next hour reviewing his notes. He thought about Lindsay's comments as he continued reading through pages and pages. He, once again, reviewed the transactions and compared them to dates and the location on the travel documents. There was an interesting pattern. Then, he spotted it. Why hadn't he noticed it before?

CHAPTER 135

This couldn't possibly be happening. Mark wouldn't have believed it if he hadn't seen it with his own eyes. Thinking he had missed something, he took one more look at the evidence. There had to be a logical explanation, something he just wasn't getting.

Rapidly flipping through the pages back and forth, stopping only to re-examine the pertinent information, the answer came up the same. He was left with accepting that he hadn't made a mistake. There was finally an explanation and it was one of the very worst possible scenarios. He let it sink in for a moment before forcing himself out of the chair.

He hated what he was about to do. He walked to David's office and stood in the doorway. David was expecting him. When he looked up, he hung up the phone and motioned him in.

"We need to talk." Mark said, closing the door behind him.

The proof, hearing the words out loud, David almost lost his balance and forced himself to sit. He latched on to the item of furniture closest to him and slid down slowly. The color drained from his face and his lips quivered. Without saying a word, he leaned forward and placed his head in his hands. He said nothing, but his upper body shook.

Wanting to give David a moment and some semblance of privacy, he walked to the window overlooking the city and stared at the lights below, not saying or doing anything. Once David regained his composure and was ready to talk, he asked how, and why?

Mark moved back to the sitting area and sat across from him. He spent the next hour sharing the details of what he had discovered.

"Is there any possibility you're wrong about this?" David questioned, pleaded.

"No, it's all there. I've examined and re-examined the evidence. The pieces connect like a carefully crafted puzzle. I don't know why I didn't see it before." He looked up at the ceiling and let out a deep breath. "Yes, I do."

David stood and walked over to his desk. He said quietly, "Why would they do this? And, how could they have been so careless?"

Mark had a puzzled look on his face. He stood up and walked over to stand by David. "You know what you have to do now."

"Yeah, I know. I just wasn't expecting this." David picked up the telephone. He hesitated for a moment, and then placed the call knowing there was no other option.

CHAPTER 136

David was standing in the lobby waiting. He labeled them the minute they walked in the door, even though they were wearing clothes similar to his. Maybe the clothes were a cheaper version or maybe not, but the men had that cop look. They did the usual protocol of shaking hands and introducing themselves, like this was any other meeting.

He didn't say much as he led them to the elevator, through the maze of cubicles and into his office that suddenly felt suffocatingly hot. He looked at the thermostat, but realized he was the only one uncomfortable. He would suck it up and get on with it.

The investigators spent the next couple of hours reading and looking through documents, and questioning Mark's evidence. It wasn't all that difficult to figure out who did it and what they did once all the documents were laid out in front of them. They were confident they had enough to make an arrest.

They gathered the originals of the evidence without saying anything. They systematically placed reams of papers and file folders in a medium size box to take back to the police station.

David watched them and contemplated how to approach the subject of timing. It wasn't worth strategizing about how to say it. They could think whatever they wanted, so he simply asked, "Can we make the arrest this evening? I'd like to get this over with."

The Lead Investigator grunted, "Not tonight. There is way too much left to do. And, the DA was clear there is no way we can be ready tomorrow without pulling an all nighter."

He almost begged, "Can we at least do this early in the morning or at the end of the day?"

The officer closed the box top and started to speak in his no nonsense tone, until he looked over at David. He responded quietly, "We'll see what we can do. I'll call you first thing in the morning? How's that?"

"Thank you. I appreciate it. I'm hoping for as little public display as possible."

"I understand." He glanced at him, picking up the box and telling him how the arrest would take place the next day.

David offered to show them out, but they swiftly gathered their things and politely declined. He walked them to the door, watching them leave and hesitating before turning back to his office. It was different this time, he felt like he was entering his own version of hell. It's where it would all take place in less than twelve hours.

David thought about her. It was late in the day and most people had left for the evening. He wondered if Lindsay was still in the office, but he couldn't call to find out. He couldn't face her, not now. He needed time and the following day would have to be soon enough.

"So, it'll be tomorrow morning before my firm falls apart. Before my…" He didn't finish the sentence, shaking his head and murmuring, "Oh well."

* * * * * * * * * *

David paused and looked out the window at the skyscraper across the way. *Why couldn't he be a doctor in a nice little family practice, working in that building?* He felt numb and dizzy with this new information swirling around in his head. He sat down behind his desk, rubbing his temples and stretching his head from side to side. He finally looked at Mark and spoke barely above a whisper, "I'm having a hard time here. Never in a million years would I have thought this. It feels so… personal."

Mark murmured quietly, "I'm sorry. I can only imagine what you're going through. It certainly isn't what I expected and I really wanted to be wrong."

David stood and walked over to the bar and poured them both a drink. He handed Mark a glass of the amber liquid without saying a word. He dropped into one of his chairs in the sitting area, ripping the tie from around his neck, and throwing it on the chair next to him. He unbuttoned the top button of his shirt and stared downward, resting his arms on the knees of his perfectly creased pant legs.

Mark didn't know what he could possibly say to make it any better. He sat quietly for a time, just being there, staring into his drink and swirling it between his two palms until he glanced at his watch and winced. He sat in silence for a few more minutes before gulping down every last drop in his glass. He whispered, "I saw you the other day. Heading to an empty cubicle, and for a slight moment, I actually wondered if it was you."

David mustered half of a smile. "I was helping a friend. Saving his son from an embarrassing situation. Let me leave it at that."

"Well, I can't believe I let my imagination run, even for a second." Standing up, he placed a hand on David's shoulder and said somberly, "I'm heading home to get some rest and you need to do the same. Tomorrow will be a tough day." He walked towards the door and turned around, "David, I am really sorry. I'll do whatever I can to help. You know you won't go through this alone."

He looked up with a forced smile, nodded and thanked Mark for his work. He continued to sit for awhile, staring at an empty picture hangar on the wall. He didn't focus on anything but that picture hangar until the sound of his cell phone startled him.

* * * * * * * * * *

His wife was calling to find out why he wasn't home for their dinner plans. He sensed irritation in her voice but it didn't matter. She would understand soon enough.

It didn't take but two words for her to realize that something wasn't right. She heard it in his voice and asked, "What on earth is wrong with you? You sound terrible."

"It's because I feel terrible. I've had one of the worst days of my life. I just found out who did it." he said quietly.

"Oh my God, who?" her voice increased to a higher octave.

"I don't want to get into it until I get home. I've got to get out of here. I'm suffocating. I'll see you in a few minutes."

He hung up the phone and was overcome by emotions he didn't easily share. He hadn't cried since his mother died so many years earlier. He was overcome by a feeling he didn't quite understand. Actually, he did understand.

He grabbed his coat and walked swiftly to the door. He looked back and thought about all the times they had shared in this office. He let out a deep breath, turned off the light, and locked the door. He would like to think tomorrow would be better, but it wouldn't. It would get much worse.

CHAPTER 137

David slowly got out of bed the next morning without the noise of a singing alarm. He didn't need it since he hadn't slept and tossed and turned most of the night. He recalled the last twelve hours, ending with driving into the garage, telling his wife what happened, and going directly to bed.

He dreaded, no he couldn't imagine the day ahead. After a shower and shave, he glanced in the mirror. His eyes were puffy and dark, and he had that overly tired, but not sleepy feeling. He ran his hands through wet hair and combed it, deciding wet would have to do.

Having a hard time accepting what he now knew to be the truth, he continued to search for reasons or explanations, but he couldn't come up with any. He was in a fog while going through the motions of getting dressed.

His wife walked into the bedroom and hesitated in the doorway, looking at the wonderful man she had spent so much of her life with. It killed her to see him hurt by someone he cared deeply about. She slowly approached him and straightened his tie and gently let him know that his shoes didn't match and he had forgotten his belt. She had a sad smile on her face as she pulled him close. They maintained the connection for a moment before he stepped back and sweetly kissed her lips, saying he had to go to his early morning meeting with the police.

He backed out of the garage and rain spit all over his car. *Why was the weather always dreadful on an already depressing day?* As if the rain wasn't enough, the tree limbs in his front yard were swaying back and forth and the sky was void of any color. He frowned at the irony of the day being gray. The kind of day to trudge through, never relive, and pretend it never happened.

* * * * * * * * * *

Arriving early with very little traffic at that hour, he parked his car and ran for the entranceway. The wind turned his umbrella inside out and he muttered some words better left unspoken.

He met Mark in the cafe and grabbed very tall coffees to get them through the hours that would follow. David mumbled that he needed something much stronger and Mark just smiled and patted him on the back, pressing the elevator button with his other hand.

As they had planned, they were in the office before the others and the suites were dark. It was early, the police were late, and David was drumming his fingers on the conference table when he wasn't walking around the room looking out the window, and fiddling with papers on his desk. He looked at his watch several times, anxious for their arrival and the ability to get this over with as quickly as possible.

It was going to be a miserable day for so many people he loved and cared about. He let out a deep breath and stared out over the city, continuing to check the time every few minutes. He almost forgot about the coffee cup in his hand, letting the liquid become lukewarm. It didn't taste good anyway and he was fairly certain his stomach couldn't handle it. He frowned and dropped the cup in his trashcan and returned to the window. His thoughts kept going back to Lindsay. He wondered when she would arrive. What would he say to her when they faced one another? He hated this.

Mark continued to sit silently at the conference table, looking over some notes about the investigation. He finally broke the silence by asking, "Have you talked to Lindsay at all?"

"No. I think it's better this way," his voice trailed off and his tone indicated he was in no mood to discuss it or anything else.

The police finally arrived, saying they had a few glitches with their paperwork and procedures, but were ready to go. They spent the next hour going over the final details of what was about to happen.

CHAPTER 138

The traffic was still fairly light in the building when David made the call. His knees were shaky as he walked slowly to his desk and picked up the phone. He took a deep breath as it continued to ring, dreading to hear the voice on the other end, almost hoping they wouldn't answer. As he was about to hang up, he heard them speak. He didn't say anything other than he needed to see them in his office right away and that it was urgent. David dropped the phone on the cradle and said nothing.

The second he walked through David's office door, his smile disappeared. His face turned red and his body temperature rose to the point of sweat instantly emerging from his pores. He attempted to wipe his forehead before it was obvious to anyone else.

David barely looked at him as he silently motioned to sit as the police officer took control. The officer went through the normal procedures to include reading him his rights and telling him he had the right to an attorney.

He dropped his head, barely acknowledging that he was listening, and mumbled slightly above a whisper, "I need my attorney." He looked up at David and pleaded, "I'm so sorry. I was going to pay the money back. I was desperate."

David shot him a look that asked for an explanation, but didn't wait for an answer. He turned and stared out the window without looking back.

The officer stopped the alleged offender from speaking, reminding him of his rights. With that, he was handcuffed and taken away.

David was left standing with his back to the door, refusing to let anyone see his eyes. He could at least control that.

CHAPTER 139

He stared straight ahead and watched the floor numbers change on the elevator, hoping it would never make it to the ground floor. He was accompanied by two men in uniform that stood quietly on both sides of him. How would anyone ever understand or believe what happened when it didn't even sound right to him? To rationalize that it wasn't embezzling, but borrowing, with a plan to transfer the money back to the firm sounded lame. But it was true, and he just needed more time to…He was finished and his life was over.

How did this get so out of control? What would it mean for the family? They were no longer safe. And, what would that monster do and who would he go after now?

The elevator doors opened and the law enforcement officials escorted him towards the front door. He hoped no one would see him, especially her. She meant the world to him and she would never forgive him. But, why should she?

His head remained down and he felt like they were in slow motion and the walk was taking forever. He glanced up when they almost reached the doorway and he saw the one person he had hoped to avoid.

Their eyes met only long enough for his face to show sorrow, mouth "I'm sorry", and then he looked away. There were no words and he stared at his feet knowing he couldn't endure seeing her like this along with everything else flooding through his mind and crashing down around him. There was nothing he could say that would make her understand anyway. She was the most compassionate person he knew and if she wouldn't understand he certainly couldn't count on anyone else.

Desperation had messed up everything and now more lives would be ruined. What would he say to his wife, his son? Then, his face flushed hot as he thought about the other problem, the fear of the danger that remained for those he loved. He couldn't be locked up, he had to stay out, he was running out of time, and he was the only one that could do this. The only one that could save them all.

CHAPTER 140

Lindsay's first thought was confusion and then shock that stopped her. Before her, accompanied by uniforms, stood her trusted friend. It was Patrick. *All this time, it was Patrick?*

She started towards him, but stopped herself, watching him walk out the door. There had to be some mistake. It didn't make any since. In all this time, beating herself up for not being transparent about the investigation and being angry with David for keeping it from him, she never imagined Patrick could be the one they were looking for. Not once, not even for a millisecond. Sure, he hadn't been himself lately, a little less reachable and slightly more distant over the last couple of months, but this. She knew him and there was no way he could do something like this. *Why Patrick?*

And that's how she discovered it was him. That's what happened. That's how Lindsay remembered it.

Nothing would ever be the same. The firm would be broken. The people in it would be different and so would she. If she couldn't believe in Patrick, she couldn't believe in anyone. How could he?

What now?

CHAPTER 141

Lindsay hesitated long enough to watch them exit the building, her dear friend in handcuffs. His life…Her life…

That's all the time she allotted to pity. *What was she missing?*

Something was terribly wrong. There were illogical pieces that didn't fit together. He didn't break rules and he certainly wouldn't commit a crime. He didn't even speed when she urged him to go faster, saying "it's against the law."

When slightly gray area decisions were discussed at work, he would always say, "we need to do the right thing", or "we shouldn't take any action that we are afraid to stand up and say we did." Heck, he didn't even like to be around people that talked about other people.

This didn't make any sense. So many questions. Her thoughts shifted to David and the devastation he would feel. She had to see him immediately. Then, she stopped herself. He already knew.

She walked briskly to the elevator as the doors were opening and slammed the button with her palm. Her movement was swift and deliberate as she stopped by her office and dropped her coat and briefcase. Without saying a word to anyone, she went to David's office.

Walking to his door, she stopped, accepted confirmation by the way he was entranced at a view of the city that, yes, he already knew. She drew in a deep breath before barging through the threshold. What did he know? How long had he known and why didn't he tell her?

She interrupted him, trying to keep her tone even, "David, what's going on here? I just saw Patrick being taken out in handcuffs."

He turned towards her with hands in his pockets, but didn't look her in the eyes. He simply stated, "It was Patrick. He was the one embezzling money from the firm."

She shook her head from side to side before she responded, "No way. That can't possibly be true. It must be a mistake. He wouldn't do it."

"Lindsay, he confessed. He did it. And let's face it, he certainly had the means." He turned back to the window.

She walked closer to David, to challenge him. "David, look at me. You know he wouldn't do this. You and I both know it. We have worked with him for years. You know him better than that. He is the most trustworthy guy you know."

"He did it," he said, as he turned around to face her.

"How did you find out?" She paused, staring at him before asking, "When did you find out?"

"I found out yesterday. The evidence supported it. I didn't want to believe it, but it's true."

"You found out yesterday and you didn't tell me? Prepare me? I've been in this with you from the beginning, leading the investigation. You don't think you should have told me? How could you?" She raised her voice and felt the anger rising. She tried to calm herself before going on, "Who else knows?"

"Just Mark."

"Just Mark," she stated with emphasis on his name. She paused, trying to manage her anger. Stepping close enough to be in David's face, refraining from the urge to do bodily harm, she said, "You and Mark discussed it and didn't think you should include me? Your Legal Counsel. So much for trust. And what about Mark? He and I have been discussing this every day and every night, and he didn't think I had the right to know?"

"Don't blame Mark. He wanted to tell you, to call you. It was my decision."

"Don't you think you should have?" She raised her voice even louder, no longer worrying about self-control, "I walk through the lobby of our building this morning, and I find one of my best friends and closest colleagues being walked out in handcuffs. You don't think you should have prepared me for that?" She paused and continued, "After all we have been to each other, you didn't trust me enough to tell me ahead of time, prepare me?"

"I'm sorry."

"You're sorry. You're sorry?" She lowered her voice to a whisper, "That is all you have to say to me?"

She stared and waited, shaking her head. David didn't answer.

She walked to the door and turned around to look back at him. "So much for our executive training - relationship building, communication. Oh, and the best part. And, probably the key to it all - trust. You are doing a terrific job at it." She left without saying another word.

CHAPTER 142

Lindsay stormed down the hall ignoring the buzz around her. She went back to her office, grabbed her coat and told Marcy she was going out. She didn't know when she would be back. Take a message.

She didn't waste any time and didn't stop to speak to anyone, running down the stairs and slamming through the exit door on the side of the building. Reaching her car, she yanked on the door, and dropped her body on the seat. Slapping her hands against the steering wheel, she felt like crying but was not going to let that happen. Get it together. She had to see him, needed answers, and needed them now. She hit the power button and the second the engine purred, she gunned it out of her parking space.

Lindsay drove faster than she should, but it didn't matter. The only thing she cared about was getting to him. There had to be an explanation and he needed a lawyer.

Then she thought of Stephanie and Andrew. She didn't know what to think. Did they know? Did they need money? Why didn't he come to her? If he was in trouble, she could have helped.

Speeding down the highway, continuing to deny the possibility he could have done this and thinking about plausible explanations, she stopped herself. She had to face the truth. He was different these days. Could he have been responsible for this?

The rest of the ride was a blur. A million conflicting thoughts about his innocence, his guilt, his family, David. She could have helped. She could have… *Stop thinking and just drive.*

CHAPTER 143

It only took Lindsay a few minutes to get to the prison visitor's parking lot. She put her car in park, cut the engine, and jumped out. She didn't know what she would say or do, but doing or saying nothing was certainly not an option.

Walking briskly into the building, Stephanie was the first person she spotted. Standing in front of her was the look of terror and a tear stained face with mascara saturating the newly formed bags under her eyes.

She saw Lindsay and rushed over to her. "Lindsay, what is going on here? What did Patrick do?" She broke down and struggled to speak through tears, shaking her head, "They won't tell me anything and I don't know what to do."

Lindsay put her arms around Stephanie and attempted to comfort her. She didn't have any answers either, but she could provide her support. "I'm here. I'll do what I can. But first, you need to answer some questions for me. Have you called your attorney? Do you know anything, *anything* at all about this?" Lindsay stepped back to look at her.

"Yes, I called Sean Mack and he is on his way. I got a call to meet Patrick here. Something about Patrick embezzling funds from the firm. That's all I know. Lindsay, he wouldn't do that. You know him. He just wouldn't do that," she answered shaking her head back and forth.

Lindsay hated to continue, "I didn't want to believe it either, but Stephanie, he confessed. And, Patrick has been different lately. Have you noticed changes in his behavior?"

"He's been more stressed than usual. He hasn't been sleeping well. When I asked him about it, he said stress at work. I didn't think much of it."

"He was more distant lately. I thought it was about you. I thought he was worried about you."

"Worried about me. What do you mean?"

"Your health. He said you were sick and the two of you were going out of town to get the best possible treatment. But he wouldn't tell me anything."

"What? Lindsay, I haven't been receiving treatment out of town and I'm not sick. I mean I had a little outpatient surgery and wasn't quite myself for a few weeks, but nothing serious. And, you know I would have wanted him to tell you if it had been serious."

Lindsay thought before asking, "Where has he been going, and why?"

"He said he was going to Philadelphia for work."

"Stephanie, we don't have anything going on in Philadelphia."

* * * * * * * * * *

Stephanie stood in silence and looked down at the floor. She said quietly, "What is happening here?" It was more of a statement than a question. She shook her head and said, "I can't believe this."

Lindsay led her to the seating area and guided her into a chair. She said, "There has to be an explanation. We will get to the bottom of this. You will not go through this alone."

Patrick's attorney walked through the entranceway and glanced from left to right looking for Stephanie. When he spotted her, he quickly walked towards them. After shaking hands, he looked from Stephanie to Lindsay.

She introduced herself as a close friend and one of Patrick's colleagues. She told him she had known Patrick and Stephanie for a long time and she was here for them.

She continued, "I should tell you that I'm also Chief Counsel of the Legal Department for the firm and was a part of the embezzlement investigation. Of course, I had no idea Patrick was considered a suspect. And, I'm here for Stephanie, not the firm." She thought to herself, *yeah, and some firm, what a great culture of trust we've built. David doesn't have enough faith and trust to prepare me for this, and Patrick is the one embezzling the money. But, let's deal with that later.*

Sean looked from one to the other, but said nothing. Lindsay assumed he thought the same thing she did about all of this. How could she not have known? And, should she even be here for this conversation?

Stephanie and Lindsay told him everything they knew, which wasn't much. He didn't offer anything. And couldn't, until he talked to Patrick.

He turned to the front desk and asked to see his client. Before walking down the hallway to where Patrick was being held, he asked if there was anything Stephanie wanted him to tell her husband?

It broke Lindsay's heart when she heard Stephanie say, "Just tell him I love him and I'm out here."

He touched her arm, and said in a low tone, "I will. I'll take care of him. We'll figure this out."

Lindsay watched Sean being escorted down the hall. She recognized him from the criminal cases he had defended over the years. He represented a couple of high profile clients involved in corporate espionage. He was a powerful and persuasive litigator. Lindsay had the feeling that Patrick was going to need it.

After what seemed like hours and a cup of coffee that tasted like sludge, Sean returned to them. He said to Stephanie, "He wanted you to know he loves you. He wants to see you."

Sean watched Stephanie walk down the hall, escort at her side. When she turned the corner and was out of hearing range, he turned back to Lindsay, "Patrick wants to see you, too. He said it's really important. Urgent. Said he has to see you before it's too late. I told him it would have to wait until tomorrow. The police won't let you see him today," he said.

"I want to talk to him, too. I'll be back tomorrow morning. I have to know. What is this all about? Can you tell me anything?"

"Lindsay, I'm not at liberty to discuss it with you. But, against my advice, I have a feeling he'll tell you himself, tomorrow. I will say, this is not exactly as it seems. It's a whole lot more complicated than that. That's all I can tell you."

She started to ask another question and he held up his hand, "I'm really sorry. I can't." He walked to the counter and spoke to the police officer at the front desk.

She nodded and dropped into a nearby chair. What was going on? What had she missed? Could she have somehow prevented all of this?

The clock on the wall was making that awful loud ticking noise and only serving to elevate the angst level she was attempting to control. Wanting to scream, to get out of there, but she couldn't. Leaving Stephanie before her sister arrived was a no.

It was getting late and there was nothing left for her to do, but wait and strum her fingers on the chair arms and shake her legs in unison. She was famished and beginning to feel weak. The room was smelly, hot and stuffy. *Where was the oxygen in the room?*

Relief flooded through her when she saw Stephanie return to the lobby and her sister enter the front door. They embraced one another and held on. Lindsay didn't want to interrupt, but touched Stephanie's arm and told her she would see her the next day. She quietly walked away.

And yes, she would see Patrick. She had to know why he did it. There had to be more to this story. This was not him. She knew him. What drove him to this?

CHAPTER 144

Lindsay didn't go back to the office. Couldn't stand the thought of it. She didn't know how to feel about the place she had worked for so long and had built such great friendships. Patrick and David had been her confidantes and her close friends. They were family. She had trusted them, and for her, trust was not easy. Now, all she felt was sad, shocked, and so disappointed.

What was she going to do? The firm would no longer be her safe haven or her home away from home. Until now, it felt more like home than her condo. She didn't know if she could stay, or even wanted to stay.

She thought of David and was sorry for him too, but she was mostly angry and disappointed in him. How could he not believe in her enough to tell her about Patrick the minute he discovered it? He had called her at night many times before. He could have at least prepared her. To see Patrick being carried out in handcuffs was devastating. That image would live on in her mind forever.

Her brain shifted from thought to thought without any focus. When she parked her car, she sat for a moment, not even remembering the drive home. She put her hands over her face and drew a deep breath and let it out. Exhaustion was the least of her problems.

She got out of the car and used all the interest she could muster to get her mail from the box and walk to the front door of her condo. An arrangement of flowers in orange, red, yellow, and white were sitting on her doorway. She picked them up and stepped inside, dropping her briefcase in the hall and carrying them to the kitchen.

The writing on the card said, *I heard about your day. Please call me if you need an ear. Or, an ear and a glass of wine. You may not have heard, but I'm a good listener. I can be there in minutes. Thinking of you, Adam.*

It must have hit the news already. Poor Stephanie and Andrew. And, poor Patrick. It was about to get messy and hurt so many people. She would find out soon enough what this was all about, but she couldn't think about it now. Not now.

She stared at the card and read it again. Adam's thoughtfulness was overwhelming. It was the tipping point that made her weep. She felt silly crying. It made her feel weak, and that was not Lindsay Thompson.

After the brief breakdown, she struggled with her judgement, determining whether or not to call Adam, wanting a friend or support or something, but didn't know if it was a good idea. This night of all nights. *Oh, what the hell.*

She picked up the phone and he answered on the second ring. "The flowers are beautiful. They made me smile, in an otherwise dreadful day. Is the offer still good? I could really use a glass of wine and a friend. I have a great wine that needs me. Come over and share it with me?"

"I'll be over in fifteen minutes. Have you eaten?" Adam asked.

"No. I haven't even thought about food. My refrigerator is stocked. Let me make us something," Lindsay offered.

"Not tonight," he said authoritatively. "I'll bring dinner."

"You don't need to do that."

"Lindsay, I insist. Please let me take care of you tonight. I know just the right meal for the occasion. Comfort food. I won't take no for an answer."

"Thank you. That would be lovely."

"Chicken Parmesan it is. I'll be there shortly."

"I love Chicken Parmesan. It is one of my favorites," Lindsay almost sounded happy.

"I know. I have listening skills, remember?" He added, "I'll see you soon."

She hung up the phone and thought about him. He was a good listener, paid attention and remembered things. What a great trait in a man. She was thinking how much he was like Patrick. Then, reality struck and brought her back. Adam had made her forget, if only for a couple of minutes. It was a couple of minutes better than she had been feeling throughout this day. She smiled at the thought of him.

CHAPTER 145

The doorbell rang and Lindsay opened it to find the man she was fighting the urge to depend upon. It would be so easy, so vulnerable. With a sweet and comforting smile on his face, he held up the dinner bag for her to get a whiff of the savory aromas escaping.

She smiled and invited him in, thinking how good it was to see him. This was exactly what she needed on this horrific day.

"It is really good to see you, Adam."

He sighed. "I'm so sorry." He hesitated and pulled her into his arms and hugged her tight. There was nothing awkward about it. This was their first real touching moment and it was warm, comforting and caring.

He stepped back, put his hands on her shoulders, and looked her in the eyes, "Now, let's have a little food and wine before the food gets cold. Please lead me to your kitchen."

She motioned the way and he walked like a man in charge. To be so in control, there was an endearing expression of compassion on his face. She followed him and poured the wine.

He eyed the dining area and noticed the table was set. He sighed, "You weren't supposed to do anything. I'm here to take care of you tonight, remember?"

"I can set the table, thank you," she said with a playfully defiant look on her face, and the feeling of happiness she didn't deserve. In fact, guilt overwhelmed her for being happier than she could recall in a long time.

Adam apportioned the food and she brought the wine. He hesitated and gestured to the candles on the table. He asked, "Do you mind if I light them?"

"Sounds wonderful. I can do it," she said, grabbing the lighter from a side table drawer.

The conversation was light and the room cozy, with wine, candles, and a fire emitting a warm glow. She was home. Something she didn't usually think about or know much about. But this felt right.

He was paying attention to her needs. He didn't mention what went on during the day. She knew he wouldn't, letting her take the lead on that conversation, if she felt like it. She didn't want to do anything to ruin the comfort she was feeling.

After dinner, Adam ordered her to the family room with a second glass of wine. She did not argue.

He cleaned the kitchen, grabbed his wine, and joined her. Afraid she might be asleep, he quietly moved towards the other end of the couch. She sensed him near, smiled faintly, and motioned for him to sit next to her.

He obediently obliged. She moved her body closer and curled her right leg under her as she faced him. She said, "Thank you for this. You have no idea what it means to me. This would classify as a really rotten day and somehow you have made it better. I can't thank you enough," she said, looking into his eyes.

"No thanks necessary. I kind of thought it might be a rough day, full of all kinds of emotions. I know how much he means to you. I could see it when you were around him."

"I don't know why he did what he did, but I do know, this is not him. There is more to this and I intend to find out what. I'm going to see him tomorrow. He asked for me. I would have done it anyway, but he asked for me."

Adam nodded. He listened. He didn't offer any advice or guidance. He just listened.

They talked for quite a while, or better said, Lindsay talked. She wasn't sure how it happened, but she awoke later to find she had fallen asleep with her head on his shoulder. She was startled to see Adam sitting next to her, reading a book. He must have read while she slept.

She had an embarrassed look on her face as she gazed up at him. He simply smiled and closed the book.

"I didn't want to wake you. You needed sleep. I made myself at home reading the book on the coffee table. Fascinating account of legal strategies," he joked. Lindsay noticed he did not look uncomfortable at all.

"I'm sorry. You must think I am a terrible hostess. I don't know what happened."

"I think you are wonderful and I am right where I want to be. You had a draining day and needed comfort, food and rest. I'm happy I could help. Now, it's time for me to go and let you sleep. You have another emotionally charged day tomorrow." He stood up to leave.

She walked him to the door and thanked him again. Adam turned and hesitated. He kissed her forehead and said he would call her the next day. With that, he simply walked to his car and waved. A trademark she was growing accustomed to.

CHAPTER 146

Lindsay's phone rang as she was pulling back the covers to get into bed. She looked at the display and picked up on the second ring. Sam spoke before she could say anything.

"Lindsay, I just saw the news about Patrick. It's all over the place. I just can't believe it. Oh my God, how are you sweetie?"

"Other than being devastated that one of my best friends could do this, I guess I'm okay."

"What in the world happened?"

"I wish I knew. I've been completely left in the dark."

Sam continued to ask questions that Lindsay couldn't answer. How could she get into the details? She didn't know any.

"Can I call you tomorrow? I just can't do this right now. I have a terrible headache, I'm exhausted, and I need to go to bed."

Lindsay hung up the phone and turned off the light. It felt good to finally lie in bed, only to find that she tossed and turned and could not get to sleep. Thinking about Adam and thinking about Patrick. Mostly, her thoughts were of Patrick, wondering how this happened. She wasn't even sure what 'this' was.

What would she say to him? More importantly, what would he say to her? How could he explain what he had done? These questions continued to swirl around in her head. She tried counting to 100, but her mind couldn't focus. Looking at the clock, it was 1:00, then 2:00. She didn't drift off until some time after that. The last thought before a little sleep was gratitude that

Adam had been there for her. She had shut out the depth of this kind of human contact that had been missing from her life. This kind of partnership. This is what she was missing.

CHAPTER 147

The day was sunny and the weather moderate, but it didn't change a thing. Lindsay couldn't rewrite history - what was done was done. She woke with the same headache she went to bed with. After coffee and an infrequent over-the-counter pain reliever, she got up enough nerve to call the office. Not wanting to talk to David yet, she called his assistant and told her she wouldn't be in. She didn't feel well and needed to take care of a few things.

Her next call was to Sean Mack to make sure her meeting with Patrick was arranged. He would meet her at the police station at 8:00 sharp.

She hung up the phone and felt a slight pain in her chest. Maybe it was too much coffee or the fact that she had no idea how to deal with any of this.

Starting to make mental preparations for a day that could only be full of surprises, her self-talk said be strong, objective, and no jumping to conclusions. Would there be any place for empathy and compassion? God, she really hoped so. She was getting ready to listen to a friend that had never let her down. *Oh, Patrick, what can this possibly be about?*

Lindsay drove into the parking lot and passed through security shortly before the agreed upon time. Taking a deep breath, she walked briskly to the front counter of the police headquarters. Hearing a creaking noise, she turned to find Sean coming out of a side door. He managed a smile that passed for a hello as he walked toward her. "It's all set. Patrick is expecting you. Remember what I told you and everything will be fine."

Lindsay smiled timidly and hesitated, "Thank you Sean. I have known him for so long, and for the first time, I don't know what to say to him. I don't even know how I'll feel when I see him."

"You'll be fine," he hesitated before saying, "You know Lindsay, I advised him against this."

"I know. But, Sean, we have to talk. There is no other way."

"That's exactly what he said, too. Well…I'll be here if either of you need me," he reassured her. "Are you ready?"

"I'm ready," she replied, and he opened the door for her and walked back to the waiting area.

* * * * * * * * *

She hesitated before stepping into the room. She had rehearsed this a hundred times in the middle of the night and now all the words escaped her. All that strategy for nothing. She glanced at him and thought, be yourself and be honest.

Patrick had his hands interlocked and his head looking down at the table. His legs were nervously jiggling up and down. He looked up and smiled weakly, motioning for her to sit across from him.

She sat without uttering a word, not even trying to hide the disappointment on her face. He sat with his head bowed. She couldn't help but notice he looked like he had aged 20 years. She didn't know if it had been over the last 24 hours or the last few months. How could he have done this, to David, to his family, to her? Tears glistened her eyes as she thought about their relationship and all they had been through. She didn't want to cry. She demanded strength. There would be no tears.

There was silence between them. There was no way she was initiating this conversation. How could he do this to her? In an odd way, she had defended him from the beginning. She had never even considered him.

"I guess you're wondering why I wanted to see you," he said quietly as he looked up at her, staring into her eyes. "I want to explain. I need to explain. It's not what it seems."

She spoke, attempting to hide the sound of her voice cracking, "I would have asked to see you anyway. I had to see you. I had to hear it from you. I just want to know one thing. How could you?"

"Lindsay, it all spun out of control and happened so fast. It wasn't supposed to be embezzling money. I was always planning on paying it back. I was hoping I could do it before anyone discovered the money missing. I just needed more time."

"More time for what? What could possibly be an excuse to do such a thing?" Lindsay raised her voice and looked incredulous.

"It's not what you think." He shook his head back and forth and didn't say anything until the words came rushing out about fear, torment, and plenty of shame. People judging...

She asked him to help her understand. She whispered, "Please tell me. What is it?"

"I'm putting my trust in you now. Don't let me down. Telling you could be very dangerous to the people I love. People that you love," he paused, looking at the doorway before whispering, "I did it for my son."

* * * * * * * * * *

Lindsay thought of many possibilities over the past twenty four hours, but Andrew certainly was not one of them. She glanced at the door and then looked him directly in the eyes and said, "Go on."

Patrick shifted nervously in his seat and leaned in towards her. He pleaded, "Lindsay, I know you don't understand right now, but...this was a last resort and I thought I could fix it, but obviously...I really need your help," he paused, "I'm desperate, I need you and your discretion, confidentiality or something like that. I'm not even sure what. I wouldn't ask, but my wife and kid may be in danger."

"Patrick, you have meant the world to me. Your family means the world to me. But, I don't know if I can promise anything, and I don't know if I can help you until I know what happened."

"You will. When I tell you everything. It will all make sense."

"I'm listening," she said in a noncommittal manner.

CHAPTER 148

Patrick told her the entire sordid story. It was almost as shocking as the fact that Patrick actually was responsible for embezzling funds from the company.

"I had no choice. This is what happened." He let out a deep breath and continued, "It involves the death of Andrew's best friend, Chad. You know the hiking trip that ended tragically."

Four months earlier, Patrick had been sitting in his office plowing through emails. His computer was set up in a way that his back was to the door. He never liked the logistical arrangement of that office, but had done nothing about it.

He had this strange sensation someone was watching him. He turned and saw Andrew's good friend, Ricky standing in the doorway. He was watching Patrick, not saying a word, and glaring down at him with an unfamiliar look on his face, a sneer.

"Your assistant wasn't at her desk. Can we talk?" He asked, without even a hello.

This was the first time Ricky had ever been to his office. Alarm washed over Patrick's face, naturally thinking something happened to Andrew. Ricky realized it immediately, and said with a frown, "Don't worry, nothing is wrong with your superstar son."

Patrick's expression immediately went to relief. Ricky continued quietly, "But, we do have a slight problem."

It was the chilling sound of his voice that made Patrick ask him to shut the door. "What's the problem?" he asked.

"It's about the accident on Lassiter Mountain. You see, it wasn't really an accident. I'll spare you all the gory details, but we need to talk about it," he said as he threw two glossy 5x7 pictures on the desk.

Patrick's face turned white as he looked without touching the pictures. He just stared, not believing what he was seeing.

Ricky eyed him carefully, waiting a moment to let it sink in. "Now, don't get all worried on me. We can fix this. It doesn't have to be a big deal. We can keep it between you and me."

Patrick couldn't take his eyes off the pictures. Two young men hiking through the woods. One shoving the other over what appeared to be a steep cliff. The other peering over the edge to watch his damage. Patrick hesitated, taking it all in, and asked in a low tone, "What do you want?"

He replied, "Not much. I'm a little short on cash and that's where you come. I need your help."

Patrick said in a measured tone, "Ricky, I can loan you money."

"I wasn't thinking of a loan."

"What exactly do you want?" Patrick slowly asked the question a second time.

"You pay for my silence." He shrugged. "It's a good deal for you."

"You can't be serious?"

"Oh, I'm deadly serious," his voice was stone cold. Then, he continued, lowering his tone, "Oops, I apologize for the poor choice of words."

Patrick stared at him for a moment without saying anything. He had watched this kid grow up. Not this person standing in front of him. This wasn't happening. He said, "You know I will loan you money, do anything for you, if you need help. But, what is this?"

Ricky shrugged without speaking.

"You and Andrew are best friends. You've been to my house a thousand times and have been like family to Stephanie and me. How can you do this?"

Dismissively, he waved and remarked, "This has nothing to do with friendship. Look at it as a business proposition. But since you asked, all of that was a long time ago. Your precious Andrew and I are into different things now. He doesn't really care about us any more. *HE* is responsible for this. *HE* has become big man on campus and, by the way, it's gone to his head. *HE* thinks he is too good for me now. In fact, I haven't seen him in quite some time. It makes all this much clearer. Easier in fact. Don't you think?"

"How much?" Patrick asked, in a harsh and cold, but monotone voice.

"I think ten million dollars ought to do it. You see, you'll be helping me get out of your lives. I want to leave town. Find a nice little island and a fresh start. Can't you see me lying on the beach and sipping those cute little umbrella drinks until the sun goes down?" he continued, "Look at it this way. I'll be out of your hair for good."

"Are you insane?" he raised his voice and then lowered it before continuing, "I don't have that kind of money. Even if I did, what makes you think I would give it to you? You altered those photos. I know my son, and he wouldn't do anything like this." He pointed his finger at the pictures without touching them.

"Are you willing to take that chance? There's more. I have a recording of them fighting before the fall. I think Andrew says something like, I could kill you." He pulled out the device and turned the volume very low before pressing play.

Patrick listened to the entire recording without uttering a word. He slammed down the end icon to make it stop. The color drained from his face and he sat motionless. Ricky let it all sink in before continuing, "I'll tell you what I'm going to do. Since this has been such a blow and I'm a nice guy, I'll give you a little time to think about it. Say, an answer by 2:00 tomorrow?"

He shook his head up and down and continued, "In fact, I'll give you another little break. I know you don't have that kind of money, but you don't have to. You have access to so much more than I'm asking for. You're the Comptroller. Shouldn't be hard for you to get your hands on ten million in a multi-billion dollar business. So here is the deal. You don't have to give me the money all at once. We can do this over time. We can work out an installment plan, say $25,000 to start. Easier that way. No one will ever find out. I get my money, and you won't get caught. You think about it. I'll be in touch tomorrow." He smiled, turned, waved behind him, and walked out.

He stopped and stepped back in, slowly transforming his expression into one that Patrick did not recognize. "One more thing. You tell Andrew or anyone else about this, and my next stop will be the police. That wouldn't be good for your son's bright future. We don't want that, do we?" he hesitated, "Or, I might have to hurt him. I'm feeling a little destructive. Think about what I said. Until tomorrow." He walked out without looking back.

CHAPTER 149

Stunned, Patrick let out a deep breath and stared at the pictures. After it sank in, he placed them in his briefcase and secured it. They had to stay there. He sat motionless in a trance, not knowing what to make of what just happened and he certainly didn't know how he was going to deal with it.

He stood and shut his office door. His legs wobbled and his hands trembled. It was an effort just to get back to his chair, putting his hands on the edge of his desk and flopping down in the chair, almost missing the seat. Thinking he might be sick, he glanced around for his trash can. He placed his head in his hands, shaking and trying to figure out his next move.

Andrew couldn't have done this. His boy would never do anything to harm his best friend or anyone else for that matter. He would never, ever commit murder.

None of it made any sense at all. He had to find out what happened, but not now. He was in a race against the clock. He had to come up with the first installment. He couldn't take any chances with his son's life. Then, he would figure it all out.

He spent a couple of minutes breathing in and out, trying to steady himself. When he was ready, he grabbed his coat and briefcase before swiftly heading out the door. He told his assistant he was leaving for the day and didn't want to be interrupted. No calls. He had an important meeting.

His mind was scrambling, trying to figure out an action plan. He was in his car barely paying attention to the traffic flying by. After a number of glaring stares from other drivers, he noticed his speed was much too slow for the traffic flow. As he drove through the city, he couldn't shake the images of Andrew committing this horrific crime. The pictures were burned into his brain.

The thought of his son killing anyone was more than he could accept. If he hadn't seen the pictures and heard the audio, he wouldn't have even considered it, and he still didn't believe it. But, was he willing to take a chance? He knew the answer.

Andrew had loved Chad and they were like brothers. He wouldn't have done this. But, there was Ricky. Based on what he had just witnessed, could Ricky be responsible for Chad's death?

Or, if Andrew was involved, it had to be an accident. Even if it was an accident, Ricky's twisted testimony could put Andrew in jail for the rest of his life. The alleged evidence appeared authentic. He would figure all that out later. He couldn't deal with it now.

Ricky's threat was so terrifying that he couldn't possibly ask Andrew about what happened. It wasn't the devil in Ricky's eyes that frightened Patrick the most. It was the rapid shift in emotions and the way he changed from even tempered to anger back to even tempered. And, he had been chilling in his declaration that he would go to the police. No reservation or doubt about that. He would do it. He was capable of anything.

If the very worst was true and Andrew did this horrible thing, how would he live with knowing this about his son? How was his son living with it, and why would he do it? It simply was not true.

He would figure out what really happened that day. But for now, he had to buy some time and had to give Ricky the money. He had no choice. His son's life was at stake and it was worth $25,000.

He had the money and could cover the amount through one of his personal accounts without Stephanie ever knowing. But he would make sure this was the one and only installment. And, he would figure a way to get it back. Stephanie couldn't find out about this until he had some answers. It would devastate her.

CHAPTER 150

Patrick drove to the bank and hesitated in his car before getting out. *Could he do what he was about to do? There was no choice.* He let out a deep breath and got out of the car, clumsily dropping his keys on the ground.

He bent down to grab them and stood up slowly, looking around and walking timidly to the door. He entered the bank feeling like a criminal. This was the only time in his marriage he had been dishonest with his wife. He kept telling himself, it was for her own good. And, it was only money.

He was relieved there were only a couple of people in line. While waiting, he thought about his next move. Deep down, he knew Andrew was innocent. But…and what if he couldn't prove it? The only simple thing in all of this was his answer to that question. He would do whatever was necessary to protect his son. And, he reminded himself, it was only money.

He had to come up with a strategy, a full proof approach to attack this. How would he keep his wife from knowing about the money? He had to solve it before she found out. No, he couldn't live with that. He had to tell her everything. No, he couldn't do that either.

He started to walk out, but stopped. Thinking back to Ricky's threat, he knew what he had to do. He looked around the bank and realized he needed a manager, not a teller for such a large sum of money. And he'd likely have to wait.

And then there was the part about figuring a way to inquire of the inner workings of electronic deposits to other banks and confidentiality requirements. He was a Comptroller, not a banker. This was new territory for him.

On second thought, not a good idea. It might raise flags unnecessarily. He had to do this on his own. All of it.

He stood around waiting and listening to annoying conversations of business being conducted, reverberating and pounding in his ears. An added irritant he certainly didn't need. He looked at the bank vault and surveyed the customers walking in. He realized he was shifting nervously on one foot and then the other like a little boy waiting in line for the bathroom. *Stop it… What if it doesn't work? What if…Stop.* One thing was clear, if he didn't figure it out quickly, he would have to do the unspeakable. At least, for a time. And he really didn't believe he could do that.

"Mr. Stephenson, please come on over. I'm ready for you now."

To his surprise, it turned out to be a much simpler transaction than he anticipated. The manager pulled up his account from college and prepared the necessary paperwork. No complications. It was almost painless. It should be, it was his own money.

All he had to do was wait until 2pm the next day. He was slightly relieved as he walked out the front entrance of the bank. His natural inclination was to look down, just in case he was being watched or filmed. Let the paranoia begin.

CHAPTER 151

Patrick's next stop was the public library. Research he didn't want to do on his own devices and couldn't do at home. He walked over to a lone computer, the greatest distance from anyone else. He started pecking away on the search engine. It didn't take long to find the police report that showed nothing suspicious. The three boys were hiking, the weather was bad, and Chad slipped and fell to his death. Andrew and Ricky tried to get to him as quickly as possible, but weren't successful in rescuing him. Tragic as it was, end of story.

If that's the way it happened, then what about the pictures? The recording? Of course, they could have been altered. The police could figure that part out rather easily. It just had to be a terrible accident and Ricky figured out a way to make money.

Patrick would go to the police, tell them everything. After all, he was being held hostage by a college boy. He was getting ready to alter their lives and make some moves that would affect his family and their futures. Ricky had to be lying and these had to be idle threats. He could end this. Yes, he would go to the police. Now.

He was closing down the browsers when his phone rang. He glared at the number and picked it up without saying anything. He listened to the other end. "What are you doing Mr. S? I see you. Not a good idea. The first move was great, going to the bank. This one, not so much. You may want to think about it. Your son's life is at stake. I don't mess around." There was a dial tone.

Patrick scanned the room, looking for Ricky, but finding no sign of him. He looked down at his ring finger and slowly twirled his platinum wedding band several times. The room was getting hot and his head was spinning.

He couldn't take a chance. Not with his son's life or the mother of his child's life. He kept coming back to Ricky, the pictures, the recording. He had been warned. Tell no one. The demand was chilling and he meant it. Ricky was definitely dangerous. Patrick didn't even want to think of all the possibilities and he wasn't about to take that chance.

He looked at his watch and hurried to his feet. He had to get home. As he drove, his mind kept going over the account of events in the police report. The more he thought about it, he was convinced there was something there.

He had to talk to Andrew without arousing suspicion. He had an idea.

CHAPTER 152

Patrick called his son and asked him to meet for lunch the following day. They agreed to 12:00 at one of their favorite pubs. It would be quiet and not too crowded during the daytime. Optimal for figuring out what was going on in Andrew's head. But for now, he would put it out of his mind, or Stephanie would know something was wrong.

He parked in the garage, turned off the ignition switch, and hesitated. Looking around him, everything neatly stacked and organized, he let out a deep breath. *Could the day have been any worse?* It took him a moment to gather enough nerve to go in.

He walked through the kitchen door to find Stephanie preparing salads for dinner. He forced a smile, kissed his wife and went to the bedroom to change. How was he going to keep this from her? One solution - end it fast.

Changing his clothes and splashing water on his face, he looked in the mirror and observed dark circles forming. He was irritated with himself for still thinking about it. The same thoughts swirling around and around in his head without any progress. He knew there was nothing he could do until the next day. He also knew there were no other options. Enough said. Get on with it. He joined his wife in the kitchen.

Pouring them each a glass of chardonnay, he actually felt like he needed it. This was usually a special time together when they caught up on events of their day, talking about anything and everything. Usually.

After setting the forks, knives and spoons in their proper location, Patrick carried the salads to the table. Stephanie brought their wine and glasses of water. She did most of the talking as they ate dinner. He was barely listening.

Patrick's mind was crowded with options, alternatives, and game plans. He felt uneasy when she asked if anything exciting happened at work. Of course he made up an answer. For him, it involved lies and then there would be more lies. They were starting to build already and he hated doing this to her.

After the kitchen was clean and they finished a cup of decaf, they retired to reading in the bedroom. He fell asleep before the end of one chapter, but it didn't last long. He woke around midnight and tossed and turned the rest of the early morning hours, continuously looking at his phone. He felt like he had fallen back to sleep around the time his alarm sounded.

Patrick rolled over and pressed his thumb on the button two times before the noise stopped. He had a sick feeling in the pit of his stomach from not getting enough sleep or worry or both. He was overly tired and wondered how he could keep this up. It had only just begun.

Lack of sleep and tossing and turning had to stop. When his wife asked about it, he said it was just work. No worries. More lies. He had to go to the office and act like nothing was wrong.

CHAPTER 153

Patrick arrived at the Pub a few minutes before noon. He had rehearsed the questions in his mind for what seemed like hundreds of times throughout the morning. It had consumed him from the moment he stepped out of the house. *Find out what really happened.*

He asked for a booth at the far end, away from the crowd and the entrance. He ordered a cup of coffee while waiting. Andrew showed up five minutes late, rushing in and telling his dad he had been stuck in traffic. He had always been punctual and a bit unnerved when he was late to anything, even lunch with his father.

They ordered and talked about basketball and classes. The season was just getting started and Andrew was busy with practice and school, leaving him with little free time. He was surprised when his father called and asked to meet for lunch with both of them having such busy schedules during the week. He feared something was wrong.

Patrick smiled and said, "I just wanted to see you. I was missing my son."

The conversation had been general and benign throughout their meal. Patrick had almost forgotten the reason for the lunch, enjoying the time with his son. After their plates were removed from the table, he became increasingly nervous to broach the subject.

He asked about Andrew's girlfriend. She was studying hard and they didn't get to see each other as much as they wanted. Their schedules weren't very flexible and there wasn't much free time for either of them. Things would slow down after the school year.

Patrick breathed deeply before the next question. He tried to appear nonchalant and asked, "How is Ricky? Have you been able to spend any time with him?"

Andrew responded in a flat tone, emotionless. He said, "I haven't seen him in awhile. We tried to get together a couple of times recently and it didn't work out."

"That's too bad. I'm sure he misses you. You guys were inseparable."

"Yeah, I guess."

"What do you mean, you guess? That doesn't sound good. Did anything happen between you?"

"Not really. The last time I was with him, he was a little strange. He went out with Melissa and me and acted like he was jealous of her. She even noticed and said something to me about it. It was really weird."

"Really? You think he is jealous of your relationship with Melissa? That is strange." Patrick hesitated as if in thought and continued, "You guys have been buddies for a long time. Maybe he is just having a hard time letting go of the past. The bond you shared, especially after what you've been through together. He really leaned on you after the accident, didn't he?"

Andrew looked down at the table before responding, "Yeah, I guess. I'm the only real friend he has left. After Chad, he became overly dependent on our friendship. Almost an unhealthy dependency. I felt it then, but there was nothing I could do about it. I certainly wasn't going to abandon him."

Andrew shifted nervously, repositioning himself on the leather chair. It was obvious he was becoming uncomfortable with the conversation, but Patrick had to keep going. "This is the first time I've heard you call him Chad. You usually say 'him'. Do you think it's getting easier to think about him? To talk about him?"

Glancing into space instead of at his father, Andrew replied, "It's still really hard. It was the worst day of my life. I lost my best friend. I'll never get over it, but I realized a long time ago that I had to come to grips with it."

Patrick took a deep breath. He had thought carefully about what he was about to say. "You never really said much about what happened that day. Have you wanted to talk about it?"

Andrew closed his eyes for a moment, and then looked directly into his father's before responding, "There isn't much to tell and I certainly don't want to relive it. It was a terrible accident. There is nothing I can do about it now. I really don't want to talk about it. I try not to think about it. I haven't made that much progress."

Patrick pressed, "Maybe you should talk about it. Get some closure so you can accept it and move on. You can talk to me."

"Dad, I've moved on as much as I can. There really is no point in getting into it."

Patrick knew he was crossing a line, but had to continue. He despised himself for what he was about to do to his son. It was manipulative, but he had to get some answers, something, anything. He continued, "I could use some closure. Chad was a big part of all of our lives. Your mother and I loved him, too. I think it would help me to talk about it."

Andrew's face changed from discomfort to empathy in a second. So typical of this kid. Above all else, he was filled with compassion, an empathetic young man that couldn't hurt anyone. There is no way he did this. He kept his eyes steady on his son, waiting for a response.

Andrew sighed in resignation, "Why now Dad? It was a long time ago. I really don't know if I can relive it. The best way I deal with it is to push it out of my mind. It's the only thing that has worked, and it doesn't always. It was a tragic accident and there is nothing we can do about it."

In that moment, Patrick saw something troubling in his son's eyes. He was hiding something. He struggled with the thought of asking him about it. He couldn't bear to know. *Oh God, please tell me he didn't do it.*

* * * * * * * * *

Andrew Stephenson stared off into space again. He had been carrying this around for a long time. A sick feeling and increasing doubt that Chad's fall had been an accident. He didn't want to think Ricky had anything to do with it, but recently, there were increasingly strange behaviors that made him more than a little unnerved. He had delicately tried to distance himself since those thoughts started surfacing. Lately, Andrew had become so concerned that, if pushed, Ricky might be dangerous enough to do something to his family or his girlfriend.

He didn't want to let his father know what he had been thinking. Nothing good could come out of it, especially with Chad gone. Andrew knew his father. He was a rule follower, a stand up guy that would be compelled to go to the police. And, there was no proof. It had to end here, remain an accident. Everyone had to stay safe. He would handle it.

He let out a deep breath and said to his father, "Okay, if it will help, I'll tell you what I remember. It was raining and the rocks were slippery. The visibility was bad and I went ahead of Chad and Ricky. Chad was between Ricky and me. He had complained of a headache a few minutes earlier, but we didn't think much of it. We told him to stay between the two of us so we could keep an eye on him."

He looked down before continuing, "Dad, I wasn't looking at him. I was trying to figure out where we would go next. That's when Chad slipped and fell and Ricky couldn't get to him fast enough. He said he did the same thing I did. He took his eyes off Chad to look around at our surroundings. That's when it all went wrong. If only I had kept my eyes on him. I might have been able to help him." Andrew kept his head down, and didn't say any more.

Patrick reached out and touched his son's hand. He hated this. He replied quietly, "I'm so sorry it happened. You can't do this to yourself. Andrew, it wasn't your fault." There was nothing left to say. He couldn't take the chance with Andrew's life, whether Andrew was involved, or not. Deep down he was almost certain his son wouldn't, no couldn't, do such a thing. He was a good, decent young man.

In that moment, he knew he had to find out the truth. He was going on the offensive and find out what really happened. He would get to know everything there was to know about Ricky.

Patrick paid the bill and they stepped outside into the bright sunlight. They walked to their cars and hugged. The lunch was draining and it ended on a sad note. They both knew it, but tried to conceal their feelings and acted like it was great getting together. Unbeknownst to the other, they both felt guilty about not being able to be more truthful. Their relationship had always been based on honesty and they had been able to talk about anything. This was different because the price of truth was too high.

Patrick left the restaurant parking lot feeling overwhelmed and worried, but determined. He would make the first payment of $25,000, and he would get his money back. There would be no second installment. He had to make sure of it. Now, he was in a race against time.

CHAPTER 154

Later in the day, Patrick returned to the bank for the cash withdrawal. He mustered the nerve only through a series of self-talk declarations - this would be the one and only installment. His next stop was Ricky.

Patrick called him from the car. He said in a flat tone, with disgust in his voice, "I have the money. Where and when do you want to meet?"

"That's good. How about now? There is a coffee shop about twenty minutes north on 95? It should be quiet and less busy at this hour." He gave him the address.

"I'll be there in a few minutes." He was ready to hang up, until he heard the next question. It was almost the most frightening part of the entire ordeal.

"Oh, I meant to ask. How was lunch with Andrew?"

Patrick jerked the wheel and almost wrecked the car. He regained his composure and asked, "How did you know we had lunch together?"

"I make it my business to know everything where Andrew is concerned. I wouldn't want to see anything happen to him. He could get hurt, you know. There are crazy people out there. Crazy enough to kill him. We can't have that, can we? It's my duty to watch over him. Keep him safe."

"You stay away from my son, you son of a…," he caught himself before continuing, knowing it would serve no purpose but to agitate him. He was absolutely certain Ricky was even more dangerous than he had ever imagined.

"Now, now Mr. Stephenson. Don't get all upset. We talked about this. It is just a business proposition. I need money and you need to keep your son free. And, you want to keep him healthy, don't you? Besides, I can't stay away from him. After all, we're best friends, bonded."

"I'll be there in a few minutes." Patrick hung up the phone. It was the calm, yet cold and calculating demeanor that was the most frightening. Ricky was enjoying this. This was not the Ricky he remembered. Something had gone terribly wrong with him, or he had been masterful at hiding it all these years.

Patrick was beginning to see more clearly what he was dealing with. He had to take a trip to Ricky's hometown and find out everything he could about him. He wasn't going to find the answers he was looking for on the internet. Up to this point, he only knew what Ricky wanted him to know.

CHAPTER 155

It was an hour later when he finally drove into the parking lot. The traffic had crawled for several miles until he reached the exit. The entire area was busier than he had hoped and too many people were dashing in and out of the coffee shop.

He parked his car away from the entrance and saw that Ricky had done the same. When Ricky spotted him, he got out of his car and walked over with two drinks. He opened the passenger door and got in, looking like they were son and father getting together for coffee.

"Hi Mr. Stephenson, I bought you a coffee just like you like it. A cafe latte skinny, with a touch of whipped cream. I started to get you that other one you like, what is it? Tall caramel macchiato with light whipped creme, but decided on the latte instead. See, I remember from the times you, Andrew and me used to stop for coffee before football games." He stared out the window, sighed and shook his head, "I really miss those days. Things were so uncomplicated then. We really had a good time, didn't we?"

Patrick almost felt empathy, felt sorry for him, almost. Something was terribly wrong with this young man. With all of this. He turned his body to face him and looked directly in his eyes. He said quietly, "Ricky, it doesn't have to be this way. I can help you. Whatever you need, money or any other kind of support. You don't need to do this. Trust me, I can help."

He shook his head and said emphatically and a little too loudly, "No, Mr. Stephenson. It has to be this way. It really does. It is too late. So, where is the money?"

Patrick didn't move or say anything for a moment. He just stared at him. Something was definitely off.

Ricky slapped the dashboard hard and said too loudly, "Where is my money?"

Patrick jumped. "Calm down. I have it in my pocket." He pulled the envelope from his jacket. Before handing it over, he attempted to reason once more. He pleaded, "Ricky, it's not too late. Let me help you. Don't do this. Think about it."

"You won't help me. You'll walk away. You're like all the rest of them. All of you. I thought Andrew was different, but he's not." His lips trembled and he looked like he might cry, until his face turned to anger. "So, it has to be this way. Give me my money, NOW."

Patrick handed him the envelope and looked at Ricky's face. He was waiting for Ricky to speak. How could he have been so wrong about this boy? All the dinners and sleepovers in their home.

Ricky stared straight ahead and let out a deep sigh. "Okay. That's good. That's a good start. Let's talk about the next installment."

Patrick said, "I'm listening."

"I think we need to step up the amount. At the rate we're going, you'll never get your debt paid. How about we increase it to $50,000 next time?"

"Come on Ricky. I don't have that kind of money lying around."

"We've already talked about it. You are the Comptroller. Money bags, a resourceful guy. I'm sure you can figure it out. Small installments, no one will ever know."

"Why are you doing this? Please don't do this."

"I have to go. I have class. You'll figure it out. I need the money in two weeks," he demanded. Looking out the window, Ricky placed his hand on the car door and said, "The next time, we'll pick a more secluded place. This one freaks me out a little." He got out and turned back to Patrick, "Remember Mr. S, not a word to anyone. Ciao, ciao." He walked away.

Patrick watched him get halfway to his car and skip the rest of the way. This was like something out of a bad murder mystery. Ricky transformed expressions and moods three or four times in this brief encounter. Patrick chastised himself for actually being relieved. Ricky was responsible for the crime, not his son. He was certain.

But none of it changed that he was in big trouble. He couldn't sustain this kind of money, and definitely had to find out everything there was to know about Ricky with a frightening sense of urgency. How could he end this? Make sure this was the last installment? He had two weeks.

CHAPTER 156

Patrick looked at his watch and felt the weight of time flying without solutions. He had to get back to the office and spend a couple of hours catching up on work that was neglected, and implement preparations for the next step.

He had to visit Ricky's hometown to get answers, like yesterday. By the time he arrived at work, he had formulated comprehensive details of his plan. He would tell David and Lindsay that Stephanie was having some health issues and they needed to go out of town for some tests. After all, she did have a little minor surgery coming up. It wasn't totally a lie. He would tell them he didn't want to talk about it. Female stuff. That would have to work for now.

* * * * * * * * * *

His first stop was Lindsay's office. He was actually nervous about asking her to join him for coffee.

At the Cafe Bar, he told her about his plans to take Stephanie out of town the next day for medical tests. Being Lindsay, she didn't pry. She simply offered assistance if he needed her. He thanked her. Everything was under control. He didn't want to talk about it, but would keep her informed.

They finished coffee and Patrick walked to David's office. One down and one to go. He could do this. He had to.

He spoke with David's assistant before going into his inner office. He attempted to remain emotionless, hiding his nervousness, his guilt. Creating lie after lie. They just kept compounding, but there was no alternative.

David stepped from behind his desk and offered Patrick a seat on the sofa. David started talking, but Patrick's mind was running a mile a minute and his heart was jumping out of his chest. He wasn't listening and he just nodded his head in agreement. When there was a break in the noise, Patrick told David the same story he told Lindsay. The details were exactly the same.

He felt the sweat dripping under his shirt. He hoped it didn't show and that David didn't see the beads of sweat across his forehead. Lying didn't come naturally to him.

About Stephanie, David was empathetic and caring. Patrick knew he would be. He told him to take as much time as he needed. To let him know if he could do anything. Patrick thanked him and excused himself. He had to get out of there.

He left David's office feeling excruciating guilt. These were his friends. He felt terrible about lying to them. It had to be over soon and there wouldn't be a need for any more lies.

He had to do what he had to do. His plan was set in motion. There was no turning back now.

CHAPTER 157

Patrick worked, or attempted to work, for a couple of hours. After several tries to read the same document, he turned off his laptop and surrendered. He wasn't accomplishing anything anyway so he decided to go home a little early. Stephanie would be happy until he told her about the emergency work trip.

He arrived at the house as she was getting out of her car. The look on her face said that she was surprised to see him. Sheepishly, she held up a grocery bag. "I thought I would surprise you with a nice romantic dinner for two. I know how stressful work has been, and this is an opportunity to take your mind off of it."

He struggled a smile, "My wonderful wife and her excellent ideas. Why don't we prepare that dinner together? How about that for romantic?"

"Wonderful. Will you open a special bottle of red, while I get the steaks ready?"

They made small talk while preparing dinner. Stephanie had been especially talkative that evening, which suited Patrick since he didn't want her to notice how preoccupied and overwhelmed he was. And less talking meant less lying.

During a break in the conversation, Patrick breathed deeply and said, "I hate to put a downer on all of this, but I have to go out of town tomorrow. Only for a couple of days. We have a problem that popped up in one of our offices and I need to be the one to handle it."

She gave him a playful, pouty look and said, "Do you have to go?"

He replied sweetly, "I wish I didn't, but yes, I have to go."

"But I will miss you."

He gave her a forced smile and hugged her to him. "It should only be a couple of days."

"Well, okay. I guess I can make it without you. But, I'll still miss you." She stood back from the hug and gave him a sweet and tender kiss.

"I love you," He said to his beloved wife.

"I love you, my darling." She smiled up at him.

They ate dinner by candlelight. The romantic setting made him think about their home. It had a warm, cozy and comfortable feeling to it. He loved their life together. Sitting at this table and gazing into her beautiful and light brown eyes, he reminded himself why he was doing this. Why he had to lie.

CHAPTER 158

The next morning, Patrick and Stephanie had coffee together before he left for the most consequential trip he would ever take. She noticed he had his first restful sleep in awhile. She commented on it and he shrugged it off, saying he finally came up with a strategy to solve a nagging problem. He was feeling better.

What he didn't say was that it was the first night he slept since the ordeal started. He wasn't sure if it was the exhaustion, the wine, or that he had a plan. He vowed to himself that he would figure out who Ricky was and what really happened on the mountain on that tragic day.

He quickly shifted the conversation to talk about her. Get the focus off him and minimize his newfound expertise in lying.

"So, what do you have on tap for today, Ms. Beautiful Corporate Attorney?" he beamed.

"I have a couple of meetings this morning. We are working through the merger I was telling you about and we're in the middle of all the legal details. Frankly, at this point, it's draining."

"You are great at the details. You'll handle it," He paused and looked at her through glassy eyes, and said, "You are an amazing woman. I hope you know I love you with all my heart."

She studied him for a moment. There was something different in his eyes, and the emotion in his voice. She walked over to him and put her arms around his neck before answering, "You are everything to me too, sweetheart. Are you okay?"

"I'm fine. I just hate to leave you today."

They said goodbye in the garage and were set to drive off in opposite directions. Stephanie was going to a meeting and Patrick was on a critical exploration that would change their lives. He had to succeed.

She rolled down her car window and motioned for him to do the same. She giggled, "Hey honey, I think you forgot your briefcase."

He made a face like he was losing his mind and smiled. "It must have been the kiss from the beautiful lady." As she was pulling away, he waved and went back into the house to grab it. He also went into the bedroom, unlocked the safe and carefully pulled out the handgun and held it at arm's length like it might discharge at any second. He couldn't imagine he would need it, but it wasn't a chance he was willing to take. He had no idea what to expect on this journey, or his future meetings with Ricky, if there were any.

CHAPTER 159

Patrick drove his car north of Washington DC. Ricky's family was from Thorndale, a small area outside of Philadelphia. The drive was only supposed to take about two and a half hours, but the heavy traffic kept him on the road closer to four. He was in desperate need of a restroom and cup of coffee.

There wasn't anything resembling a cafe bar in this little town. He stopped at a local gas station, featuring good gas prices, outdoor toilets, and bad coffee. At that point, taste didn't matter. With drink in hand, his first stop was the public library. It was time to find out about the Henderson family.

He had considered that Ricky might follow him, a risk he had no choice but to take. Being out of town was something he could explain, if Ricky called or checked on him. A business meeting, conference, or meeting with one of their offices. It still left him feeling uneasy, not knowing exactly what Ricky was capable of.

He hoped to obtain what he needed without making too many stops and talking with too many people. This small town reminded Patrick of a place where everyone knew everyone, and their business. That might work to his advantage later on, but now was all about piecing the puzzle together and filling in the blanks.

He was counting on getting all the information he needed while in Thorndale. He didn't want to have to make a trip to the Division of Vital Records. It was five hours from Philly and he didn't have five hours to waste.

Thinking back on the conversations he had with Ricky about his family, there was rarely any talk about his parent or siblings, only that he had a fairly normal childhood. He had two older brothers and an older sister. When there was mention, it was mostly about his sister. He said she was the world to him.

Patrick sat down at the computer terminal and accessed Henderson. A fairly common name and a couple of hundred entries emerged. He couldn't remember Ricky's mother's name, but remembered his father was Chuck.

He retrieved the record of one Charles Henderson, but it couldn't be the right one. The man died sixteen years earlier. He started to search further down the list, but for some reason kept reading to find he was married to Kathy Henderson. Memory jogged - it was Ricky's mother. She was a couple of years younger than his father. The next discovery was more perplexing.

He queried the name Kathy Henderson. To his surprise, she too, was deceased. He kept searching until he found a picture of her. There was no doubt it was Ricky's mother. It had to be. This was getting more strange with every new detail. Patrick shouldn't have been surprised that Ricky had the capacity to lie about his past. *How did his mother die?*

He spent the next few hours reading. He was deep in research when the librarian told him they were getting ready to close for the evening. He was welcome to return the following day. They opened at 9:00AM. Oh, he definitely would be back. He had only just begun.

On his way to the hotel, he grabbed takeout at a local deli. He ate dinner and called Stephanie as he normally did while away. He told her the trip was going fine. They were solving some issues. He ended the call as quickly as possible. The lying thing was gut wrenching. And, he needed a good night's sleep. The following day might just save, or destroy his family.

CHAPTER 160

Patrick left the hotel early in the morning and stopped at a local diner a couple of miles away. He asked for a table in the back and pointed to one facing the entrance. As he wolfed down an egg white spinach omelet and drank dark roasted coffee, he couldn't help but scan the room and parking lot for any sign of Ricky. Paranoia. A terrible thing.

Eager to get started, he was back at the library when the doors opened. The same petite middle-aged woman let him in that closed him down the night before. He smiled and she smiled back. Neither of them made small talk, other than a quick hello.

That was fine by Patrick. He wanted as little contact as possible. Just like the day before, he sat behind one of the computers at the far end of the room for day two of his detective work.

He began by inputting the name Kathy Henderson. The previous night's search didn't reveal much, only that she was deceased. Over the next hour or two, he attempted query after query. He finally found what he was looking for and shock didn't adequately describe it.

Kathy Henderson committed suicide fourteen years earlier. Two years after Chuck's death. Ricky would have been about seven years old at the time. *What happened to her and where had Ricky been all this time?* Finding these answers had to shed light on Ricky and his childhood.

He continued looking into her background. Nothing grabbed his attention, until he reached the part about children. Chuck and Kathy had two children, Ricky and Kaitlin. Ricky had said there were two older brothers, but there was no mention of other boys.

After a couple of hours, he was left with more questions. Hoping the remaining ones could be answered through other means, he finally gave up and opted to use the internet on his tablet. *Yep, paranoia is a terrible thing.* He made the necessary preliminary notes, gathered the information he had copied, and drove back to the hotel.

He continued his search on Kathy Henderson. There were a number of articles on her life and death. He looked at her obituary. It talked about survivors, among them Ricky and Kaitlin. Instead of flowers, the family requested contributions to the Noble Home for Women.

Patrick searched for information on the Noble Home for Women. The website homepage included pictures, points of contacts, and a summary description of their mission. It was finally coming together and becoming more clear what he was dealing with.

He picked up his phone and made a call. It would be his first stop the next morning. Both chilling and satisfied, he was finally getting closer to the answers.

He looked at his watch. It was getting late and he had missed dinner. He was hungry, but decided on sleep instead. The next day would be another early one and he had to get information and get home as soon as possible. Another plan that had to work.

CHAPTER 161

The Noble Home was a sprawling facility at the end of a long drive laced with trees on both sides. The landscape was a colorful bouquet, a kaleidoscope of sorts surrounded by deep green grass. It was stunning and immaculate, accompanied by a manmade lake staged to the left side of the front entrance. There were stone benches placed in various locations simulating the look and feel of a sanctuary.

The facility reminded Patrick of a large southern mansion. The exterior was white with black shutters and the front entrance was an expansive porch that covered the width of the home with thick round columns supporting the structure. The porch housed rocking chairs with rose colored seat cushions and pillows, contributing to formal and grand, not institutional.

Ms. Feinstein was waiting for him. Patrick shook her hand as he stood back and looked at the exterior of the facility. He had rehearsed his lines a thousand times before this moment.

"This certainly is impressive, Ms. Feinstein," he smiled at her.

She pursed her lips and said, "Thank you. Please call me Nancy. We take great pride in our facility and the work that is accomplished here." She motioned him towards the front entrance, "Shall we, Mr. Stephenson?"

His gentlemanly manners solicited her to lead the way. "And, you can call me Patrick. I am anxious to hear all about Noble Home. I've a vested interest in people struggling and needing the support you provide."

"You've come to the right place. The work we do here is critically important. And everyone on staff cares deeply about it, about the people we serve," she said as she led him down the hallway and into a room with her gold name plate on the door.

Her office was furnished in a traditional setting with an antique desk as the focal point. The room had one wall of encased bookshelves to the right of the desk. At the other end of the room, there was a sitting area with Queen Anne furniture and antique rugs strategically placed on Brazilian hardwood floors. A soft floor lamp illuminated a dim, comforting light.

Ms. Feinstein ushered Patrick over to the sofa and sat across from him. The boundary of separation was an oval shaped coffee table. She carefully sat down and pulled her three quarter length skirt tight around her legs. Her eyes peered over her reading glasses. She couldn't help but notice he was younger than she expected. And quite handsome.

"Let's have some coffee, and I would love to tell you about us. We are quite proud of our success rate in changing the lives of many women who start out with no hope for a future. With others, we try to give them the best life we can while they are here. We become like family to them, caring for them. Unfortunately, there are those few times when we haven't been so successful. As you know, we weren't so successful with Ricky's mother," she said as her voice trailed off and she shook her head to the right and left before looking down.

Patrick studied her response for a moment before saying, "Ricky doesn't talk much about it, but I wish he would. I think it could help him. As I told you on the phone, he is like family to us. There have been numerous occasions when he started to tell us about her, but he would stop himself, become emotional, and shut down. My wife and I want to help him." Patrick paused and continued, speaking softly, "I'm sorry. I digressed."

"Oh please don't apologize, I completely understand."

Patrick cleared his throat and continued, "My intentions for the visit are to talk about the foundation. As I mentioned on the phone, my firm is interested in establishing one in the name of Kathy Henderson. As part of our philanthropy work, we look for the right opportunities, personal ones. Being the CFO, I can influence these types of decisions. Ricky's relationship with our family led me to the Noble Home."

He smiled before continuing, "As you can imagine, we have a number of opportunities and only attach our name to the very best. So far, I'm quite impressed. But before making any decisions, I would like to gain an understanding of your facilities and operations. Make sure this is mutually beneficial for the Noble Home, as well as our Company."

"Excellent. We'll be happy to share whatever we can with you," Ms. Feinstein paused and continued, "And maybe we can offer some insight on Ricky as well."

"Thank you," he said quietly, looking down at his hands.

She nodded, gave him a moment, and said, "About our staff. For starters, there is minimal turnover. We are very good to our employees and we have strict expectations concerning performance. In fact, the nurse that worked with Ricky's mother is still here. I'll talk to her and see if there is anything she can share with you. Of course, you understand, we must be careful about violating any patient privacy. But maybe there is something we can do to help you with Ricky. We'll figure it out."

She called for her assistant to bring in coffee. It was arranged perfectly on a sterling silver coffee tray. Napkins, fine china, and an assortment of sugars and cream. They paused while preparing their coffee and waiting for the assistant to shut the door behind her.

They talked for over an hour. Patrick was impressed by her dedication and their mission. To give women an opportunity and address their medical needs with the dignity they deserved. Treating their illness like any other type of condition requiring medical treatment. There were varying ranges of need in the facility, but many were women searching for appropriate medication and therapy that could lead to hopeful and fulfilling futures.

The facility really was spectacular, but Patrick had a hard time staying focused and engaged in the conversation. At any other time he would find it fascinating and would be interested in doing whatever he could to help. But this was a matter of his family's future.

It was beginning to look like a dead end until Ms. Feinstein took him on a tour. When he met Kathy's former nurse.

* * * * * * * * *

Ms. Feinstein introduced Patrick to Joyce, explaining that his firm was hoping to create a foundation in the name of Kathy Henderson. "Please spend a few minutes with him and bring him back to me when you're finished talking." She smiled and politely excused herself.

Joyce looked like she could be in her late sixties or maybe seventies. Who can even identify accurate age anymore? She was a small framed, little woman of about ninety pounds. Her silver hair was pinned up in a little bun, reminding Patrick of his favorite elementary schoolteacher. She had a pleasant smile and was friendly.

He began the conversation by attempting to woo her. He followed rule number one according to his mother's charm school. The first thing you do is ask questions to show interest in the other person. He did and she talked and talked. He listened and nodded his head up and down in agreement.

She offered him coffee and he accepted. He smiled to himself. If he kept taking them up on their coffee offers, he would float away or need a bladder repair.

Most of the conversation was about the general operations of the facility. He was looking for the appropriate opening, without being obvious, to focus on Kathy Henderson. He had a hard time getting her there.

She was a talker, going on and on about this and that. He occasionally nodded. She finished her coffee and offered him more, but he politely declined. He couldn't possibly consume any more.

She asked about his family. Finally, a perfect opening to steer the conversation to Ricky. He gave her the general background before broaching the topic he was really after.

He said carefully, "My son Andrew is best friends with Kathy Henderson's son. That's how we developed an interest in your facility. Her son, Ricky, is like family to us. What happened to his mother broke our hearts. I'll never forget the first time he talked about her and talked about her death."

He shook his head back and forth and sighed. He continued, "We all cried together. Ricky is like a son to my wife and me." *God, please forgive me.*

Joyce sadly nodded in agreement. "It is a very sad story. I still believe if she hadn't escaped from here, she would be with us today. It's a shame she left. She didn't take her medications with her, and undid all the progress she made. It was moment after moment of weakness and hopelessness that finally took her life."

"Yeah, that's what Ricky's uncle told him, and he shared it with us." More lies.

"That poor little boy. He and his sister were so small. Just awful. His mother left those two lovely children behind. They were shipped off to foster care. Separated. As I recall, she was adopted by a nice middle class family by the name of, let me see if I can still remember, Watkins," she barely took a breath, "I never did hear what finally became of him. I believe he was shipped from foster home to foster home last I heard. Tragic for those children."

"That's what Ricky said. He didn't like to talk much about it. Didn't know her diagnosis. Evidently, no one ever told Ricky all the details." Patrick appeared to be in thought, pausing before continuing, "What happened to his mom exactly? We need to get a general understanding if we are establishing a foundation in her honor."

She hesitated, "Oh, I'm sorry, I can't release any of her medical condition information. You will need to talk to Ms. Feinstein."

Patrick hesitated. *Take it easy. This could be it.*

He responded with disappointment in his voice, "No problem. As you can imagine, I have two interests here. I'm interested in the foundation, but I have a deep vested interest in Ricky. I want to be there for this young man. I really think we can help him."

Joyce didn't say anything for a moment. She looked around the room like she was afraid someone could be listening. She leaned in and said, "I probably shouldn't be telling you this, but if it will help us with the foundation and at the same time help Ricky," she thought before continuing, "Oh, what harm can it do if I can help." It wasn't a question.

She continued, "This tragedy is one of those that stayed with me after all these years. We could have helped save her and it affected so many lives. She suffered from severe depression, and she felt hopelessness about her future, about life. It was a shame. We really thought we could help Kathy with the right medications and the right treatment and environment. She was doing very well here and seemed to be getting better. She even told us this was the only place she had ever felt at home. Something changed, caused her to digress. Then, she…I can't think of another word at the moment but snapped." She shook her head in sadness, reflecting on Kathy's life.

Patrick asked, "Did anyone else in the family have similar emotional or mental challenges? Maybe we could also provide their story as part of the foundation."

"Kathy's great grandmother killed herself. I always wondered about Kathy's children. Some disorders and their connection to genetics, present in other family members. Research is showing the disorder may be genetic, but the research is…there is still so much to learn. You said Ricky is doing well?"

"Ricky is good. Healthy. I don't know much about Kaitlin since she doesn't live in our area, but I've never heard Ricky say anything to the contrary about her." Patrick had all the information he was going to get or need from Miss Joyce. He looked at his watch and stood, telling her he had to get to another meeting. He thanked her for help and indicated they would be in touch about the foundation.

She led him back to Ms. Feinstein's office. In that awkward departure moment, she hugged Patrick rather than shaking his hand. Miss Joyce was off and running. She was a sweet little lady. He was ashamed of himself for deceiving her.

* * * * * * * * * *

Ms. Feinstein walked Patrick to his car. He told her she would be hearing from their firm as soon as they could get some of the financing issues out of the way. He felt good about the possibilities, but it would take some time to pull it all together.

He smiled and thanked her again for taking the time with him. It had been very beneficial. He would be in touch.

The guilt was racking up. Lies, lies and more lies. It was heart-wrenching. This was an honorable facility accomplishing great things. He was sorry Kathy Henderson wasn't able to get the help she needed. It was a tragedy, and for a second and more times than he deserved, he almost felt bad for Ricky. Patrick was certain he had inherited his mother's genetics, or much worse. What about Kaitlin? What next?

* * * * * * * * * *

Pulling out of the facility driveway, he hesitated, thinking about his next move. He had gained a better understanding of what he was dealing with, but the news was not good. Ricky was a danger and he was desperate.

And, then there was the sister. Where was she and who had she become? He glanced at his watch and winced. He needed to get back home, but he had an idea. One more stop.

CHAPTER 162

Patrick returned to the town library for a place to sit and continue his research. He walked directly to the computers and pulled out his tablet. He had to look her up. It might be a dead end, but what other choice did he have? He searched the name, Kaitlin Henderson.

Another twist. Kaitlin was twenty three years old, and survived by Jake and Mary Beth Watkins. She died in Philadelphia approximately a year earlier. There were no details. His first thought was suicide.

He couldn't contact her parents until he had a plan. He needed to know about her death and her relationship with Ricky. He couldn't shake the feeling that he might be involved. He would have to make another trip. Ugh, he was so running out of time.

His concentration was interrupted by the sound of his cellphone. Ricky's name and number filled the screen. He felt dread as he answered, "What do you want?"

"Well, hello to you too, Mr. Stephenson. Is that any way to talk to your son's best friend and your business partner?"

Patrick felt the heat flush through his face. With fear in his voice that he could not hide, he repeated, "What do you want?"

Ricky ignored the question. He said, "So, you are out of town. Where are you?"

"It's not your concern where I am. I'm working. And, how do you know I'm out of town?"

Ricky laughed, "I told you, we're partners. I make it my business to know about you. About Andrew. Where you are? What you're doing?"

Patrick ignored the question and said flatly and emotionless, "What do you want?"

"I'm a little short on cash. I need another installment and I need it sooner than I thought," he said with a strange, slightly shaky tone in his voice.

He hesitated and sighed, "How much?"

"I need $50,000. Let's say by next Friday."

"What? I can't get my hands on that kind of money, especially on such short notice."

"Of course you can. We've talked about this. You have access to all kinds of money. Comptroller of our little bank. My apartment. Next Friday. Don't disappoint me." His voice was low and cold as he hung up.

Patrick stared at the phone without being able to focus. Tired, nauseous, and his chest hurt. What was he going to do? Maybe it was time to give up and go to the police. *Could he take that chance?*

No. There was no way.

He would have to do the one thing…the tipping point. He had desperately hoped it wouldn't come to this, but what other choice did he have?

CHAPTER 163

Patrick spent the next few hours of the drive thinking about borrowing the money. He couldn't use any more of his family's funds so he had to figure out a way to get the money from the firm. He couldn't risk going to anyone and he only needed it for a small period of time anyway. He would reimburse the company when he received his next bonus. He hated it, but it was the only way. He rationalized his actions. It was only a short-term loan and it wouldn't hurt David or the firm.

He would get to the office early and make the transaction to a bank in another town. A nearby big city. That's how it would have to be. He had been dreading this last resort alternative since the blackmail began. Details were finalized by the time he pulled into the garage.

He sat in his car and put his head against the head rest. He needed a moment to get a grip on his emotions. What happened to him and that wonderful and peaceful life he so desperately wanted back? He looked in the mirror and all he saw was deep fear and sadness. The gaunt face and bruised eyes. He breathed in and out for a few seconds. He grabbed his suitcase, manufactured a smile on his face, and walked through the kitchen door.

* * * * * * * * *

"Hello sweetheart. I'm home," he spoke loudly.

"Hi darling." She walked in from the back of the house. On her way to him, she picked up two glasses of white wine from the counter. As she got closer, he could smell her perfume and shampoo and it was intoxicating, almost making him forget what was happening to them.

She handed him the wine as she kissed him on the lips. Her action was obliging and endearing. He had called from the car and told her he desperately needed a drink. His trip had been exhausting.

He looked around. The table was set and the room lit by candlelight. He grinned sheepishly and asked, "What have I done to deserve this?"

She put down her glass and put her arms around his neck. She leaned in so close he could feel her breath. "Because you are a wonderful husband. I feel like pampering you for an evening."

He kissed her gently and again more sensually before speaking, "I love you so much. I don't know what I would do without you," he hesitated before continuing, "I will never let anyone hurt you, my love."

She stared at him for a moment and cocked her head sideways. She asked, "Are you okay? Honey, what's going on with you?"

He faked a laugh and a smile. "Nothing. I'm just tired and so glad to be home."

She kept her attention on him and thought she saw a tear in his eyes. "Hey, are you really okay?" she asked, stepping back and looking deep into his eyes.

He smiled. "I'm fine. Very happy to have you and a little tired and drained all at the same time."

"Okay. You would tell me if something was wrong, wouldn't you?"

He didn't hesitate, he couldn't hesitate. "Yes dear."

"Okay. Why don't you take a quick shower and then dinner will be ready."

He picked up his suitcase and carried it to the bedroom. He dropped it by his closet door and stared at it. It contained the evidence he desperately wanted to disappear.

He removed his shoes and sat on the bed. He put his face in his hands and sobbed. He couldn't believe this was his life. He got up and stepped into the shower. It wasn't so much to feel refreshed as it was to wash off the filth and grime.

CHAPTER 164

The next morning Patrick had coffee with his wife before rushing out of the house. He told her he had an early meeting and didn't have time for breakfast.

He was uneasy entering his office suite at that hour. It was dark and too quiet. Maybe it was because no one else was around. Or maybe it was more about what he was going to do. He immediately went to his desk and turned on the computer. While waiting for the financial system to boot up, he walked to the kitchen to make coffee.

By the time he returned, his knees were weak. He felt sweat running down his face and the heat underneath his shirt. He sat down behind his desk and undid his tie. He felt like it was restricting his air flow. He had to get a grip. *Breathe in, breathe out.* He had to think. The first attempt, he just couldn't do it.

* * * * * * * * * *

There were several attempts at different times followed by the same result. Scavenging multiple places throughout the building to make it happen. He kept telling himself he would pay the money back. He was just borrowing it. He stepped away, paced the floor reminding himself there were no other options, and went back to the computer, another computer and another computer. More attempts.

Finally after completing two withdrawal transactions to the bank account he opened, he shut down the system. Mission accomplished.

Dazed, numb and sitting quietly at his desk, he jumped as Lindsay walked into his office and surprised him. She looked at him awkwardly and apologized. "I'm sorry. I didn't mean to startle you. Are you doing something you shouldn't be doing?" she teased.

He stuttered, "Ugh no. I think I've had too much coffee, and I didn't sleep very well. I'm a little on edge."

She had a concerned look on her face. "Are you okay? You haven't been sleeping well for awhile now."

"Yeah, I'm good. It's just the stress of everything. Too much going on. It will get better."

"Do you feel up to joining me for a drink? Maybe a decaf or a tea? I was hoping to get a little Patrick time. I've missed talking to you."

"I've missed you too. I'll grab a decaf." He almost welcomed the distraction. He had to get out of the office.

CHAPTER 165

Patrick and Lindsay approached the Cafe Bar and he saw David enter the building. He was walking swiftly to the elevator without looking up.

Patrick felt a rapid increase in his chest as he looked to his left and saw him. He quickly turned away, hoping David hadn't noticed as he rushed Lindsay into the Cafe Bar. He wasn't ready to face David, not yet. He had to come to grips with what he had done, even though he was just borrowing the money. That's hardly a crime he kept telling himself.

Lindsay and Patrick spent the next thirty minutes talking about things, nothing in particular. Just things that friends talk about. He almost forgot about Ricky, Andrew and the money. He enjoyed this special friendship, a precious bond that made work more fun, even comforting at any other time.

Lindsay was one of the most powerful and strong, yet empathetic and tender women he had ever known. Men found her fascinating, even sexy in a subtle way. Patrick understood why, but it was different for him. She was a dear friend that felt more like family. *God, why hadn't he confided in her?*

The thought of all of this made him sick to his stomach. Not only was he cheating David, but he was lying to Lindsay. If she knew what he had done, she would never forgive him. Trusting relationships were core values and meant everything to him. *He hated this.*

CHAPTER 166

"And THAT is how it all began," he said to Lindsay, sitting behind bars and prison walls. He told her he had to make three more withdrawals before it caught up with him. He swore he was planning on returning the money, when he received the next year's bonus, and the next year after that, and…

He pleaded, looking directly into her eyes, "I swear to you. You know me." He paused before continuing, "It was my son. I had no option."

Lindsay stared into space and paused for a long moment before looking at him. She said softly, "You could have come to me. I would have helped you."

"Lindsay, you couldn't. You don't have the kind of money Ricky was talking about. And I wouldn't bring you into this horror. Besides, he threatened to ruin Andrew's life if I told anyone. By that time, I knew he wasn't stable and was even more concerned he might kill Andrew for distancing himself. My research didn't uncover a diagnosis, but he definitely has serious problems and is dangerous. Of this, I am quite sure," his voice cracked, as he continued to stare into her eyes.

There was silence between them. Patrick assumed the conversation was over and that would be the end. She had a right to know the truth and hear it from him. He was further broken by the reality that he may never have the chance to talk with Lindsay again, but the time had come to get on with it.

Dreading her departure, but mustering strength that didn't really exist, he said, "Thank you for coming. I couldn't bear to let you think I'm capable of this without knowing the truth, my motivation behind it. I am so sorry. I know you have always believed in me and I've let you down. I wish I could take it back, but I can't."

"Where is Ricky now?"

"I have no idea. This may not be over. I'm afraid of what he might do. He may still ruin Andrew's life. Lindsay, I think he is capable of anything."

There was more silence between them before Patrick said quietly, his voice trailing off, "You can go now. I just had to let you know the truth." He studied her for a moment, thought he saw a flicker of something he recognized in her eyes that he knew all too well and said softly, "There is one more thing. I have no right to ask this, but I need someone to tell Stephanie everything and help her. She may need some legal representation for Andrew, with Ricky still around. I don't know how this will play out. I'm sure you'll find this ironic, but you are the only person I trust. Will you talk to her? Help her? Be there for her?"

Lindsay stared back at him for a moment. Without saying a word, she stood and walked to the door. She put her hand on the knob and hesitated. She couldn't walk out on him. She had known him too long and he had meant too much to her. She knew he wasn't an embezzler. She knew him better than that. He wouldn't have done this, except to save his family. Desperation.

She leaned her head against the door. She breathed deeply, turned around and walked back towards her dear friend. Facing him, she said, "I can't imagine what you've been through. I know you, Patrick. You wouldn't do this unless you thought there was no other way. I'll help you."

His hands covered his face and he choked out the words. "Thank you. I couldn't handle this if Stephanie didn't have someone to turn to. She needs your strength. Someone that cares about her and Andrew as much as you do with the resolve that only you have."

"Of course, I'll be there for Stephanie. But, that's not what I mean." She sat back down and smiled faintly before saying, "I'm talking about you. I'm going to help you. So, what do we do now? We need a game plan."

* * * * * * * * *

Patrick sat motionless in the metal prison chair, stunned and processing before lifting his head to look up at her. It was the first moment he didn't feel alone and hopeless since this all started. "You're willing to help me after all this? Why would you do that?"

"I believe you when you say you were planning to reimburse the company. Now, we just have to find a way to get you out of this mess, so you can pay back the money."

"I don't even know what to say, but thank you. For believing in me, trusting me, when I didn't even deserve it," his voice cracked and lowered as he continued, "You have always been an amazing friend." He tried to turn away before she had the chance to see him wipe tears from his eyes.

She placed her hand on his and said, "You would do the same for me." With a forced cheerfulness, she continued, "Okay, let's get down to business. We have work to do. Where do we go from here?"

They spent the next few minutes talking about the information Patrick gathered. The lies about Ricky's parents and his siblings. The serious emotional challenges and the foster homes. It kept coming back to Ricky's sister, Kaitlin. "I don't know why I feel this, but something tells me Ricky is involved in Kaitlin's death. I have no basis, but I can't shake the feeling."

"Well then, I better take a trip to Philly and search for the truth. I'll find out what happened to Kaitlin, and we'll go from there. I'll leave tomorrow morning."

They finalized their plan, but Lindsay didn't let on that she was apprehensive. She didn't know if she could successfully execute it, but they didn't really have a choice.

Before she left Patrick, she tried to reassure him. Give him hope. Or, maybe she did it for herself because she needed to hear it. She hugged him and held on for an extra second, while she tried to wipe tears from her eyes without him seeing. She told him not to worry. They were going to figure this out. He could count on it, on her.

What she didn't say was that she was really worried. About him, Andrew, and Stephanie. What was Ricky capable of? She had little time and had no idea what she was walking into.

CHAPTER 167

Lindsay called David to tell him she needed a couple of days off. There was no chit chat. Direct and to the point. Told him it was an emergency and she had to go out of town and couldn't get into the specifics. Her voice was firm and it did not come across as a request. David didn't push for any details and the conversation was brief.

"Take all the time you need," he said quietly. She was up to something and it wasn't hard to figure out that it likely involved Patrick. He opted not to broach the subject since she was more than a little upset with him already. He knew he had to address their last conversation, but it wasn't the right time. They both needed time.

CHAPTER 168

Lindsay woke early the next morning and joined the commuters on the highway. With coffee in hand, she settled in for what she hoped would not be more than a three hour drive. That would place her in position for her first conversation at the appropriate time.

She had spent much of the evening doing research into Kaitlin Henderson's life. Kaitlin and Ricky had been separated after their parents' death. While their mother was in the Noble Home, they were staying with relatives. After her death, where did Ricky go?

Her first stop was the last address she could find for Kaitlin Henderson. It was an apartment complex on the outskirts of Philly.

There was little traffic, inviting her to drive faster than she should. She stopped once for food, coffee, and a bathroom. The timing was perfect and she rehearsed what she was planning to say to the office manager.

When she arrived, she sat in the car for a couple of minutes taking in her surroundings. The apartment complex was upscale. It felt more like a condo community than apartment living with grounds that were carefully manicured. The pool area was expansive, with a variety of lounge chairs, tables with umbrellas, and an outdoor tiki bar. It felt like a tropical paradise tucked away in a Philly suburb.

Hadn't Kaitlin been in med school? The rent was more than an average mortgage. *Note to self, where did the money come from?*

Lindsay took her time getting out of the car and walking to the office entrance. There were few cars in the parking lot. She assumed most of the tenants were at work or school. There was a local university and med school a few miles away.

As she tentatively opened the door, a twenty something young man was sitting behind a desk, busily texting on his phone. He looked up and smiled as she walked toward him. *Let's go Lindsay, showtime.*

CHAPTER 169

"May I help you?" The young man didn't wait for an answer as he continued, "If you're looking for an apartment, we don't have any vacancies at the moment. I can put you on a waiting list and you can complete an application."

"Well, that's disappointing. I'm new in town and I need a place to live, like yesterday," she smiled and leaned on the counter facing him.

"I'm sorry I can't help you. We rarely have vacancies in this complex. Even the waiting list is fairly long," he said apologetically, putting down his cell phone and looking at her.

"That's really too bad. I had my heart set on it. I started a new job here and I'm in a hotel. I can't stay there much longer. Any ideas about other places of this…caliber? This complex has the look and feel of community. It's the kind of place I'm looking for. As a single woman, I need a place that feels safe and secure." She tried charm.

He pointed to his left and said, "There are some fairly nice apartments about two miles from here that you might like. I think they may have some vacancies. The only down side is all the college students, so it might be a little rowdy and noisy at times."

"Oh no. I can't do that. I need a quiet place to research and write. I'll be teaching at the school and I don't think it would be appropriate to live surrounded by students. How long is the wait? Is there any chance I could get in here within the next few months?"

"There are a few names on the list. I can't make any guarantees, but you're welcome to complete an application and see what happens."

Lindsay appeared to be thinking before she answered, "I guess I better keep checking around first. I'm getting a bit desperate. I may come back."

"I'll give you my card. You can give me a call and let me know how the search is going. I can put your name on the list and then you can come in and fill out an application. I don't normally do it that way, but I'll see what I can do." He paused before continuing, "Maybe, my manager might be able to help since you're a professor at the university. I'll be happy to talk to her." He smiled.

"Thank you. I really appreciate it. You have been very helpful." She extends her hand. She starts for the door, but hesitates and turns back around. "I should have asked before. I just made an assumption the answer is no. Do you have many students that live here? Doesn't really look like a complex geared for students."

"Not many. We've only had a couple and they are in the med school not far from here. They are busy and aren't around much."

"Med school. Isn't that a coincidence? That's where I'll be teaching. I'm a psychology professor," she continued, "If you tell me their names, I'll see if they are in any of my classes."

At first, he didn't know if he should answer. Then, he thought it might be good for the girls. She could be one of their future professors. Might help to know her. Not to mention, she seemed harmless, and very pretty. "Cynthia Lewis and Charlene Jackson. Both are in their third year."

She looked around. "Nice place for med students. Times have changed. I remember when I was in school. I barely had two dollars to my name. I wasn't fortunate enough to live in a place like this. Impressive." She tried to act nonchalant.

"Yeah, me too. I've had to earn every dime I ever had."

"It's hard. I still remember like it was yesterday. I really struggled," she said, shaking her head. *Keep him talking.*

He responded, "My family didn't have much money. I had to take out college loans and I'm still paying on them. And, probably will be forever."

Lindsay smiled. They were bonding. She casually walked back towards him. "I know how you feel. It took me a long time. Keep working hard. You'll get there." A little bit of positive reinforcement couldn't hurt. She said, "I guess these med students had it better than you and me."

"These girls have been fortunate. They both came from money. Cynthia's dad is a judge. Almost made her move a year ago. Some things happened that were tragic, very hard for Cynthia to get through. You may hear about it. It still feels fresh to everyone around here. Cynthia's roommate died in the apartment." The Office Clerk said, as he suddenly became more talkative. Boredom was working in her favor.

"Her roommate died here? That's terrible." She looked, actually was, horrified. She looked down and back up at him. "What happened? If you don't mind me asking."

He hesitated and then thought, why not? After all, being a psychology professor at the school, she would hear about it anyway. What could it hurt? He answered, "It was awful. I probably shouldn't talk about it, but it's not exactly a secret. She killed herself."

His mood changed. As the Office Clerk continued to talk to Lindsay, he looked more upset than she would have expected for an acquaintance. There was almost a physical reaction. Lindsay recognized the signs. There was more to it and she intended to find out exactly what it was. How well did he know her? Were they friends, or what was their connection?

"You know, you can talk to me. I've dedicated my life to helping people. It's what I do for a living." Lindsay softly reassured him and continued, "What can I do to help?"

It was obvious he was thinking about whether he should go any further. But, he wanted to talk to her. He took a deep breath and said, "Kaitlin left a note about school being really difficult and feeling an unbearable amount of stress, feeling hopeless and depressed."

Lindsay attempted to appear surprised. She said, "I'm so sorry. I've completed a lot of research on depression and the impacts on the person and the people they love. It's just terrible." Shaking her head, she continued, "Such a tragedy. If only we had known, we might have been able to help her."

"I know. I wish she had been able to get the help she needed. She didn't get the chance." His voice dropped off and he looked out the window. There was silence between them.

Lindsay's voice was barely above a whisper, "Me, too. I wish I had been here to help. But, maybe I can help those that were left behind." She paused and continued in a conversational tone, "What about her roommate? I'm surprised her roommate would be able to stay in the same apartment after an awful experience like that."

"She couldn't. Cynthia moved to another building. The building next to this one, with a new roommate." He nodded and pointed in the direction of the change in residency. "Another med student. She said she didn't know why, but wanted to be closer to the office. To feel safer." He couldn't seem to stop. She was easy to talk to. "I'm sorry about going off on a tangent. I probably shouldn't have talked about this. I've said more than I should."

"No, no don't be sorry. I'm sure Cynthia will be in some of my classes. You may not realize it, but you're helping her. It gives me some insight. I can pay attention to any possible signs of trouble for her. I've observed too many people go without help when they needed it. I can provide support, if she needs it." Finally, some words streaming out of Lindsay's mouth that weren't lies. This was awful. *Remember, the plan.*

He seemed to relax. "Would you like a cup of coffee? I made a fresh pot a few minutes ago and almost forgot about it." He said as he lifted the pot in her direction.

"I would love one. Black, please. We can have coffee and chat some more. Why don't you tell me more about Cynthia and Kaitlin? I don't want to intrude, but I certainly want to be available to Cynthia."

He handed her a coffee mug and offered her a seat on the couch, next to floor to ceiling windows overlooking a wooded area. He sat in a chair across from her and continued talking. "I had only been working here a few months when it happened. I would see both Kaitlin and Cynthia around the complex. Kaitlin used to take walks in the woods on the side of this building and sit over there." He pointed to a bench with a couple of side tables and chairs, two bird feeders, and a mini flag that displayed a variety of colorful bouquets. His desk had full view.

He continued, "She would sit for hours and read and take notes. She was a beautiful girl. Kind. So caring. I used to glance at her sitting on that bench and think how I wished I could be more like her. She was obviously bright and seemed to have it all together. Little did I know what was going on inside her head."

"You said there was a letter she wrote, saying she was under a tremendous amount of stress. Were there any other signs of problems or challenges? Did you ever see her with anyone besides Cynthia? Like maybe a boyfriend or a friend?"

"I didn't know of any boyfriend. She was too busy with school for anything like that."

Lindsay just knew there was more. He had observed Kaitlin more than he let on. He might have even had a thing for her. She proceeded cautiously. "Did she ever have visitors that you know of? Any of her family visit her?"

"Oh yeah, I almost forgot about him. A brother. He visited occasionally. Good looking guy. They looked alike. That's how I first figured out it wasn't a boyfriend. I believe his name was Ricky."

* * * * * * * * *

Of course, it was. Lindsay's face showed no emotion, other than interest in their conversation over coffee. She tried not to be obvious when she asked, "Were they close? Did he come around often?"

He looked puzzled by the question. Weren't they supposed to be talking about Cynthia, not Kaitlin? "Why do you ask?"

Be cool Lindsay. She shrugged and said, "I was just wondering about him. If he ever saw signs of instability or depression. Too bad. He might have been able to help her, or maybe he was helping her."

"I don't know anything about their relationship, other than he visited occasionally. Why all the questions about Kaitlin? I thought you were interested in helping Cynthia."

"Oh, I'm sorry. I didn't mean to intrude. I got the impression you were fond of Kaitlin and I thought you might like to talk about it." She was taking a chance. "You should talk about it. Don't worry, I'm discreet," she said with an endearing smile, "But, I certainly don't want to pry."

He studied her for a couple of seconds, weighing what to say next. He bit his bottom lip before continuing. "I liked her," he said as he looked down at the floor. "She was nice to me. We used to talk and I was starting to really like her. We went out a couple of times for beer and pizza. Never really went any further than friendship. There wasn't enough time. Her life was over before I had the chance to get to know her."

"I'm sorry. I can't imagine how that felt for you. Tell me about her. If you want to." *Careful, let him talk.*

He had a faint smile on his face as he glanced out the window in the direction of the bench, Kaitlin's study spot. "She talked mainly about school and a little about her family. She was a good conversationalist, a great listener. We shared stories about our wacky families and our tragedies. She told me about her parents dying and her getting adopted at a really young age. She and her brother were separated early in life. Were sent to different foster homes. She was fortunate enough to be adopted, but she said he wasn't."

He paused and continued, "She said something about her adoptive parents not being able to take both of them at the time. I don't remember her saying why. That left him going from foster home to foster home throughout his childhood. They recently reconnected and he didn't even have an opportunity to get to know her. How awful it must have been for him."

Lindsay tried to show empathy. She couldn't shake the feeling. Ricky was involved in Kaitlin's death. She knew it. If he was capable of killing Chad over jealousy, he was capable of killing his sister.

"Who found Kaitlin in the apartment?" Lindsay hesitated and showed genuine concern with her next question, "Was it Cynthia?"

"Yes," he responded quietly, shaking his head and looking down.

"Has she ever talked about it?"

"Nope. I mentioned it to her one time and her reaction was beyond terrified. I thought she was on the verge of a breakdown. When it first happened, she had a friend stay with her. The friend stopped by the office one day and we talked. She said Cynthia was having nightmares and refused to speak about it at all."

Lindsay was convinced Cynthia knew more. She knew something or suspected something. She was frightened and Ricky was definitely involved. She had to talk to her, immediately. Something had to be done about him. Her thoughts shifted to Andrew. Patrick was right, he might be in serious danger.

"That poor girl. I can't imagine what she has been through. I'm sorry I've taken up so much of your time," she said as she looked at her watch.

"Oh, it's no problem at all. As you can see, I'm not that busy and I've enjoyed talking to you." He smiled.

She smiled back. "Me, too. When I start my work at the university, I'm sure I'll have Cynthia in classes. I'll keep an eye on her. You probably don't realize it, but you have really helped her today." She hesitated for a moment before writing down a phone number and a name. "Uh, here's my phone number in case you get an opening for one of the apartments or you want to talk or you sense trouble for Cynthia. I might be able to help her, or you. Well, you think about it. Thank you for the coffee." She said goodbye and left the office.

Lindsay walked to her car and got in. She looked at her watch again. It was getting late and it wouldn't be long before dark.

Not wanting the Office Clerk to see her loitering around the property, she left the complex to wait for the sun to go down, and to hopefully get to Cynthia. She parked across the street, strategically positioning her vehicle to see both the entrance to the complex and the parking lot of her apartment building. The rest was just a matter of waiting.

CHAPTER 170

Click, click, click. Lindsay continued to press the buttons on her electronic device, flipping through text and picture after picture.

If she didn't recognize Cynthia by the online photos, she had a view of the apartment and could identify her going in. But the pictures should do it, large scale, good visual clarity. They displayed an athletic looking girl of medium height, with shoulder length brown hair and what appeared to be dark eyes.

Lindsay had been searching on the internet to find out anything she could on the girl. As luck would have it, she typed in the name and several pictures popped on the screen.

Cynthia was a very talented tennis player in high school and a decent one in undergraduate school. She even had a couple of local tournament victories attached to her name, along with a number of other awards.

Lindsay could relate to college athletes. They were a special breed to be able to balance sports and the challenges of academia. She thought about altering the strategy and changing their upcoming conversation to tennis, but decided against it. Stick to the plan. She was confident it would work.

Successfully finessing Cynthia to open up was the only way. There was one thing she knew for sure, it wasn't suicide. She was convinced Ricky did this to his sister, and Cynthia knew something, suspected something, or knew too much.

CHAPTER 171

Lindsay sat in the car for the next half hour rehearsing her script. A little after 6:00, she saw a car enter the complex and drive slowly to a parking space in front of Cynthia's apartment. The young girl sat for a moment and looked around before getting out with her backpack, probably full of what Lindsay assumed to be medical books. She walked quickly and didn't waste any time getting the key in the door and slamming it shut.

It was definitely Cynthia. Dread overwhelmed Lindsay momentarily, but this was a confrontation that had to take place in person. She couldn't take the chance of talking by phone. She had to see her reaction, her fear. She was certain it would be there.

Lindsay moved to the lot, parking out of sight from the office. Giving Cynthia time to settle in, she rehearsed the script one last time.

She walked to the front door and knocked timidly. At first, no answer. She knocked again and Cynthia opened the door slightly. They were facing one another. The chain was on the lock.

She took in a deep breath. *Make it good Lindsay. Just get in the door.* "Good evening. I'm a new professor of Psychology and Psychiatry at the University. The Office Clerk said you might be willing to speak to me about living in this community. I am new in town. I'm thinking about renting an apartment here. We might be neighbors."

She frowned at the thought of the Office Clerk, but the mention of psychiatry professor peaked her interest. She relaxed slightly, "What would you like to know?"

"I was hoping you would share your opinion about living here. What do you think of this complex? I'm looking for a quiet place. I'm working on my latest book and I need a place with minimal distraction."

"It's very quiet here. I'm a student and I study most of the time when I'm home." She offered a slight smile and said, "In fact, I'm studying to get into a psychiatry residency."

Lindsay's face broke into a big grin. They could bond. "Really? What a coincidence. I begin teaching next semester. Bad timing, but I'm in the middle of this book and trying to move to a new area all at the same time. I would like to get settled now and focus on getting the final draft to my editor. I don't know anyone, or where to live, eat, shop, or anything else. I'm feeling a bit like a fish out of water at the moment," She talked without taking a breath.

Then, she paused in hopes of an invitation. She proceeded with caution and a backup plan. "Well, thank you for your time. I'll be going. I'm sure I'll see you at school. Maybe even class."

Cynthia thought for a second. Why not? She might be in one of her classes in the future. She asked, "Would you like to come in? I just made a fresh pot of tea. I have a few minutes before I have to study. We can have tea and I can tell you whatever you need to know about the area."

Lindsay thanked her before asking, "Are you sure? I don't want to disturb you. Wouldn't be good for a professor to keep students from studying." She smiled, teasingly. *So far, so good.*

Cynthia laughed, "Oh, no problem. Please come in." She removed the chain from the lock and stepped aside.

CHAPTER 172

Lindsay entered the apartment. There were no textbooks or notebooks, pizza boxes or other takeout containers littering the furniture or the coffee table. It was well decorated and organized, neat and clean. Mature surroundings with sophisticated taste. It looked like something out of an Ethan Allen store.

"Your home is beautifully decorated. You have splendid taste," Lindsay said as she appeared to glance around the living room.

"Thanks. I would like to take credit but it's really the result of searching through a ton of magazines. I've been on my own for quite some time and my parents helped finance the furnishings. And, then there were roommates with similar tastes."

"Roommates? Aw, I remember those days. They were really fun. I was never lonely. Do you have roommates now?"

"Just one. I meant over the years," Cynthia said. Lindsay thought she saw a slight flicker of something. Remembrance. Fear. Pain.

"Yeah, I never lived with more than one roommate. I considered the possibility, but was worried it would be too much chaos. Of course, I had to have one. We didn't have much money."

Cynthia smiled and offered Lindsay a seat. She excused herself to get the tea. The kitchen was not visible from the living room, making the next step easier.

Lindsay waited until she could hear Cynthia gathering cups and saucers before stepping quietly to the front door and examining the latch at the bottom for extra security. She winced as she quietly slid the medal to the locked position and returned to the couch. She waited until they were both seated and sipping tea before she made her next move.

"This is very good tea. Thank you for inviting me in," She paused and turned to face her before continuing. She spoke softly, "I don't want to alarm you, but we have to talk. I know you were Kaitlin's roommate. Please don't be afraid. I really am here to help."

The fear registered across the girl's face. Her mouth gaped open and the tea cup abruptly stopped before touching her lips. She regained her composure and slowly placed it on the coffee table in front of her.

Lindsay continued with the soft tone. "This conversation may save your life. I need to talk to you about Kaitlin and her death. I need some answers. I know it was ruled a suicide, but I don't believe that. I want to talk about the brother she left behind. Ricky Henderson."

* * * * * * * * *

Cynthia looked startled and panicked. She glanced at the front door. Lindsay said, "Don't be frightened. I'm not here to hurt you."

Cynthia's lips quivered, she stood and stepped away from the couch, "Who are you and why are you here? Please leave."

Lindsay continued, "Cynthia, I promise I'm here to help. You don't realize it, but you really need my help. And, I need yours. I know what you have been through and I think you want to hear what I have to say. I can put an end to this nightmare. I have information about Ricky that you will want to hear. He has a history of violence. He has killed before. I think he is a danger to you."

Cynthia's lips changed from quivering to trembling, she started crying and shaking her head from side to side. She pleaded, "Look, I don't want to get involved in this. I'm trying to get my life back together."

"I know, but you are already involved. We both know what happened. I wish there was another way, but I desperately need your help."

"My best friend died in our apartment and I can't get the vision out of my head. I live with it every day. I can't help you. And there is nothing you can do for me."

"Cynthia, I'm very worried about anyone who has contact with him. That has or had a relationship with him. Ricky is blackmailing a dear friend of mine. A very kind and decent man that doesn't deserve this. Ricky likely murdered a young boy and is framing my friend's son. He certainly would come after you if he thought you knew something. Anything. I need to know what we're dealing with. Trust me. I am trying to put him away."

"Go on," she said in a measured tone, attempting to calm down.

"Since Kaitlin was your best friend, I'm assuming she told you about the deaths of both parents. Her mother killed herself when the children were very young." Lindsay continued, "Ricky was in a number of foster homes. I didn't know the extent of his emotional issues until recently. He didn't stay in one foster home for very long. No one offered up any explanation, other than he was a 'troubled' child. The system made it sound like he was troubled, but it was more than that."

"What does that mean?" Cynthia said in a shaky voice.

"It means he has a history of emotional issues. He is paranoid, obsessively jealous, and violent. Who knows? Probably psychotic. We think the trigger is a feeling of what he perceives as rejection, abandonment. He becomes violent and wants to hurt, to destroy anyone in his way. We didn't figure this out until it was too late. He had already killed."

"What happened?"

"People close to him started noticing odd behavior patterns. It was discovered that his mother had a history of psychiatric issues. His foster care parents all realized something wasn't right. The system required a number of evaluations and consultations. He has a personality disorder, perhaps antisocial personality disorder. In the past, he underwent treatment, therapy, and was placed on medication to control his behavior. As long as he stayed on his medications and engaged in a treatment program, he seemed to function."

"Why are you telling me this? I haven't seen him since Kaitlin died. I don't know where he is or what he is doing. I talked to him a few times when he visited Kaitlin, but that's it." Cynthia was lying.

Lindsay didn't fall for it. She continued, "Did Kaitlin say anything about him? Mention his issues?" She looked directly in her eyes, "Cynthia, he is a danger to himself and to others. There is no telling what he will do when backed into a corner. Did I mention he has killed before? He will do it again. No one is safe, especially you. You are a liability to him. Don't you realize that? You know too much."

"I already told you. I don't know anything about him," she said, this time even less convincing. Lindsay could see that she was breaking and the reality was sinking in.

She moved closer. She said quietly, "I think you do. Cynthia, if you don't let me help, this could turn out very bad for you."

"I can't talk about any of this. You don't know," she trailed off, shaking her head back and forth and stepping away from Lindsay.

Lindsay demanded, "Cynthia, you have to. Don't you care about justice, about Kaitlin's memory? You can't let him get away with this." She raised her voice, "He will kill you. Maybe not today or tomorrow, but what about next week or next year? He WILL kill you. Even if by remote chance he doesn't, are you prepared to spend the rest of your life looking over your shoulder? Do you have the stomach for that?"

"Why are you really here?" She gasped for breath. Tears emerged from her eyes.

"I told you," Lindsay replied in a low, pleading voice. "Let me help you."

"You aren't a psychology professor, are you?" she asked with resigned panic in her voice. The tears were flowing.

"No, I'm not. I'm a lawyer, but you have nothing to be afraid of. I'm on your side." Lindsay handed her a business card.

"What do you want?" she whimpered.

"Cynthia, I couldn't help Kaitlin, but it's not too late for you. You have got to trust me."

"Trust! I can't trust anyone. I can't talk about it. You were right about one thing. He will kill me. You weren't there when he threatened me. He meant it." She started trembling and sobbing again as she stumbled towards the nearest chair.

Lindsay caught her before she fell, putting her arms around her. The young woman broke down, crying uncontrollably. She kept crying, "I can't, I can't. He will kill me. He will kill my mother and my father."

She led her to the couch and held and rocked her back and forth in her arms. She said in a soothing voice, "It's going to be okay. He won't go anywhere near your family, I promise. But, we have to act quickly. We will put him away forever and this nightmare can end for you. We have to get this monster off the streets before he harms anyone else. You do know that, don't you?" Lindsay sat back and put her hands on her shoulders. She stared deep into her eyes, "Don't you?"

She finally gave in and nodded, looking drained and exhausted. She calmed slightly and started regaining her composure. She had been living with this torment for so long. "How can you protect my parents and keep them safe?"

"As soon as you tell me everything, the police will be sent to their home. But, you have to talk to me."

Cynthia whispered, "I'll tell you everything. I can't go on like this any more."

* * * * * * * * * *

In that moment, Lindsay felt many emotions, but none more potent than relief. She could help Cynthia and Patrick. It would finally be over.

She asked, "He killed Kaitlin, didn't he?"

"Yes."

"Do you suspect he did or do you know?"

"I know," she said emotionless.

Lindsay took a deep breath, before asking, "How do you know?"

"I saw him standing over her. But it was too late. She was already dead." She resumed crying, talking about her friend. "He poisoned her and made her take pills. When I walked into the apartment he was staging it to look like suicide. I caught him by surprise."

"But, he didn't kill you."

"I suspect it's because I disrupted his plan and he needed it to be suicide. He told me he would kill my family and me if I uttered a word. There was nothing I could do for her. He knew he had sufficiently scared me. He visits me from time to time and calls to let me know he is watching my every move. Says it's a reminder. He sends notes about watching my parents. He knows too much about them and their whereabouts for it to be an idle threat."

"That doesn't totally explain why he didn't kill you. You were a liability in his plan."

"Before all of this, we would talk when he came to see her. We started developing a friendship. I think he even liked me. I liked him back then. He could be very charming."

"Or maybe his plan was to scare you to the point of silence. And then come back and kill you after some time passed and no one would suspect him. And, you weren't a threat to his self esteem. Cynthia, what do you know about him and Kaitlin?"

"In the beginning, they were thrilled, almost euphoric about finding each other and their long lost relationship. For the first few months, they spent most of their free time together. Getting to know each other. At that point, it was amazing. Then, Kaitlin started talking differently about him and trying to distance herself. It was all very strange."

"What did she say about Ricky?"

"She thought he might have issues like their birth mother, or worse. He wouldn't admit it to her, so she was limited in her ability to help him. She was worried. Thought he might be depressed. Over time, she became concerned he was much worse than their mother, maybe even dangerous. She hated to do it, but she stopped taking his calls. She was frightened. Too frightened to help him. He showed up a couple of times and she made excuses not to see him. I guess he finally… snapped."

Lindsay's suspicions were correct. She asked, "What do you mean?"

"That day. When I walked in on him, he was distraught, looked disheveled. His eyes were wild, darting around the room like a crazed person. A mad man. He had killed her with poison, with pills. It was over and he had made it look like suicide. The bottles were open and he had placed them by her right hand. She was lying still on the carpet. He was talking to her. He said something like, 'It didn't have to be this way. Look what you made me do. Just like Chad. You didn't leave me any choice. Why do people make me do these things?' That's what he…" Cynthia stopped talking.

"Go on. What did he do next?" Lindsay urged her to continue.

"Then he said the most bizarre thing. He started crying and sat down next to her, holding her hand. He said, 'I didn't want to kill you. I love you. Other than Andrew, you're the only person I ever loved. But, you both betrayed me. Abandoned me. And now you want to put me away.'

"He wasn't making sense. He was talking fast and rambling. Then, he saw me. I tried to get out of there, but he grabbed my arm, and led me to the couch. He was surprisingly gentle with me."

"What happened next?"

"He told me I shouldn't have come home. He paced and said he had to think for a minute. Figure out what to do. Then, he sat down beside me. He told me why he had killed her and admitted that he had killed before. Almost like he was rationalizing his behavior. Thinking I would agree. I listened. I tried not to talk, other than sympathize with him. I agreed with him. Told him they left him no choice. I was desperate. I didn't know what else to say. I prayed he would leave."

"Go on."

"He said his sister wanted to leave him. She was just like everyone else in his life. He became angry and talked about how she was the lucky one. She had been in foster care and was adopted into a family. He was shuffled from one home after another. She never tried to find him. She never cared about him and she was trying to abandon him once again. He had gone to the trouble to reunite with her after all this time. They could be a real family and this was his thanks."

"You said he had killed before. Are you sure he said Chad? What did he say about him?"

"It was definitely Chad. I will never forget how he spit out his name with such emphasis. Something about Chad taking away his best friend, Andrew. Said Andrew was his brother and the only family he had other than his sister. He had no other option. Chad made him do it." She shook her head and stared at the wall in front of her. "I tried to talk to him. Calm him down. Act like we were friends. I even tried to placate him and continued to repeat he had no choice. I was terrified he would kill me."

"Did he say what he did to Chad?"

"Yes. He told me the details. He said it was on a camping trip with Chad and Andrew. He drugged Chad enough to make him a little off balance. When Andrew wasn't looking, he pushed him off the mountain. He actually bragged about it."

"Anything else you can think of?"

"That's it. I've had periodic visits from him. It's terrifying. Unnerving. Sometimes he acts as if he cares about me. Like he wants some kind of relationship with me. Other times, he is more distant and calls his visits friendly reminders to keep my mouth shut. But, he always knows what's going on with me," she sighed and said, "That's all I know. Can we please get the police over to my parents? And how about me? He will come after me."

"Now, it's over. Your worrying is over. You and your family will be taken care of. I need to make a couple of phone calls. I'll take care of everything." Lindsay embraced Cynthia, allowing her to break down and release the terror she had been holding in for so long.

She hadn't expected all of this. Her goal had been to save Patrick and Andrew, and get Ricky off the streets for killing his sister. Cynthia's story gave her an idea.

＊ ＊ ＊ ＊ ＊ ＊ ＊ ＊ ＊

Lindsay walked to another room, rapidly punching digits on her phone. There were two calls to make. Her first was to the police back home. Her second was just as important, an edgier one that would impact everyone. The one that had to work. She was on the phone for a few minutes, working out details and logistics. *Yes, it had to work.*

While hitting the end call button, Lindsay headed back to the living room to check on Cynthia. She hadn't moved from the couch, rocking back and forth with her hands wrapped around her knees staring straight ahead. Lindsay went to her, warmed her cold tea, tried to talk to her, but there wasn't much of a response. Feeling guilt and certainly some amount of responsibility, she told herself this was necessary. It was the only way to end this, for everyone.

If the day concluded as Lindsay hoped, Cynthia would be a vital player, avenging the actions of the disturbed young man Ricky had become. And, she and her family would be safe with immediate police protection.

Time seemed to stand still waiting for Cynthia's parents. Lindsay was getting nervous about the time, pacing back and forth, glancing at her watch every few seconds. Finally, two very frightened people rushed through the door and Lindsay briefly spoke before power walking out. She had to get back.

CHAPTER 173

Lindsay drove faster than she should, but she had to get there. It would soon be over if everything worked as planned.

Her next stop was Patrick and Stephanie's house. Patrick was still in custody, but she wasn't there for Patrick. She was there to pick up Stephanie.

Not long after they left, Andrew pulled into the driveway of his parent's home. He hesitated in the car, expecting a text. When the text came, he went to the front door and let himself in.

About ten minutes later, Ricky pulled into the Stephenson's driveway. Andrew had called to hang out like old times and Ricky was super hyped about it. He really missed his company and devouring Mrs. Stephenson's food while they watched basketball. He couldn't remember the last time they did this. He was thrilled to think he might have his old pal back. Just like the old days, the two of them hanging out like brothers. Maybe he would rethink everything and figure out how to make amends.

He was fidgeting at the front door with his hands in his pockets. He was humming a song he heard on the radio. He couldn't remember the last time he felt this way.

That is, until Andrew answered the door and stepped aside for him to enter. There was no smile, no hug. Ricky immediately thought something was wrong. Andrew had a strange look on his face, like he wasn't happy to see him. Ricky admonished himself to stop. His mind always went there. He had to stop it. Maybe Andrew was just tired. His mood would improve over the basketball game. They both loved the game.

Instead of cranking it up and bringing out the food, Andrew turned off the television. He motioned for Ricky to sit on the couch.

Ricky looked puzzled. "Hey, what are you doing? I thought we were watching the game. It should be on any minute. I'll tell you man, I've really missed this. Feels like old times," Ricky said smiling and stretching his arms on the back of the couch.

"Miss me? Do you miss Chad?" Andrew asked with a directness as he looked him in the eyes.

"What are you talking about? Of course I miss Chad." Ricky's smile slowly disappeared.

"I know what you did. The question is, why did you do it?"

"What are you talking about? What do you think I did, and why are you acting like this? I thought you wanted to watch the game." Ricky had a look of panic on his face.

"You killed him. You killed Chad. But, why?"

"I don't know what you're talking about Andrew. I loved Chad. You were there. You know he fell off that mountain."

"Really? Is that your story?"

"Is that my story? Are you kidding me right now?" Ricky stared at Andrew for a moment. "I can't believe you would even think I'm capable of such a thing. What's going on here?" Ricky's voice turned from panic to anger.

"We're going to talk. Just you and me. I don't want to watch basketball or anything else with you. We're not hanging out, Ricky. Not anymore. Not ever. I found out about you. What you are capable of." Andrew was sitting on the other end of the couch from Ricky. There wasn't enough space between them.

Andrew turned sideways and resumed the direct look into Ricky's eyes. He continued steadily and emotionless, "When did you become a cold-blooded killer? How could you do this? I loved you, man." He shook his head back and forth before continuing. "I didn't want to believe this about you. Who you really are."

"Andrew, don't do this," Ricky pleaded.

"Friends tried to tell me something wasn't right with you. Even Melissa, and she sees the good in everyone. She was afraid of you, but she certainly didn't realize you were a killer. She was uneasy every time you were around. By the way, I have some good news. We're getting married and I want you to stay away from her. You see, after what you did, there is no place for you in our life. We are finished."

"Just like that. After all we have been to each other, we're done. We were like brothers and now we're done. You're just walking away." His voice was masking the repressed rage.

"Yes, we're done. I've wanted to distance myself from you for a long time, but I was scared of what you might do. To me, my family, and even yourself."

Ricky stood and faced him, his body trembling. The rage boiled on the verge of eruption. His face turned crimson. His eyes transitioned to wild fury. He looked as if he might explode and then he calmed momentarily, trying to get himself under control. He looked around the room, shaking his head, and pleaded, "You don't mean it. You know I wouldn't do anything to harm Chad. It's the girl talking. She is just a girl. I'm sure it's her filling your head. I don't blame you."

"Stop. It's not her."

He begged, "You don't want to end our relationship over a girl. She doesn't love you. I love you man. She'll break your heart. What about all those times we talked about it? You, Chad and me. We said girls would come and go, but we're forever. You're seriously breaking that pact?"

Andrew raised his voice, "This is not about her. You killed my best friend. You're crazy. When did you become a monster?" He hesitated before going on with a coldness in his voice, "And I don't want anything to do with you. Don't you get it?"

At that moment, Ricky snapped. He screamed with a hatred and rage that he could not control. "I loved you. You were my best friend. This is how you treat me. I thought when Chad was gone, things would be better. It would be you and me forever. Brothers until the end. But no, you're just like the rest of them. My dad, my mom, my sister. You're no better than my sister."

Ricky quickly surveyed the room. He found what he was looking for. He reached to his left and grabbed the silver based lamp and ripped it from the electric socket.

Andrew stepped back and away from Ricky before saying "What are you doing? You're crazy."

"Am I crazy? Did you just ask me if I'm crazy?" Ricky stepped towards him. His face became distant and there was nothing left of him. He raged, "You're right. I'm crazy and I'm doing what I should have done a long time ago. I thought if I got rid of Chad we could be best pals again, but no, that wasn't enough. That wasn't enough for you. When you started spending time with her, you changed. You had to get involved with her. I should have known you didn't really care about me. You would leave me, too. Now, I have to take care of you, just like my sister and Chad. You leave me no choice."

Andrew was stalling. He needed to hear it. He softened his tone. "Ricky, what did you do to Chad? To your sister? You killed them, didn't you? Tell me. I can help you, if you'll let me."

Ricky was violently shaking his head back and forth with tears streaming down his face. "I had to get rid of them. I didn't want to, I didn't want to, but I had to." He cried, "Chad was in the way and my sister wanted me out of her life. I didn't want to kill her. I had to." He made a sniffling noise and used his shirt sleeve to wipe the tears. He swayed back and forth like he might drop to the floor before regaining his balance. "And now, you," he whimpered. "You and her. The only two people I've ever really cared about, and you both want me to go away."

Ricky suddenly stopped crying and his face twisted into a strange looking rage. "You are going to get your wish. I'll be out of your life for good. This ends here and now." He stepped toward Andrew, lifted the lamp base, and swung like he was trying to connect on a third strike ball that knocked him off balance.

Andrew swiftly ducked out of the way at the same time two police officers barged in from the back of the house and slammed Ricky to the floor. They read him his rights and cuffed him before lifting him to his feet. He was stunned, sweating and his body was trembling. His hair was matted to his forehead and a few of the longer strands covered his eyes, but he didn't seem to notice or care. Unaware of what was happening, there was nothing but a hollow look as they carried him out.

CHAPTER 174

Andrew watched the police put Ricky in the back of the car. He walked into the bathroom without a word. When Stephanie and Lindsay rushed in from the garage door there was silence except for the heaving sound coming from the hall bathroom. When Andrew walked out, his face was expressionless and drained of color.

The sight of him broke Stephanie's heart. She went to her son, put her arms around him, and walked him to the couch. Neither said anything for a time. Stephanie held him in her arms and gently rocked back and forth. She could feel his tears soaking through her shirt.

Lindsay grabbed a throw and draped it around them before going to the kitchen to make tea and sandwiches. While the water was boiling, she looked at her phone, displaying a missed call from Adam. She swiped the notification to an answer on the first ring. Speaking in a low voice, she summarized what had happened. He said he wanted to see her and would pick her up for dinner later that evening.

She returned to the living room to find them still holding on to each other. They said they weren't hungry but she insisted they try to eat. She served the tea, placed the food on the ottoman, and embraced them before leaving. Pausing at the front door, she looked back with a sense of relief, but only for a second. She knew this was not over. Not yet. She locked the door behind her and let out a big sigh. What a day. Lindsay had one more call and one more stop to make.

CHAPTER 175

The minute her car engine was on, she grabbed her phone and entered the number for Patrick's attorney. She told him everything that happened, the specifics of Ricky's confession, his arrest, and every other detail she could remember. She had to see Patrick immediately and asked that he please make it happen.

It wasn't long before Sean called her back. He had taken care of everything and agreed to meet her there. She could see why he was considered one of the best, an ability to make things happen quickly.

Parking in the correctional facility parking lot and thinking about what she would say to him, there should have been a feeling of triumph or at least relief, but there was only sadness. They still had a long way to go to free Patrick from this crime he actually committed. She stepped out of the car and walked briskly to the entrance, hoping this would be the last time she ever processed in and out of this facility.

She was quietly seated in the visitation room when Patrick was escorted in. He was unable to talk to Stephanie before Lindsay arrived. "It's over," she said and smiled at him.

"What does that mean exactly?"

"Ricky admitted to killing Kaitlin and Chad. Andrew got the confession out of him."

Lindsay spent the next few minutes telling Patrick how it unfolded while they waited for his attorney. Sean had been negotiating an unusual agreement with the district attorney to get Patrick back home to his family immediately. After fast talking, promises, influence and persuasion, Sean's work led to Patrick's bail.

Lindsay drove Patrick to his home. He wouldn't let her call Stephanie to let her know the good news. He wanted to surprise her. When Lindsay pulled into the driveway, Patrick looked at her with grateful, loving and tearful eyes. "I can't thank you enough for what you've done for me, for us. I don't even know what to say that can even come close to letting you know how much this means to me. How do I make it up to you?"

"You already have. The look on your face. We've been through so much over the years. That's what friends do for one another. I love you Patrick and I trust you. I have never doubted your intention to reimburse the money. I know you. For now, get in there and see your family. We'll talk tomorrow. Besides, I have a date to get ready for," she said with a wink. He hugged her and wiped his eyes.

She watched him walk up the front steps. By the time he inserted the key in the lock, the door opened and Stephanie stepped outside and leaned in, hugging and kissing him. He twirled her around and held on tight. Before entering the house, they both turned and touched their hearts twice and waved to Lindsay.

She responded with a wave and double tap of her own heart. The minute she exited the neighborhood, she looked at her watch and accelerated speed. This was becoming a habit she had to break. Later. She was in a hurry. A date with a wonderful man.

CHAPTER 176

Adam arrived at Lindsay's home at 6:30 sharp. His thing about punctuality was refreshing. At her request, they had reservations at the Grille. The familiarity of the atmosphere was warming and seeing Sam would provide a level of comfort she desperately needed.

When she opened the door, he handed her a box of her favorite dark chocolates and took her in his arms and held her close. This time she held tight and didn't want it to end.

When he let go, she stepped back and looked at his eyes smiling down at her. "I really needed that. Thank you. What a day!"

"I can only imagine," he said, shaking his head. He stepped inside and asked, "Is there anything I can do for you?"

"You're doing it. Just by being here." She smiled, gestured a thank you for the chocolates and placed them on the hall table before closing the door behind them.

* * * * * * * * *

Adam and Lindsay arrived at the restaurant fifteen minutes before their reservation. Samantha saw them as they entered, engaging and talking with one another. They made a beautiful couple. She waved and motioned them to the bar and ordered three glasses of Prosecco.

They clinked crystal and talked until their table was ready. Lindsay told her all about Ricky. It wouldn't be long before the news would be splattered on every local network. There would definitely be bad publicity for the firm, but that was nothing compared to the carnage of those suffering from Ricky's crimes.

Sam led them to the table in the back corner which just happened to be the most romantic setting in the entire restaurant. She winked at Adam and walked away to get them one of her finest bottles of Bordeaux. Lindsay looked suspiciously at Adam and he admitted to selecting the table, wine and dinner menu ahead of time. He knew it was a little presumptuous, but he hoped she wouldn't mind.

She wouldn't have it any other way. It was exactly what she needed, especially after the past few grueling days.

They were into their entrees when they circled back to more discussion about Ricky. Lindsay told Adam everything. All of the sordid details.

"How did you come up with the idea to entrap Ricky?"

"It was something Cynthia said about him. He had told her there were only two people in his life he had ever loved, Kaitlin and Andrew. They both were deserting him and he had to do something about it."

Lindsay continued, "Then it hit me. Since he killed Kaitlin for trying to get away from him, Andrew might be our best shot at ending the nightmare. So, we devised a plan for Andrew to reject him. We were lucky it worked."

Lindsay told him about calling the police and talking to Stephanie and Andrew from Cynthia's apartment. The police and Stephanie initially opposed the idea of using Andrew to set up Ricky. But he insisted, reminding them he was twenty one and capable. He was all in and this was the one thing he could do for Chad.

Reluctantly, they agreed. It was, after all, to take place in a controlled environment with the police in the next room. Andrew's childhood home where he and Ricky had shared many hours and a lifetime of experiences.

"And that's how it all went down. The past forty eight hours. Can you believe it?" She said it more as a statement rather than a question.

"Impressive. A brilliant plan. Not to mention, you saved Patrick's family."

"He would have done the same for me."

"Did you ever, even for one minute, think he could have done this?"

"It never entered my mind."

"What about paying back the firm?"

"I know you may not understand this, but I believe in him. It probably sounds a little crazy, given what he did. I know him and would trust him with my life."

"No, I get it. I'm not judging. He was desperate. And desperate people do things that are completely uncharacteristic for them. Actions they would otherwise never consider. It becomes survival."

"That's exactly it," she said, nodding her head. She thought for a second before continuing, "And, like we talked about in the workshop. Patrick and I have a relationship and it's built on trust. It would even take more than this to break it."

Adam smiled and raised his glass like a toast. He said, "You are an excellent student."

She raised her glass, winked and responded, "I had an outstanding teacher."

The gesture led to a penetrating look between two people that were out of practice. Maybe there was a little uneasiness creeping in between them. They both could feel it, the conversation was changing to a much more personal one.

Adam grew quiet for a second. Almost pensive. A master at conversation, and he wasn't sure how to introduce his feelings. There was a silent awkwardness between them until he spoke. He was looking down at his wine glass and twirling it in his fingers. The wine had legs. A good Bordeaux.

Lindsay experienced an uneasy, unexplainable feeling of nervousness. *Oh no, what was he about to say?*

He started to speak, and then hesitated before continuing, "What you did was brave. Not to mention, being an empathetic friend. I'm proud of you."

She started to interrupt, but he put his hand in the air to stop her. "There is more I would like to say. Let me do it while I still have the nerve. It's not just that I admire you. I guess what I'm trying to say is that I am really starting to care about you. It's new territory for me. Something I haven't experienced in a very long time. As a supposed communications expert, you would think I would be more eloquent in my declaration." He laughed and she detected a bit of a quiver in his voice when he said, "What I'm trying to say is that I am falling for you."

It wasn't exactly what Lindsay was expecting, but she was not surprised either. Searching carefully for the appropriate words, she looked down before responding. It felt like minutes, not seconds before she looked back up, staring directly into his eyes. "How to say this." She sighed. "Adam, I'm flattered."

"I think I hear a 'but' in there," he interrupted, trying to lighten the conversation.

"Yes, there is a 'but'. I think you should know, I'm not very good with commitment or relationships. In fact, the thought terrifies me and I have steered clear of them for a long time now."

The surprise and the disappointment was evident in his eyes. This wasn't what he expected, nor wanted to hear. He looked down at his plate, attempting to hide the disappointment.

She started to speak when Adam interrupted again, "I'm sorry for making you uncomfortable, for blurting out my feelings. I didn't mean to pressure you. I should have known. I listened when you described what you went through with your fiancee. It must have been horrific."

"It was. In fact, I decided then, I couldn't take the chance of getting seriously involved and hurt like that again. I shut myself off from those kinds of feelings."

He looked hurt, shaking his head and looking down. He said quietly, "I'm sorry for putting you in this predicament. I…"

It was Lindsay's turn to interrupt. She said, "No, don't be sorry. That's the way I felt, until now. I have been fighting my feelings for you. I've looked for ways to keep myself from getting involved."

She paused, searching for the right words, and gathering the nerve to say them. To utter them would mean there would be no turning back. It would be out there and it would be real. She took a deep breath and continued, "The truth is, I feel the same way about you. Something Jack said, God, I can't believe I'm listening to Jack now, but I want to stop running scared and live, not just exist. I want to try, and I want to try with you. That's all I can promise."

Relief washed across Adam's face. "That's all I can ask. I'll make a promise to you, too. I won't pressure you into anything you aren't comfortable with. We can take this at whatever pace you want. But, I'll say this, we had a connection from the first time we met and I think we might be on to something really special here. I don't want to miss that opportunity."

He smiled sheepishly and reached across the table and placed his hand over hers. They both shared relieved smiles for a moment.

He asked, "Are you in?" to which she replied with a smile, "I'm in."

CHAPTER 177

The start of a new chapter, the beginning of a new adventure. Adam and Lindsay spent the remainder of dinner talking about their interests, feelings, and even fears. They talked about their dreams and what they wanted to experience, to share.

"What is the biggest priority on your bucket list for travel?" he asked, with an excited tone to his voice.

She answered without the need to think, "A two week trip through Europe. All of it. Take in everything. And, not take one call or email from the office."

"Ah, very nice. I've travelled extensively in Italy, been to Spain and England, but that's about it in Europe. Good one."

"What is on your bucket list for travel?"

He thought for a moment, smiling and tapping his finger against his upper lip. He answered, "Oh, I have many trips on my list. I like the Europe idea, but my first priority is a safari."

"Ooh, that's a good one, too."

There was an excitement enveloping them, the process of getting to know someone new. After dinner, they went back to Lindsay's for coffee and dessert. They were becoming much more at ease with one another as they talked late into the evening.

It was midnight before either of them knew it. There was an obvious awkward moment of determining what to do next. Adam made the first move.

"I need to get going. It's late and I have to do some research tomorrow. I'm up against a tight deadline on my book," he said, as he stood and they both walked towards the door.

Before reaching for the doorknob, he turned back and gazed at Lindsay. He took her hands into his and eased her into his arms. They looked into each other's eyes and he kissed her gently and then more passionately. He stepped back, lightly placed his hands on her shoulders, and smiled at her. In an attempt to reassure her, he said, "Don't be afraid. We're in this together. I'll be here, by your side."

She sighed and asked quietly, "Oh Adam, what are we doing?"

"We're getting in the game. Look Lindsay, we don't know where this road will take us, but I know how I feel about you and I'm dying to find out," he smiled and opened the door. He touched her chin and said, "Don't worry so much. At least we have a leg up when it comes to mastering communication skills. There was this training program that changed our lives. In many more ways than one." His smile transformed into a grin that accentuated those adoring dimples.

"This could be one wild and crazy ride."

"I'm counting on it. I wouldn't miss it for the world." He kissed her again and left. He would definitely be back.

CHAPTER 178

The lives of Patrick, Stephanie and even Andrew were beginning the transition to a new normal for them. Stephanie was disappointed, and sometimes angry that Patrick hadn't turned to her when they should have been going through the ordeal together. Things might have been different if he had believed in her strength and trusted enough to lean on their partnership.

On some level, she understood why he couldn't turn to anyone. He was desperate and overwhelmed with fear for his family. And, he was attempting to protect his wife from experiencing the almost unbearable fear, worry and concern he had dealt with all this time. After all, she was a mother. And, she loved him for that.

Judgment day was good to them. Patrick's punishment included probation, community service with the Noble Home, and a restitution agreement to repay the money he owed the firm. He was granted the maximum degree of leniency due to the circumstances of blackmail and that he was able to produce an accounting ledger illustrating a payment plan. Of course, Patrick had a payment plan. After all, it was Patrick. The plan was comprehensive, detailed and showed projected payments and timeframes based on future bonuses and salary increases clearly demonstrating the intent to borrow, not embezzle money.

CHAPTER 179

The thought of Patrick's first face-to-face encounter with David was one of the most difficult tests he would have to endure. But, it was something he had to do. Just the two of them. To look him in the eyes and tell him just how sorry he was turned out to be almost as terrifying as the entire tragedy. Until he saw David's face.

David had defended his colleague, even spoken on his behalf. It was the relationship. Even without the evidence, David believed him.

Patrick would never commit such an egregious act for his own personal gain. As strange as it may seem, David's image of Patrick was still based on their foundation of trust. He would have staked his life on Patrick's intent to reimburse the firm. He knew Patrick that well. He was a good and decent man. Yes, even a man with integrity, but a desperate man.

Patrick was much more than a little surprised by David's reaction. He asked him, "Why have you been willing to do all of this for me? Even though I was always planning on reimbursing the firm, I still did it."

"Because I know you. You're a good man that found himself in a desperate, terrible situation. No one really knows how they would have handled what you went through. We might say we would have handled it differently, but would we? I don't know the answer to that. Your family was in grave danger and there is no doubt in my mind that you did what you thought you had to do, and yes, you were planning on paying back the money."

"I still did it."

"Look, what you went through was awful. People react in ways that are almost outside of themselves when they're in real trouble. I still believe in you. It's like Adam said in the workshop about the rules of trust."

"That seems so long ago. I don't even want to think about it. I blew so many of those rules with my actions, regardless of the motivation," Patrick said, shaking his head and looking down.

"Patrick, this is one of those moral dilemma things, so stop being so hard… you have to forgive you. I just wish you had trusted me enough to come to me. I could have helped. Or Stephanie or Lindsay. We could have helped. But, I also understand the high stakes you were facing. It was about your child, your family."

"One of the worst things about this entire mess is that I've let down the people I love the most. Now, I have to figure out a way to repair the damage," Patrick said with resignation in his tone.

David could see the torture in his face and there was no doubt that he would battle with this for a very long time. He responded in a reassuring tone, "I'll give you the Adam textbook answer. Because you already have a relationship with us, some level of trust may be damaged, but it hasn't been destroyed. Look, trust is a continuous process. In this tragic situation, it was challenged, tested. But, it's not irreparable. We know why you did what you did. Of course, there were other ways to approach it, and I wish you had. But, we also know that your intention was not to hurt us."

"I know, but I still did it, and that's the part I have to live with. Determine where to go from here."

"I have faith in you. You'll know what to do next."

"I've been thinking about it and I know where to start. Maybe those relationship skills I learned in the workshop will come in handy after all." Patrick glanced away for a second before looking back at David. "I'll admit, I wasn't all that supportive in the beginning. By the time we reached the end, I understood the value and the merits of what we were trying to accomplish. That toolbox of behaviors may seem basic, but when things get challenging… priceless. And, it's certainly timely and applicable to my situation."

David asked, "What's your plan?"

"My first move is to put my life back together, to work on the relation-ships that were damaged." Patrick paused and contemplated for a moment before continuing, "I'll focus on making them right. I'll use my new arsenal of communication techniques and the rules of trust to do that." He actually gave David a look that might have resembled a faint smile.

"It sounds like a good start." David returned with a tentative smile that only took a second to turn into a big grin. He said, "For someone who fought the workshop most of the way, you certainly appear to have bought into the principles."

"You're right. It is another thing I was wrong about. Adam's work with us made us better. I should have been more attentive from the beginning."

David nodded his head in agreement. "This is going to all work out."

There was a momentary silence. They both hesitated, but somehow knew where the conversation was headed. It had to be addressed. They could not longer avoid it so Patrick broke the ice.

"Well, I can't thank you enough. I don't know how I will ever repay you for believing in me. I'm beyond grateful for your forgiveness." Patrick looked up at David, with a quiver in his voice.

David shrugged and said, "It's purely selfish. I still think you are a great asset, one of the best in the business. I'm hoping we can put all of this behind us and maybe get back to work?

Patrick looked surprised. He hadn't thought through the possibility until that moment. He hesitated before saying, "David, I appreciate it, but I can't work for the firm anymore."

"What do you mean? I want you at the firm. We just talked about trust. A long standing relationship I still believe in."

"I can't do it. Too much has happened. Regardless of the circumstances, I won't be as credible as a leader. I don't know how we make people under-stand. What I did is not okay, regardless of the reason."

"We'll make people understand. I'm not saying it will be easy, but it's worth it. You were planning on paying the money back. They know you. They believe in you. It doesn't have to be this way," David pleaded. He had not planned for this reaction, but deep down, he knew Patrick was probably right. He just wasn't ready to accept it.

Patrick adamantly shook his head in a manner that said no. "It's too late. I can't go back. I can't do that to you, to the firm. You deserve better out of a CFO. People will not understand."

David looked out into the distance and didn't say anything for a moment, and then asked quietly, "What are you going to do?"

"I don't know. I'll have to figure that out." He paused, let out a deep breath and said, "David, I am so grateful to you. I owe you my life. I will never forget all that you have done for me. If you ever need me, all you have to do is call."

"Then come back to work."

Patrick turned his head sideways and smiled at him. "That's the only thing I can't do." His voice trailed off for a second, "You know I can't do that. But, your willingness to have me back means everything to me. I don't deserve it. As I said, if you ever need me for anything, I will be there for you. Count on it."

David didn't want to leave it this way. He searched for words, for options. He simply asked, "Is there anything I can say to change your mind?"

Patrick shook his head. He couldn't say anything. There were no more words. They both knew it was time to move on. They embraced and held on a little longer than normal, neither of them wanting the other to see tears. They departed knowing they would see each other again. It was time to start over.

Patrick watched him walk away. He wiped the tears from his eyes and shielded them with sunglasses.

He owed David his life. He hoped their relationship would continue. He only hoped he could support David, the way he had been supported. Gratitude was a powerful pill. And isn't trust complicated?

CHAPTER 180

David walked to his car with blurred vision and thinking about what they had been through over the last few weeks. His major life experiences flashed through his mind. He lived his perspective on life in the gray space. Things just didn't seem to fit neatly into a tidy little box. He had experienced more than once how desperation had driven decent people to drastic behavior, completely out of character.

David sat for a few minutes reflecting. His disappointment about Patrick hadn't sunk in. It stung, but he wouldn't realize the full effect until he returned to the office. The executive team meetings without him, the late night conversations and a cocktail in his office. Seeing Patrick and Lindsay sharing time and a drink at the coffee bar. Getting over it would take time. It had become a way of life.

But, there was something else bothering him. Something left unfinished. His thoughts shifted to his life's work. The firm he loved so much. It had meant everything to him. Now, it was being tested.

His executive team seemed to embrace Adam's work with them and it may have slightly changed some. For a couple, it was transformational. The majority bought into just how critical their relationship building would be for survival, and for long term success. It added a new element to the work environment. A feeling of connection. A new energy.

He hoped it would stick. It was still fresh and they were caught up in the honeymoon phase. The real work was ahead of them. There would be conflict and plenty of tests along the way. The difference would lie in exercising the staying power, the day-to-day reinforcement.

The success would be determined in the days and weeks ahead. Could they continue to emphasize the value of their relationships in those moments when the stakes were high? Egos tested? Could they communicate through turmoil and conflict? Would they trust enough to make the tough decisions for the benefit of the firm? And, would that be enough?

He thought back to the numbers and the strategic plan ahead. They might have a shot. They had taken a critical first step, but only time would tell. He sighed, hit the ignition switch and drove off, all the while wondering. Yes, only time would tell.

CHAPTER 181

Andrew experienced tragedies that people shouldn't have to experience at such a young age. He watched his father act in desperation, attempting to save him from the destruction of Ricky's creation. A victim of moral dilemma. And, he lived through the loss of his two childhood best friends and the dreadful truth about one of them.

But, he was resilient and would continue to build his life around creating loving relationships. He intended to finish college, marry the woman he loved, and become the new Assistant Basketball Coach for the University. He would have the opportunity to help mold and shape young boys into fine men.

Andrew couldn't shake the feeling that something was left unfinished and he just couldn't get Ricky out of his head. He had to see him. His fiancee tried to talk him out of it, but he went anyway. He had to go.

CHAPTER 182

When Andrew entered Ricky's room at the facility, he was shocked at what he saw. Ricky barely looked up. His face was gaunt and he looked twenty years older. He was a shell of the guy he once knew.

"Hi Ricky. How are you doing?" he asked, not knowing what else to say.

Ricky was sitting in a chair, staring at a wall at the other end of the room. He was looking at his university's banner. The noise of Andrew entering the room startled him. He looked up, confused, almost like he didn't recognize Andrew. "I'm fine. What do you want?" His voice was distant as he looked back at the wall.

Andrew hesitantly walked over and sat next to him. He whispered, "Nothing. I just had to see how you're doing. To tell you, I'm sorry about everything."

"I'm fine. Don't worry about me. I understand now," He spoke without emotion and continued to stare at the wall.

Not much else was said. Andrew attempted to think of things to say, but mainly they sat in silence. Andrew couldn't pick himself up to leave. Not yet.

He hadn't forgotten the awful and tragic things Ricky did. Yes, he killed, but he couldn't help feeling sorry for him.

The boy never had much of a life. It was doomed for disaster from the start. He never experienced real love or the caring and comfort of a family. He didn't comprehend relationships. He spent his life being deserted.

His mental and emotional issues weren't fully detected until it was too late. No one really knew when or how it escalated into a delusional state.

He was sentenced for his crimes, and would live out his days incarcerated in a court-ordered psychiatric hospital. The emotional breakdown at Andrew's parents house left him vacant. Extensive testing, observation and multiple forms of therapy would determine if the condition was permanent.

The remainder of his life would be confined to the four walls of his room, having his special needs attended to. It was almost ironic he would receive the level of care his mother couldn't. If she had stayed in the Noble Home and gained the necessary tools to deal with her pain, maybe she wouldn't have ended her life. And, it could have all turned out differently.

There were no words spoken for quite some time. When he could bring himself to leave, Andrew stood and said goodbye to Ricky. Walking down the halls, he thought about all the other people in desperate need of help. How many people struggle through intense pain and danger, and they live through it all virtually unnoticed? Until they harm themselves or someone else. The tragedy comes when it is too late.

He wished he had been able to help Ricky. Get him the care he needed. If only he had known the truth. If only... He got in his car and called his fiancee. He told her he was on his way.

* * * * * * * * * *

From several floors up, Ricky watched the window, waiting for Andrew to reappear and walk to his car. His eyes flickered when he saw him. When the vehicle was moving slowly out of sight, he turned away. He walked to the faraway wall, touching his school banner. He traced the letters with the fingers of his right hand. He smiled.

CHAPTER 183

Adam was safely tucked into his seat in first class of the airplane. He was sipping a glass of white wine as the flight attendant announced they could resume the use of their electronic devices. There went his excuse. He sighed and grabbed his laptop from his briefcase. He had work to do. A deadline to meet.

He was making the final revisions to the draft of his second book. This one was about relationship principles for executive teams. The methodology used teaching through the application of recent case studies and the main attraction was Thurmond and Hollingsworth.

He was thinking about them as he was writing. The time with the executive team had been fascinating, and he was overwhelmed with gratitude that David granted approval to use them as a focal point for one of the case studies in the book.

He closed his eyes and thought for a couple of minutes back to the beginning of their work together. His first thought was the beautiful and sexy Lindsay walking into the room for the first time with an aura of power. He opened his eyes abruptly. *Stop. Thoughts of her would have to wait. There was work to do.*

He regained his composure and focus, but with a smile on his face. It didn't take him long to determine what to write as an introduction about this team. He began typing.

The case study of Thurmond and Hollingsworth demonstrated the three key components to the success of any professional, as well as personal relationship. There were many unexpected twists and turns along the journey for this team. But, we'll get to that later. First, let's examine the three components of relationship success that were put to the test: how to build and maintain relationships, how to use appropriate communication tools and skills in a high stakes, emotionally charged environment or conflict situation, and how to build, instill, and restore permanent trust in our relationships.

It sounds basic and simple, but it was complicated. We were dealing with the complexities of human beings. As if that was not enough, the circumstances were more challenging for this firm on the verge of collapse on an urgent timetable. The executive team was assigned one very specific goal - to save the company.

This was an interestingly new challenge for a team that had been a thriving business. In the past, they could afford to be creative and innovative without making financially based decisions. The money was flowing. Relationships were good enough. They didn't have to be tested because nothing was really at stake. It's easier when things are good.

But, times changed. For the first time, they found themselves thrust into a high stakes game of possible winners and losers. They had to figure out how to navigate through the challenges and relate to one another for the firm's survival. It was urgent and it was critically important.

How did it change them? At first, it didn't. They suffered through the painful realization of the new world they lived in. Similar to most groups of people in this situation, they thought about themselves and self-preservation kicked in. They exerted a protectionist attitude for their Departments above the firm. There was no common goal to work towards or to relate through.

I remember the first time I met them. There was this mesmerizing and stunning executive that walked into the room that almost took my breath away. Adam smiled and then frowned, Ugh - no, delete. Not appropriate for this book. But, it was fun typing it. Made it feel real. Do over. Yes, it made him smile.

The first time I walked into the room, there were several executives at the refreshments table talking about this and that. Nothing unusual. But, as you are about to find out, they were an extraordinary group of people. When they started seeing each other as human beings, with challenges and vulnerabilities, and changed their narratives by looking at their similarities as opposed to *their differences, the transformation of culture began. It wasn't nirvana, but it was a beginning.*

Adam spent the next couple of hours typing in a trancelike fashion. He was focused as he introduced the players and wrote about their strengths and vulnerabilities as a way of understanding their team dynamics.

And, then there was Lindsay and her process of change. It was the start of a romantic interest after all these years. She had struggled for so long with the idea of commitment and love. But, not this time. She was going for it. No excuses. Let's hope he is worthy.

We can all hope for new beginnings. Adam smiled. He couldn't write that, not in this book.

He continued his work and the next part of the story was particularly difficult to reduce to writing. It was about changing the lives of so many people. He wrote,

The next part of this story will demonstrate trust beyond your wildest dreams, in both personal and professional settings. It is a story of tragedy that will blow your mind. It has elements of relationships, effective and ineffective communication, and every facet of trust you can think of. There is good, bad, and there is desperation and moral dilemmas. At the conclusion, I'll leave you with a question - what would you do?

It's a story of a close relationship between Patrick and Lindsay and the many casualties along the way. It is about a murder, blackmail, embezzlement, and what to do with all the fallout.

Adam spent the next few minutes recanting the story as he remembered it. As he typed, he still couldn't believe all that had happened. It would make a better novel than a non-fiction book on relationships, communication, and trust. Oh well. He would leave that to the novelists.

"Sir, may I get you another drink?" the flight attendant interrupted his thoughts.

He didn't hear her at first and then realized she was talking to him. "Just coffee, please. Black." He smiled and looked back at his laptop.

Normally, he might have gazed a little longer at a flight attendant so easy on the eyes. Not now. Things had changed. A great many turn of events had occurred in the last few weeks.

He smiled, sighed and shook his head. He returned to his writing.

So, what does this story tell us? That Lindsay and Patrick have a solid foundation or this would have turned out much differently for everyone. Without Lindsay's help, the tragic story would have ended even worse than it already did.

And then there was the part that Adam couldn't write about. Once again, he typed and deleted it. He wanted to see it in print, no he needed to. It made it more real.

CHAPTER 184

Adam pressed the power button on his laptop and closed his eyes. He leaned back in his seat and thought about Lindsay. He missed her already.

He thought back to the airport and her. This felt safe and warm, but exciting. Maybe he was finally home. It made him realize he had spent too much of his life alone, and what he had been missing. Not that his life was empty, it just wasn't as fulfilling as it could be. Yes, he wanted this to work.

He spent the previous night with Lindsay. Their first night together. It wasn't one of those caught up in the moment, frenzied and can't wait to get your clothes off times. There was nothing haphazard about it. They weren't entering into it without conscious thought and talk about the implications to their relationship. They weren't taking anything for granted.

The night began with all the traditions of a romantic evening. Dinner, wine, candles, and soft music. As they approached coffee and dessert, the nerves were elevated. The conversation was a little more tentative. They both knew the next step.

When she took his hand and walked him slowly to the bedroom door, he could hardly breathe. He knew he would walk out of that room a different man. His life was about to change. The door closed and he fell in love with her.

She was even more breathtaking than he had imagined. It was tender and caring, and loving. Maybe even a little clumsy, at first. Nervous feelings were difficult to overcome. And, then the exploration of a new beginning.

They held each other all night, too alive and exhilarated to sleep. They may have fallen in and out of sleep, but mainly they talked. He could still smell the scent of her hair and her perfume. He hoped he could carry it with him a little longer.

They didn't really talk about his upcoming trip. He couldn't tell her much. There were classified aspects that could not be discussed with anyone. But, he could say enough for her to realize she was uneasy, maybe a little worried.

The following day, he would be on a plane in route to a very small, remote country halfway across the world. What was he doing and where was he doing it? He couldn't say. He called it nation building, telling Lindsay it was a politically sensitive project, but he left out the part about danger.

Adam's client was the State Department and the mission required his top secret security clearance. This project wouldn't be as dangerous as his work with the CIA. After all, he reminded himself this was nation building. And, he was one of the negotiators for the good guys.

He had experienced many of the bad things going on throughout the world. Too many. Some he couldn't talk about. He wasn't scared, but he hadn't really thought much about it before. Things were different now. He had someone he cared about. Someone he had to think about. At some point, maybe even be responsible for, if he was lucky.

He remembered how she looked when she walked him to his gate. Her beautiful hair was silky and shiny and her eyes sparkled. The skinny leg jeans and form-fitting sweater accentuated her curvy, but trim body.

She hugged and kissed him before letting him go. Before entering the airplane, he turned and waved. He had never experienced that feeling before.

CHAPTER 185

Lindsay waved back and smiled, not taking her eyes off of him. She adored that impish grin and smile she had become accustomed to. She blew him a kiss and watched him disappear inside. She couldn't remember a time when she was happier. She couldn't wait until he returned home. Then, her smile disappeared.

She stopped herself. She was thinking about his upcoming work. It was more about what he didn't tell her. This was not a project without danger. For a fleeting moment her thoughts went back to her former life. *Please dear God, not again. Please, please, not again.*

Words from the Author and Discussion Guide for *When Truth and Lies Collide: The Power in Connection, Communication and Relationships*

Thank you for taking this journey with me. I hope you'll appreciate learning through the story. This methodology was designed for those of us who can't quiet our brain long enough to sit back, relax, grab a great read, and indulge in a robust cup of coffee or drink of choice (depending on the hour). If you are like me, your conscience keeps telling you "no" to relaxation, and "yes" to learning. Well, I've taken a shot at giving you the best of both worlds.

1. What was the dilemma for Thurmond & Hollingsworth? How did the workshop's focus on relationships, communication, and trust change them? Why are such basic principles so complicated?

2. The first principle in the workshop introduced building and maintaining relationships. What were the main points? Do you agree? Why or why not? Additional thoughts?

3. What happened as a result of the gut wrenching exercise when the participants described a tragedy that impacted their lives? How did it make you feel?

4. What were the key moments that caused a shift in the executive team's behavior? Why? How?

5. The principle - communication. In the story's illustration of communication in the budget planning session, what was the first mistake?

What were they instructed to do about it? What action(s) changed behavior and response when they reconvened?

6. The principle - trust. What were the main points? Discuss the concept of trust and how it relates to the group of people in the video. What initiated the beginning of a change in culture? How did the story of Deniese make you feel?

7. Give an example of a trusting relationship that went bad for you? What happened? Was it restored, or how could it have been restored?

8. What steps did the Thurmond & Hollingsworth team take to ensure the experience and impact of the workshop would not be lost and forgotten when they retreated back to their offices and hectic schedules?

9. Do you believe this team of executives will be successful? Why? How? Will it be enough? What do you think happened to them?

10. What did the principles in the story teach you about connections and relationships? What about Lindsay and Patrick?

11. Moral dilemma: If you were Patrick, what would you have done?

12. Moral dilemma: If you were Lindsay, would you have helped Patrick? Why? Why not?

13. What emotions and perspectives did this story evoke in you? Why? Would you change anything in your life because of this experience?

ACKNOWLEDGEMENTS

The principles in this book are not new shiny objects, revolutionary, earth-shattering, or complicated, but may be transformative when applied collectively to build relationships. I leave that part up to you - I am a continuous work in progress. Perfection isn't possible and self-improvement isn't always easy.

The concepts weren't originated by any specific teacher, but a culmination of interpretations from diverse backgrounds too many to name. Most aren't even aware of their influence that impacted the theme - building a culture, system, infrastructure, or whatever term suits you that results in people working together. Connection!

There have been many coaches, mentors, years of experience leading teams and people, as well as playing on successful and unsuccessful professional and athletic teams that led to this. Experiences have been both good and bad, shaping my beliefs and perspectives along the way. Some of the mentors are other authors, colleagues, friends, family, and senior leaders that taught me - principles I extracted to incorporate into my toolbox, and other habits and leadership techniques I elected not to commit to action.

To many friends that were willing to read this, even at the "less than readable" draft phase, thank you. I know it must not have been easy. Even though you aren't named, you are so very special and I am indebted to you and your feedback.

To Deniese Kelly's son, your mother was an inspiration that touched my life. We worked together, befriended one another from both coasts, and I had the opportunity to know this amazing person. When she was battling cancer and my father was dying, she reached out and provided such comfort to me. I'm sure you are an exceptionally fine young man. You have a great role model. We miss you Dee!!!

And to my special aunts, uncles, and cousins, you know who you are, and I love you with all my heart. I'm never alone because of you, and you're not alone either.

To my mother, thank you for pushing me to always do better and strive for success, and occasionally perfectionism. It helped shape me and made this possible. You never, ever let me feel unloved.

To my father, he knows how I feel. He was the one that said, "I know you, and you can do anything you set your mind to." I never forgot that and it became my stretch goal in every life circumstance. You are with me every day!

ABOUT THE AUTHOR

PS Kellihan has spent over sixteen years as a senior leader for a Naval Command of over 18,000 people throughout the United States, Europe, Africa and Southwest Asia. With more than twenty years of leadership experience with Navy, Army, and Coast Guard commands, a substantial amount of her time has been focused on re-engineering and transforming cultures and infrastructures, policies and processes, roles and responsibilities, and navigating through command and control operations for organizations.

She performs a wide range of consulting, speaking, and training engagements throughout the country at national conferences and other world class organizations on a variety of topics. Her extensive experience in leadership, coaching and mentoring a diverse collection of individuals and teams, and her passion for connection and relationship building through a system approach dates back to playing collegiate basketball. She was inducted in the Christopher Newport University Hall of Fame in 1990.

She is president and founder of RaiseUp LLC.

PSKellihan.RaiseUpLLC@gmail.com